PURSUING
GOD'S
PRESENCE

A 365-DAY DEVOTIONAL

#1 *NEW YORK TIMES* BESTSELLING AUTHOR
MIKE EVANS

TimeWorthy
·BOOKS·

P.O. Box 30000, Phoenix, AZ 85046

Pursuing God's Presence
Copyright 2018 by Time Worthy Books
P. O. Box 30000, Phoenix, AZ 85046

US Hardcover: 978-1-62961-180-8
Canada: 978-1-62961-182-2

This book is dedicated to my beloved
Jerusalem Prayer Team partners
who have dreamed the dreams with me.

FOR SOME, it is the gentle light of dawn seeping through the windows; for others, it is the cry of a baby, the smell of coffee brewing, or the raucous blare of an alarm clock. However you may awaken to face each new day you have the assurance that God is there. What joy it is to know that His love is everlasting, His faithfulness eternal!

The prophet Isaiah reassures us of God's presence:

> "'Fear not, for I *am* with you; Be not dismayed, for I *am* your God. I will strengthen you, Yes, I will help you, I will uphold you with My righteous right hand.'" (Isaiah 44:10 NKJV)

The most important thing you can do is spend time in the Word of God, and devote time to meditation. It is there you receive wisdom for the day ahead, and hope for tomorrow.

This book is a tool to inspire you, to give you strength for the day, to cheer you, and to bring you delight. The psalmist wrote, "Delight yourself also in the LORD, And He shall give you the desires of your heart." (Psalm 37:4 NKJV)

My prayer is that God will use the daily readings within these pages to strengthen you, help you, and uphold you with His righteous right hand.

In His grace,

JANUARY

JANUARY 1

For our present troubles are small and won't last very long.
Yet they produce for us a glory that vastly outweighs
them and will last forever!
(2 CORINTHIANS 4:17, NLT)

WHAT FORCE within propels us forward with the determination that there is so much more to which we can look forward? That this life is not all there is; that there is more just beyond the curtain? As Believers, we experience what can perhaps best be described as homesickness. Singer/songwriter Squire Parsons caught the essence of that feeling when he wrote the beautiful song, "Beulah Land":

> I'm kind of homesick for a country
> To which I've never been before.
> No sad goodbyes will there be spoken
> for time won't matter anymore.
> Beulah Land, I'm longing for you...[1]

Mankind is naturally hard-wired to seek God. You will find Him when you turn away from sin and place your faith and trust in Jesus Christ as your Lord and Savior. He is the Way, the Truth, and the Life. Spend time learning of Him through His Word, the Bible.

JANUARY 2

He has made everything beautiful in its time.
Also He has put eternity in their hearts, except that no one
can find out the work that God does from beginning to end.
(ECCLESIASTES 3:11 NKJV)

BLAISE PASCAL, a famous French mathematician, philosopher and physicist made this assertion: "There is a God shaped vacuum in the heart of every man which cannot be filled by any created thing, but only by God, the Creator, made known through Jesus."[2] Sadly, all too often men and women try to fill that vacuum with things that will only kill, steal, or destroy[3] —drugs, alcohol, sex, pornography, thrill-seeking.

Like the innate ability of a carrier pigeon to find its way home, or a salmon to make its way back to its spawning grounds, or a swallow returning to San Juan Capistrano, Believers are inexorably drawn toward home. With eternity in our hearts, we are enticed by all that awaits us. Until we reach the place where Jesus awaits, you and I will be homesick for heaven.

Several times each year, I travel far from home. At some point during the trip, my heart always turns toward home and I long to be there with my wife and family. There is a yearning deep inside the heart of every Believer to be at home with the Father—a desire greater than any other.

JANUARY 3

When you pass through the waters, I will be with you; and through
the rivers, they shall not overwhelm you; when you walk through fire
you shall not be burned, and the flame shall not consume you.

(ISAIAH 43:2 ESV)

AS A BELIEVER, have you endured what you might call a "fiery trial?" If not, at some point in your walk with God, you will. One thing you will not have to fear is that He will take you aside and leave you there. Jehovah assured David in Psalm 23:4, "Even when I walk through the darkest valley, I will not be afraid, for you are close beside me. Your rod and your staff protect and comfort me."

The apostle Peter wrote in his first book, chapter 5, verse 7, "Cast all your anxieties on him, for he cares about you." It is sometimes difficult for us to remember while in the deep throes of apprehension that God is always ready and willing to shoulder our problems. All we need to do is ask for His help.

King Hezekiah, the twelfth ruler of Judea, was extraordinarily pious. When Sennacherib, the king of Assyria, dispatched a threatening letter to Hezekiah he was so upset that he tore his garments and went to the temple. There, in the presence of God, he spread the letter on the altar and prayed:

O Lord God of Israel, the One who dwells between the cherubim, You are God, You alone, of all the kingdoms of the earth. You have made heaven and earth. (2 Kings 19:15 19 ESV)

When you are faced with trouble, when problems arrive on your doorstep, spread them out before Jehovah God and call upon Him.

JANUARY 4

Call to me and I will answer you, and will tell you
great and hidden things that you have not known.
(JEREMIAH 33:3 ESV)

JEREMIAH, the Old Testament prophet, faced trying times, not only in his personal life, but in events surrounding his beloved country. As he looked about him, it seemed that things were going from awful to even more awful. It would have been easy for his hope to completely evaporate as he pondered where he might find the help so badly needed. Perhaps Jeremiah even wondered where God was in all the upheaval.

Then God reassured His servant that all he had to do was call upon Him, and He would answer. Jehovah reminded Jeremiah that not only does He know the future; He holds it securely in the palm of His all-encompassing hand.

The prophet was uplifted and cheered by God's comfort and hope during both a national and a personal predicament. Jeremiah 33:3 reminds us that God knows all, sees all, and is in control of all.

Our heavenly Father doesn't promise that troubles will not come, but He does promise that He will walk through them with us. And, after all, it is in the valley that He restores our soul.

JANUARY 5

But he said to me, "My grace is sufficient for you,
for my power is made perfect in weakness."
Therefore I will boast all the more gladly of my weaknesses,
so that the power of Christ may rest upon me.
(2 CORINTHIANS 12:9 ESV)

SEVERAL OF MY BOOKS hold accounts of my difficult childhood and of my father's abuse—to the point of nearly having been strangled to death. Because of my experiences, I've been able to offer support and comfort to others who find themselves in a similar situation.

Sometimes we find ourselves walled in on all sides, seemingly with no place to turn for escape. We simply must remember that God is in control. There is no wall He can't topple anytime He wishes. So why doesn't God simply remove the wall and let us go free?

In Genesis, Joseph, son of Isaac, discovered why. The little tree that Jehovah planted beside a wall made the decision to stretch its limbs toward the sun and to push its roots deep into God. Season after season, it kept growing and bearing fruit where it was planted—in the pit or in the prison. One day, its branches ran over the wall into the palace courtyard.

The greatest joy we will ever know comes after we have grown bigger than the problem, and even our offenders can find rest in our shadow and be nourished.

JANUARY 6

*For You, Lord, **are** good, and ready to forgive,*
And abundant in mercy to all those who call upon You.
(PSALM 86:5 NKJV)

AFTER JACOB'S DEATH, his brothers, fearful that perhaps Joseph now would hate them and pay them back for the evil they had done him fell down before him in fear. Joseph responded:

> You intended to harm me, but God intended it for good to accomplish what is now being done, the saving of many lives. (Genesis 50:20 NIV)

The purity and beauty of Joseph's character is so forgiving, so persevering, so loving, and so completely Christ-like. We look at him longingly and ask, "Could I ever be like that?"

The answer is yes! Joseph was not some one-in-a-million, incredible man. It was that Joseph appropriated the grace of an incredible God. He learned to receive grace for his own sins and weaknesses, just as he learned to appropriate God's grace for the offenses committed against him.

My friend, difficult times don't last forever. As did the apostle Paul, continue to press toward the goal for the prize of the upward call of God in Christ Jesus. (See Philippians 3:14.) Don't give up; beyond the valley is a mountaintop.

JANUARY 7

He who dwells in the secret place of the Most High
Shall abide under the shadow of the Almighty.
(PSALM 91:1 NKJV)

PSALM 91 brings Corrie ten Boom to mind. It was once my honor and privilege to share lunch with her at a hotel in Texarkana, Texas. Most might think she and I met by accident, but I know it was a "God moment."

Over a bowl of soup, I asked, "Who is your favorite Bible character?" She smiled and replied, "King David, and my favorite Psalm is the ninety-first. God gave me that Psalm on my birthday, while I was in Ravensbrück [Nazi prison camp]. It was April 15, and I said, 'Lord, this is my birthday. I would like a birthday present.' And He whispered, 'YOUR PRESENT IS PSALM 91.'"

Then she quoted the first verse. "'Whoever dwells in the shelter of the Most High will rest in the shadow of the Almighty.'" She went on to explain, "Living in that shelter—*that hiding place*—means living before an audience of one and seeking Christ's affirmation above that of the world."

For those who may not know, the home of Casper ten Boom and his daughters Corrie and Betsie in Haarlem, Holland became a hiding place for Jews escaping the Nazis during World War II. Her family successfully saved the lives of 800 Jewish men, women, and children.

JANUARY 8

He who dwells in the shelter of the Most High
will abide in the shadow of the Almighty.
(PSALM 91:1 ESV)

IN DESPERATE NEED of a space to conceal their "visitors," the ten Booms engaged one of Europe's most respected architects, also in hiding in their home. They knew him only by his code name, Mr. Smit. That elderly wisp of a man freely gave of his time and energy to design and direct workmen who built a room so secure that the Gestapo never found it.

Once the room was completed, "guests" rehearsed again and again getting into the hiding place quickly until they could vacate the home's lower floors to safety inside the compartment in less than two minutes. Corrie practiced stalling techniques to delay anyone who might come in search of the hidden Jews. The ten Booms were able to save the lives of 800 Jewish men, women, and children until the family was arrested. Casper died shortly after his incarceration; Corrie and Betsie were sent to the infamous Ravensbrück where Betsie later succumbed due to her ill treatment.

When the psalmist wrote of a "secret place," he was declaring a truth expressly to us as Believers. If we dwell in the secret place of the Most High, Jehovah is obliged to shelter us; He has promised to protect us. Do you need a hiding place? You will find peace and safety in the eternal Hiding Place.

JANUARY 9

I will say of the LORD, He is my refuge and my fortress:
my God; in him will I trust.
(PSALM 91:2 NJV)

LATER, AFTER HER DEATH, I thought of Corrie's dream during those terrible war years, and by faith flew to the Netherlands to visit the clock shop and follow God's leading. As I walked around the shop, I asked about viewing the home's upstairs, where those eight hundred Jews had been hidden and saved during the Holocaust. The owner advised me that the door was kept locked, as the area was only used for storage. My heart broke. I felt that the Ten Boom clock shop should be open as a testimony to the world of the love of a Christian family for the Jewish people.

As I stepped outside onto the sidewalk, I prayed, "Lord, I want to buy this house and restore it. If it is Your will, please help me." That evening, I again sought God regarding my desire to fulfill Corrie's wishes.

The next morning I awoke confident in God's answer. I returned to the clock shop and asked the owner if he would sell the shop to me. Just as he refused my offer, the clocks in the shop began to chime the noon hour. He turned to me and asked if I knew what day it was. I mentioned the day of the week. "No," he said. "That is not what I meant—today is April 15, Corrie's birthday. In her honor, yes, I will sell the shop to you."

When God gives you an assignment, be assured that He will give you the tools to complete what He has called you to do. Perhaps we all need a plaque to remind us: "Please be patient; God isn't finished with me yet."

JANUARY 10

The heavens declare the glory of God;
And the firmament shows His handiwork.
(PSALM 19:1 NKJV)

PSALM 91 is a wonderful song of God's precious protection over His people. Reading through the chapter, it is soon evident that God doesn't promise we will never find ourselves in tight places, in desperate situations, or be exempt from trouble or affliction. It *does* promise that God will walk with us through each trial and tribulation.

The story is told of an early American Indian tribe with a unique method of transitioning their youngsters from that of childhood to Brave. After thirteen years of training in every aspect of becoming a warrior—hunting, scouting, riding, and survival in the wilderness—the young man would spend an entire night alone in the forest, presumably away from the scrutiny and security of his tribal family. On the night in question, he would be blindfolded and led deep into the dark woods several miles from the village.

When he removed the blindfold, he found himself alone in the black night, surrounded by strange sounds. Each time a twig snapped, he imagined a dangerous animal stalking him. After what seemed like an eternity in a sleepless night, the first rays of sunlight penetrated the forest. Looking around, the boy spotted the path that would lead him to safety. As he started forward, he was utterly amazed to find his father, armed with a bow and arrow, sitting near a tree a few feet away. The father had been keeping watch all night long.[4]

We can rest, assured that our Heavenly Father is keeping watch—every night, all night long.

JANUARY 11

God is our refuge and strength,
an ever-present help in trouble.
(PSALM 32:7 NIV)

THE PAGES OF SCRIPTURE are rife with descriptions of God's divine protection. The list is long and the stories always amazing: Daniel was lion food; the three Hebrew men were fire fodder; Moses was cargo in a reed boat; David was a giant's bull's-eye; Elijah was a king's nemesis; the list goes on and on. In each instance, God provided supernatural protection; He safeguarded His children.

Let's look again at Psalm 91:1: "He who dwells in the secret place of the Most High shall abide under the shadow of the Almighty." (NKJV)

Like the psalmist, the Believer has a choice to make: Dwell in the "secret place" or walk in the counsel of the ungodly and stand in the path of sinners.[5] The place of Psalm 91 is a place of safety and protection, a place where we are totally dependent on God. It is a place of strength for the obedient; the only true sanctuary.

All the blessings of God are available to the one who "abides under the shadow of the Almighty." And all you need do is ask for that protection.

JANUARY 12

Humble yourselves, therefore, under the mighty hand of God
so that at the proper time he may exalt you...
(1 PETER 5:6 ESV)

THE TRIALS AND TRIBULATIONS of the apostle Paul led him through valleys deep and dark. Through it all, the illustrious disciple remained humble, pliable, and useful in the Kingdom. He knew that God's grace was sufficient to keep him. When Paul was under a great weight, he fell on his face and poured his heart out to the One who could lift the load. The secret of his powerful walk with God was his Radical Humility. Like John the Baptist in John 3:30, Paul knew that: "He [Jesus] must increase, but I must decrease."

Humility is seldom easy for one distinctly and individually called by God. Few, if any, of us could testify of being struck down and blinded by God at our conversion as was Paul. He could have boasted of how he was THE called-out one. He could have worn his superiority like a mantle—demanding the choice seat at banquets, commandeering the best chariot for his travels, claiming the only first-class cabin on the ship. He could have, modestly of course, boasted of his superiority.

Paul could have certainly bragged about his accomplishments. Instead, he remained honorable, principled, and humble in the sight of God and man. His ministry was, as yours should be, that of a true apostle, characterized by meekness, truth, and love.

JANUARY 13

The humble will see their God at work and be glad.
Let all who seek God's help be encouraged.
(PSALM 69:32 NLT)

GOD BLESSED Paul's ministry. Unlike the false prophets that flourished in his day, Paul did not often draw huge crowds, nor was he welcomed as a hero. Rather, Paul lived a life of physical danger:

> Five times I received from the Jews the forty lashes minus one. Three times I was beaten with rods, once I was pelted with stones, three times I was shipwrecked, I spent a night and a day in the open sea, I have been constantly on the move. I have been in danger from rivers, in danger from bandits, in danger from my fellow Jews, in danger from Gentiles; in danger in the city, in danger in the country, in danger at sea; and in danger from false believers. I have labored and toiled and have often gone without sleep; I have known hunger and thirst and have often gone without food; I have been cold and naked. (2 Corinthians 11:24-27 NIV)

Despite those hardships, Paul could still say with great love and confidence: "For when I am weak, then am I strong." (1 Corinthians 12:11 NIV)

At any time, Paul could have taken the easy path, but he chose to be humble. As you labor to be a genuine child of God, strive for humility. It comes when you honestly assess yourself in light of God's Word. When you do, you will live your life in God's life-changing favor.

JANUARY 14

*The salvation of the righteous is from the Lord;
he is their stronghold in the time of trouble.*

(NLT)

IN 1978 the late Jamie Buckingham, international author and columnist, invited me to accompany his group on what had become for him a regular trek through the Sinai. It would be an unforgettable journey through the desert—one filled with sand, sun, scorching heat, scorpions, and a stunning example of God's presence. Lying on my back on the hard, rocky ground one night, my eyes were filled with the sight of countless stars in the heavens and the wonders of creation. I understood firsthand how David must have felt as he watched over his father's sheep in the hills of Judea.

It must have been there that he sang the first words of Psalm 19. Perhaps he, like me, was lying on his back staring in awe at God's handiwork, so much more visible in the darkness of the desert. But it is often in the night hours, in the rocky places, that God reveals His power and presence to His children.

It was on a cold, dark night outside Bethlehem that He announced the birth of a baby. It was not written on parchment, but heralded by a host of angels who lit up the dark sky and gladdened the hearts of a group of shepherds with their song.

It was a personal invitation to come and see the Christ child, the Messiah, the Savior of all mankind. It was proof yet again that while the Creator hung the stars and planets, the sun and moon in the skies above, His message was, and still is, carried by men and women of faith.

JANUARY 15

The next day John saw Jesus coming toward him, and said,
"Behold! The Lamb of God who takes away the sin of the world!
(JOHN 1:29 NKJV)

THE ANGELS HERALDED a message that should resonate in every heart: "Come and see! Go and tell!" After seeing Mary, Joseph, and the Baby Jesus, the shepherds excitedly shared the message with others. What is that message? It is the one of God's overwhelming and eternal love for all mankind.

Emmanuel: God with us—always and forever. Jehovah carries our burdens, our struggles. He bears our grief and sorrow and bids us rest in Him. He forever lives to make intercession for us.

In Matthew 11:28-30, Jesus assures us:

Come to me, all who labor and are heavy laden, and I will give you rest. Take my yoke upon you, and learn from me, for I am gentle and lowly in heart, and you will find rest for your souls. For my yoke is easy, and my burden is light. (ESV)

God freely offers forgiveness, love, peace, and hope. Hear and heed the message of those who saw Jesus for the first time, and then carry it to those who need to know His joyous love.

JANUARY 16

As for you, you meant evil against me,
__but__ God meant it for good...
(GENESIS 50:20 NASB)

IN OCTOBER 1982, a member of my ministry team and I were on our way home in a private plane piloted by a friend. We had just completed taping a television special, *Israel: America's Key to Survival*. As we neared our destination, one of the engines of the plane malfunctioned, and we could smell smoke and fuel; the lights on the instrument panel blinked out, and suddenly we were flying blind in a dark sky. As I rebuked the Destroyer, my team member began to pray, "Angels of the Lord, undergird us...angels of the Lord, undergird us."

Twenty-one minutes later we landed safely at an airport near Fort Worth. When the pilot looked over the plane, we were astonished to learn that one engine had broken loose and was totally drained of oil. We had truly experienced the power and presence of God on that flight—an absolute miracle.

The following morning, a ministry partner, Mrs. Obel, called the office and reported to my secretary that the previous night she had been awakened from sleep and was impressed to pray that the Lord would undergird me wherever I was. All she could pray for thirty minutes was, "Angels of the Lord, undergird Mike; angels of the Lord, undergird Mike." What Satan meant for evil on that dark and starless night, God turned to good.

In your time of need, no matter where or when, our God hears our prayers.

JANUARY 17

For I, the LORD your God, will hold your right hand,
Saying to you, 'Fear not, I will help you.'
(ISAIAH 41:13 NKJV)

IF YOU HAVE EVER experienced a miraculous intervention—maybe you remember the time, place, and circumstances. Perhaps God intervened to prevent a catastrophe and you never knew it. Someone somewhere may have been impressed by the Holy Spirit to pray for you, just as one dear lady prayed for me that dark night as my friends and I were suspended in a crippled airplane somewhere between heaven and earth.

Psalm 91:11-12 reminds us just how precious we are to our Heavenly Father:

> For He shall give His angels charge over you, To keep you in all your ways. In their hands they shall bear you up, Lest you dash your foot against a stone. (NKJV)

What a beautiful picture! Angels commissioned by God the Father to watch over and protect you, His child.

JANUARY 18

It is I; be not afraid.
(JOHN 6:20 KJV)

JUST AS DAVID REVELED in the awe of God's power and presence in the night sky while tending his father's sheep, so did the apostle Peter see a miraculous expression of God's power and presence in the darkness of a storm.

Matthew 14:22–34 teaches a lesson on the authority of our Lord over creation. Jesus had spent a long and physically draining day of exhorting, instructing, and healing a vast assembly of people. He then fed both soul and body of the hungry multitude. In His humanity, Jesus must have been exhausted.

As night slowly descended upon the Sea of Galilee, Jesus then sent His disciples across to the other side. Matthew tells us it was the "fourth watch of the night," or from three until six AM.

Jesus heard the distant cries of His disciples who were battling a fearsome storm. Rising from His prayers, the Son of Man laid aside His human exhaustion and assumed His role as Lord and Master of the waves. He strode down to the water's edge, stepped onto the stormy sea as if it were dry ground, and walked out toward the wallowing craft. Jesus then reached out a hand to reassure them, "Be of good cheer! It is I; do not be afraid." (Verse 27 NKJV) Immediately, the disciples realized that their fears were unjustified when compared to the power and presence of Jesus.

As a child of God you must grasp that same understanding: Jesus has not forsaken His children in the midst of the storm; He is ever present, ever powerful, and loves us unconditionally.

JANUARY 19

Now is the time of God's favor, now is the day of salvation.
(2 CORINTHIANS 6:2 NIV)

JEREMIAH WAS A PROPHET ordained by God to deliver a message of judgment to Israel, an unappreciated job at best. Unfortunately, his message was not designed to win friends; he was to simply speak only "Thus says the LORD." (See Jeremiah 15:2.) Jeremiah did exactly that; he pronounced judgment and destruction on Israel because of their sins. He warned, "I [Jehovah] will cause anguish and terror to fall on them suddenly" (see verse 8).

But Jeremiah's message was not totally one of devastation, for God always provides a way of escape for His people, a glimmer of hope in a dark world. He promised, "If you return, Then I will bring you back; You shall stand before Me (see verse 19).

The reaction to Jeremiah's message was to be expected; the people were incensed. Plans were made to cast him into prison without possibility of reprieve. The prophet reacted much as you or I might have: He vowed to stop preaching and began to complain.

Then in Jeremiah 15:19–21, God makes the promise of His power and presence. He reminds Jeremiah that he has been promised the power of God, the security of the Holy One of Israel to defend against those who threaten him.

God's favor can accomplish what your greatest talents and abilities cannot—unlocking doors you may think are locked, eliminating hurdles hindering your advancement, presenting unexpected openings, and bidding you to develop new associations. Seek to stand before God in sincerity and submission; offer His grace and favor to others; enjoy favor with God.

JANUARY 20

And he said, "Please, show me Your glory."
(EXODUS 33:18, NKJV)

WHAT AN AUDACIOUS REQUEST Moses had made of God! The Father, who has promised to hear and answer our cries, must have been saddened by such an appeal. It seems to be verified by His response to Moses in verse 20: "But He said, 'You cannot see My face; for no man shall see Me, and live.'" God, however, had a plan to grant Moses' petition.

Unlike Moses, my encounter with the divine was not something I had requested. At the age of 11, I had a divine encounter with God's Son. My earthly father had strangled me and left me for dead. I cried out in the dark, "Why was I born?"

Suddenly, the Lord appeared to me. I saw the nail scars He bore. He spoke to me and said, "Son, (a word I had never heard from my earthly father) I love you, (a statement I had never heard from him), and I have a great plan for your life."

Moses is the only man in the Bible to have asked to see God; yet with his dynamic request, he stood head and shoulders above all other men and women in the Bible. It was surely the sincere longing behind the petition that touched the heart of God and moved His hand to grant the desire of Moses' heart.

Jeremiah 23:13 reminds us, "And you will seek Me and find *Me*, when you search for Me with all your heart." (NKJV)

JANUARY 21

There is no fear in love; but perfect love casts out fear,
because fear involves torment.
(1 JOHN 4:18 NKJV)

MOSES HAD FAVOR with God, and the Creator of the universe responded. How did he feel after making such a bold appeal? Did he tremble at the audacity of his entreaty? Moses had a sustained track record with God. He knew Jehovah to be faithful. He had seen His glory in the burning bush, in the fire and cloud, in the parting of the waters of the Red Sea, in the salvation of an entire people during the solemn and fearful Passover. Moses was sustained by faith; he knew his God.

Moses' favor with God had been earned in the fire of adversity and the cloud of spiritual union. Moses refused to allow fear to rob him of stepping into the very presence of Jehovah. As the apostle Paul wrote in 1 John 4:18: "There is no fear in love; but perfect love casts out fear, because fear involves torment."

Moses established a bond before he sought a glimpse of the Almighty. He was not a beggar who had to grovel at the back door of the throne room, seeking but not expecting an audience with the Lord of the manor. No, Moses was a son who had access to the front entrance, an open door because he had favor with God. You and I have that same privilege. Ask to see His glory in your life.

JANUARY 22

And the LORD said, "Here is a place by Me, and you shall stand on the rock. So it shall be, while My glory passes by, that I will put you in the cleft of the rock, and will cover you with My hand while I pass by."
(EXODUS 33:21–22 NKJV)

MOSES HAD AN ENCOUNTER with the Creator and Sustainer, a personal encounter. He was hidden away by God, covered by His hand—cherished, protected, blessed, and highly favored!

Moses saw not the God of judgment, not the all-consuming fire; he basked in the presence of a God who loved the man He had chosen to lead His people, the one upon whom rested favor with God.

Just as I peeked between my fingers for a glimpse of God when I was 11, so Moses must have peered between his fingers from his hiding place in the cleft of the rock, his senses consumed by the glory of the Creator; his heart filled with awe for the character and power of Jehovah. Moses was transformed by the overwhelming love of God.

When we realize our place in Christ, you and I are forever changed. We can rest assured of his power and presence in our lives.

JANUARY 23

For you died to this life, and your real life
is hidden with Christ in God.
(COLOSSIANS 3:3 NLT)

THE PICTURE OF MOSES hidden in the cleft of the rock is
a perfect illustration for us. We have been placed in Christ Jesus
by God the Father. We have been adopted as His child into a place
where His glory is revealed.

In Exodus 33:19, God reveals what we can expect as His child:

> Then He said, "I will make all My goodness pass before you,
> and I will proclaim the name of the LORD before you. I will be
> gracious to whom I will be gracious, and I will have compassion
> on whom I will have compassion." (NKJV)

God was not obligated to allow Moses to see His glory; it was
because God had poured out His grace freely. Moses was allowed
to see the glory of Jehovah, not so that he could boast of his relationship, but that he might be transformed.

When Jesus "became flesh and dwelt among us, and we be-
held His glory, the glory as of the only begotten of the Father,
full of grace and truth" (John 1:14 NKJV), it was for the express
purpose of redeeming mankind so that we might be transformed
into His image. Jesus exhibited "all the fullness of the Godhead
bodily" (see Colossians 2:9 KJV)—mercy, grace, forgiveness, love,
joy, peace.

In the gift of Jesus Christ, God the Father wrapped up everything He is and everything He wants us to be.

JANUARY 24

*Blessed **are** the poor in spirit:*
for theirs is the kingdom of heaven.
(Matthew 5:3 kjv)

THE BEATITUDES present a picture of what the life of the Believer should be when we allow God to live in and through us. That is what the Beatitudes are about—God showing through. It has always been God's purpose that when He entered our lives, He would be allowed to so fill and control us that He would show through. We should not simply pretend to be what God has called us to be, but Christ should shine through our transparent lives... like a lamp that glows when connected to a power source.

The truth is, we can't simply "act" our way through life. There is no way we can achieve God's purpose and receive God's abundant blessings if we are simply playing a role. The Father wants the world to see, not us, but the image of His Son shining through us.

Would it be a burden or a blessing if Jesus were to come to visit you today? How would your activities differ from every other day? Would it change the way you treat others? Conduct business? Live your life? Yet we may often boast that Jesus lives within us. When we pause to consider that the Beatitudes are a picture of the attributes of Christ, we should lay aside Self and allow Him to develop those characteristics in our lives. We should live every day with the knowledge that Jesus *has* come to reside in our "earthly houses."

JANUARY 25

And all these blessings shall come upon you and overtake you,
because you obey the voice of the LORD your God...
(DEUTERONOMY 28:2 NKJV)

THERE ARE THOSE who view serving God as a negative. If
you ask, they will gladly list all that is forbidden to the Christian.
They single out the "thou shalt nots" instead of the blessings that
pursue the Believer.

British Bible scholar Dr. G. Campbell Morgan wrote:

> "Blessed" is therefore a condition—such a condition as to create
> a consciousness, which is the consciousness of a perfect peace,
> and a perfect joy, and a perfect rest. All these things are included
> in the condition of Happiness! That is God's will for man.
>
> That is the Divine intention for human life. Sorrow and sigh-
> ing are to flee away; He will wipe away all tears. Happiness and
> joy are never to flee away; He will never banish merriment and
> laughter. [6]

Jesus delivered a sermon to His followers that painted a dia-
metrically opposed picture of Yahweh—a God who wanted His
followers to be blessed. His desire was to see them live a life filled
with contentment, happiness, and enjoyment.

JANUARY 26

In Your presence is fullness of joy;
at Your right hand are pleasures forevermore.
(PSALM 16:11 NKJV)

AS A YOUNG SOLDIER barely old enough to join the U.S. Army, I spent fourteen months in South Korea on a mountain the Koreans called Wonton-ni. Wandering around the mountain early one morning, I experienced the overwhelming presence of God settling over me, flooding me with the burning desire to be a man of righteousness and integrity. Joy unspeakable filled my soul, and like Samuel of old, my spirit whispered, "Speak, Lord, for thy servant heareth." (See 1 Samuel 3:10 KJV.) Finding a secluded spot, I sank to the ground and tears rained down my face as the Holy Spirit gently reminded me of Jesus' words when He had appeared to me as a child.

When you are wounded and hurting, sit silently before the Lord. Can you feel His peace as it steals over you, calming your spirit? That sweet presence surrounding you is the omnipresent Father. The Lord of the universe, the God of all Creation, is delighted with you!

The purpose of the Old Testament book of Zephaniah was to deliver a letter of hope to the Israelites who were surrounded by a seemingly impossible situation—to bring hope when all seemed lost. The prophet was anointed to paint a picture with words to a discouraged and depressed people.

His message: All is not lost. God knows you and loves you! Listen closely and hear His song of deliverance.

JANUARY 27

You make known to me the path of life;
in your presence there is fullness of joy;
at your right hand are pleasures forevermore.
(PSALM 16:11 ESV)

GOD IS A GOD OF JOY, and we are invited to enter into His joy! We have become Believers with benefits—forgiveness, faith, and a future with Him in eternity. Judgment has been replaced with joy; hell has given way to heaven; struggle has been supplanted with serenity. Yes, my friend, Almighty God rejoices over you with gladness!

When a need arises, the Believer does not have to crawl on his hands and knees to seek an audience with the King of Kings. No, as His children, we have access to our Father's throne room anytime. I'm reminded of the picture of John F. Kennedy, Jr. as a child playing under his father's desk in the Oval Office of the White House. John-John had access to his father because of sonship. Just as his father's face was filled with joy when his little boy peeked around the door in his office, so our heavenly Father's face is filled with gladness when we come "boldly before the throne of grace." (See Hebrews 4:16.)

I believe the principal response in God's presence is gladness. There, we can find gladness for all eternity.

JANUARY 28

And whenever you stand praying, forgive,
if you have anything against anyone, so that your Father
also who is in heaven may forgive you your trespasses.
(MARK 11:25 ESV)

CONSIDER THE BAND OF SOLDIERS who were kneeling at the foot of the cross of the crucified Christ casting lots for his garments. Did those men even know the name of the Man into whose wrists and feet they had just driven spikes? Were they aware whose side the sword of one of them had pierced? Were they aware that His name was Jesus and that He was the Lamb of God, the One God had loved before the foundations of the world were even laid? It is likely none knew just how much they would need the forgiveness offered by the One hanging above them. They simply heard: "Father, forgive them, for they do not know what they are doing." (Luke 23:34 NIV)

Astonished, the soldiers momentarily halted their grisly game and looked heavenward. They were accustomed to hearing screams and curses, pleas of innocence, entreaties for mercy, appeals for water, but a prayer for forgiveness? Unimaginable.

The Man on the cross had prayed for the soldiers, pleading for God's forgiveness for their actions, just as He intercedes today for you and me!

JANUARY 29

*For You, Lord, **are** good, and ready to forgive,*
And abundant in mercy to all those who call upon You.
(PSALM 86:5 NKJV)

NONE UNDERSTOOD that Jesus had taken on the role of advocate, defending the actions of those who had wronged Him. His teachings of "Love your enemies, bless those who curse you, do good to those who hate you, and pray for those who spitefully use you and persecute you,"[7] were more than mere words; they were a lifestyle. It was an act of the will. It was Radical Forgiveness at work.

Jesus taught that there was a relationship between forgiving and receiving God's forgiveness:

> And whenever you stand praying, if you have anything against anyone, forgive him, that your Father in heaven may also forgive you your trespasses. But if you do not forgive, neither will your Father in heaven forgive your trespasses. (Mark 11:25-26 NKJV)

The prayer for forgiveness on the cross was not meant to be the last act of a dying man; it was an example for His followers. As they had been forgiven, so were they to forgive those who sinned against them. (See Matthew 26:9-13.)

This is profound forgiveness. It takes extreme courage to exercise that kind of forgiveness. But doing so will bring an abundance of God's blessings into your life, and will free you to be healed both emotionally and physically.

JANUARY 30

*The Spirit of the Lord **is** upon me, because he hath anointed*
me to preach the gospel to the poor; he hath sent me to heal the
brokenhearted, to preach deliverance to the captives, and recovering
of sight to the blind, to set at liberty them that are bruised.

(LUKE 4:18 KJV)

GOD IS A GOD OF DELIVERANCE. His redemptive plan
is to save and deliver. Luke 4:18 is a microcosm of the purpose of
Jesus on earth. He had gone to Nazareth, and the chapter tells
us that it was His custom to go to the synagogue. Once there, the
Torah scroll was presented to Jesus, and He began to read those
above words from Luke 4 that can also be found in Isaiah 61:1.

All of mankind was in a perilous situation when God sent His
Son to deliver His creation from the wages of sin and to provide
the gift of eternal life. Perhaps the greatest message within the
pages of Scripture is that of deliverance:

Noah was delivered from the flood; Isaac was delivered from
becoming a sacrifice because God provided a ram; Esther and
her people were delivered from the wicked Haman; Daniel was
delivered from the lions' den; his friends—Shadrach, Meshach,
and Abednego—were protected in the fiery furnace; Jonah was
delivered from the belly of a big fish; and David was delivered
from Goliath. Jehovah had dramatically rescued each one from
a desperate situation.

He is still in the business of rescuing His children from snares
that confront us.

JANUARY 31

But I am poor and needy; Make haste to me, O God!
You are my help and my deliverer; O LORD, do not delay.
(PSALM 70:5 NKJV)

OFTEN DURING my ministry I have been in perilous situations, but I never imagined that my beloved son would endure such danger. Michael was in Israel in early August 2014. It was then that he emailed me the following:

> Today while on a fact-finding trip to the front line of the conflict between Israel and Hamas a mortar fired by Hamas narrowly missed our vehicle. Most of the time mortar fire is too small to set off the early warning system, so we had no idea it was coming. A short distance down the road the mortar struck and exploded. It is likely I would have been hit had we not stopped to minister to a group of Israeli soldiers in an open field. I left the area feeling that God had delivered me today.

Jehovah's frequent deliverance is not just an element of Old Testament stories; it is as real today as it was then. The psalmist penned in Psalm 144:1–2:

> Blessed be the LORD my Rock, who trains my hands for war, and my fingers for battle—my lovingkindness and my fortress, my high tower and my deliverer, my shield and the One in whom I take refuge, who subdues my people under me. (NKJV)

FEBRUARY

FEBRUARY 1

So [Naaman] went down and dipped seven times in the Jordan,
according to the saying of the man of God; and his flesh
was restored like the flesh of a little child, and he was clean.
(2 KINGS 5:14 NKJV)

IN THE EARLY 2000s after having written three books,
despite all my efforts I could not find a publisher. The books were:
God Wrestling, The Prayer of David: In Times of Trouble, and *The
Unanswered Prayers of Jesus* (based on John 17).

Yet, the Holy Spirit prompted me to write another book. I
reminded God that there were three unpublished manuscripts
languishing on a shelf in my office—as if He didn't know that. The
Spirit of the Lord replied, "I told Naaman to dip seven times. If I
tell you to write seven books, obey My voice."

"Yes, Lord," I replied and in eleven days wrote the first draft
of *Beyond Iraq: The Next Move*. When I had the published book in
hand, I called my daughter Rachel and asked if she would go to
New York City with me to promote the book. She accepted, and
the next morning we boarded our flight. As soon as we checked
in to our hotel, we each took a stack of books and began to make
the rounds of the various television studios.

Sometimes, it is necessary for us to take that first step. Naaman
had to step into the waters of Jordan as an act of obedience before
God obliterated his disease. Step up, step out, step in today; God
is ready and waiting for you to move in His direction.

FEBRUARY 2

Trust in Him at all times, you people;
Pour out your heart before Him;
God is a refuge for us. Selah
(PSALM 62:8 NKJV)

THE SUNDAY we were in New York City, Rachel and I attended Times Square Church where my dear friend David Wilkerson pastored. After the service, I asked him to pray with me about the launch of the book as we had had no success in securing television shows or interviews. Even after the prayer, a question remained: Should we stay in the city or pack our bags for home? We decided to stay one more night.

The next morning my phone rang. The caller identified herself as a producer for Neil Cavuto's show on the Fox News Network. Over the next several months, scheduled appearances on sixty-one programs—television and radio—came my way. By June, *Beyond Iraq* had sold 53,000 copies, and in July it hit the *New York Times* Bestseller list in the top ten.

It was the opening of a floodgate of books for me. Why? Because God reminded me that His ways are far above man's ways! That is as true for you today as it is for me.

FEBRUARY 3

For the law was given through Moses,
but grace and truth came through Jesus Christ.
(JOHN 1:17 NKJV)

JESUS WAS DIFFERENT from any man who has ever walked the earth. He was, if you will, a revolutionary. He presented a gospel of grace radically different from the legalism the children of Israel experienced under the Law of Moses given to him in the Sinai. Both the scribes and Pharisees had added onerous obligations and frustrating rules and regulations, while the Pharisees were obsessed with outward behavior, and an unerring attention to their views of right and wrong.

These scribes and Pharisees in attendance watched Jesus closely and were thinking of how they might trap Him. They walked headlong into a perfect opportunity for Jesus when He spotted a man with a withered hand in the crowd; they offered only condemnation.

Despite the palpable contempt emanating from His detractors, Jesus walked up to the man and spoke these words, "Arise and stand here." Jesus told the man to stretch out his hand, and it was fully restored!

The people nearby understood the Mosaic Law and its constraints: The Old Testament prophets reminded the Israelites of their sins; Christ offered righteousness through His blood, and grace as an alternative to the legalistic nature of the law that He had come to fulfill.

It is because of God's grace in the person of Jesus that you can have eternal life.

FEBRUARY 4

For by grace you have been saved through faith,
and that not of yourselves; it is the gift of God,
not of works, lest anyone should boast.
(Ephesians 2:8 nkjv)

GRACE HAS OFTEN been defined as "God's unearned favor."
It is as vital to His character as are mercy, compassion, and generosity. Each of us is unworthy of our Heavenly Father's abundance,
but in His unwavering love for us, He is eager to forgive our sins
and trespasses and regard us as favored sons and daughters.

Perhaps the greatest expression of grace can be found on Golgotha, that lonely and bloody hill on the outskirts of Jerusalem.
It is there that grace kissed the earth as God's plan of redemption
unfolded. It is the silver cord that links the past and present to
all eternity.

It is the bridge that spans the great divide between earth and
heaven. It is the covering that wraps the gift of justification—the
declaration that you and I have been pronounced "Not guilty,"
and are able to stand before God just as if you had never sinned.

FEBRUARY 5

May God give you more and more grace and peace
as you grow in your knowledge of God and Jesus our Lord.
(2 PETER 1:2 NLT)

GRACE IS GOD'S sudden, calming presence during the stormy seas of our lives. We hear his voice; we take the step. There are three things we must never forget about grace:

1. It is not based on works. We cannot *work* our way into heaven.
2. It is undeserved.
3. It is endless, eternal.

In this "pull yourself up by your own bootstraps" society in which we live, it is difficult to grasp the understanding that a life filled with God's grace is indicated by liberty, not by slavery; by gladness, not apathy; by happiness, not fear. Our responsibility is not canceled by grace—whether it is reading the Bible, praying, or serving others; it is simply the oil that keeps friction at bay and reminds us constantly of God's love for His children.

It is all too easy to allow our lives to become dominated by fear that we have failed God or fallen short of His expectations; to believe that we have broken covenant with the Father. It is Jesus who has fulfilled the law and offered us His abundant and all-sufficient grace that falls on us from above.

As beloved children of God, surrounded by His grace, you and I have favor with Him. The most joyful people in the world are those who surrender daily and allow God's grace to govern their lives!

FEBRUARY 6

Then God saw everything that He had made,
and indeed it was very good.
(GENESIS 1:31 NKJV)

FOR TOO LONG we have sought the pot of gold at the end
of the rainbow, the perfect marriage, or the world's concept of
beauty. We have failed to understand and recognize how precious
and delightful we are to the God of all Creation.

Author C. S. Lewis wrote:

We were made not primarily that we may love God (though
we were made for that too) but that God may love us, that we
may become objects in which the Divine love may rest "well
pleased".[8]

The God of the universe formed Adam and Eve for the specific
function of fellowship. He receives pleasure from you and me.
That is difficult to understand—especially for me, a man who, as
a child, suffered abuse and feelings of worthlessness at the hands
of my earthly father. To realize that God takes pleasure in me has
been overwhelming.

Ephesians 1:5 reveals a great truth:

God decided in advance to adopt us into his own family by bringing us to himself through Jesus Christ. This is what he wanted
to do, *and it gave him great pleasure* (NLT, emphasis mine).

Meditate on these verses and revel in the knowledge that you
are loved—completely an unconditionally—by a great and loving
Heavenly Father.

FEBRUARY 7

For the LORD takes pleasure in His people;
He will beautify the humble with salvation.
(PSALM 149:4 NKJV)

YOUR ARRIVAL on this planet gave God great pleasure. He was under no obligation to create mankind, but He chose to do so in order that He might have fellowship with us. You and I have a distinct purpose: living to give pleasure to God. Could anything be more satisfying and rewarding?

How can we possibly bring pleasure to God? Psalm 147:11 provides an answer: "The LORD takes pleasure in those who fear Him, in those who hope in His mercy." Fear of God means having a reverential awe of His power and glory.

God takes great delight in our worship, which is so much more than mere words or music; it is our very existence. It is everything we do and everything we say. It is reading the Word, praying, worshipping, sitting in silence before Him, or partaking of communion in remembrance of our Savior. Adam worshipped with his sacrifice in the Garden of Eden; David worshipped with his harp and lyre on the hillsides of ancient Israel; Jesus bowed His body in worship and surrender in the garden of Gethsemane.

Each was a very special moment dedicated to the One who takes pleasure in our sacrifice, our song, and our submission.

FEBRUARY 8

Teacher, this woman was caught
in adultery, in the very act.
Now Moses, in the law,
commanded us that such should be stoned.
But what do You say?
(JOHN 8:4-5 NKJV)

FORGIVENESS is literally a matter of life and death for the forgiven. We find that truth in the book of John chapter 8, and the story of the woman taken in adultery. Jesus had spent the night on the Mount of Olives and had risen early to make His way to the Temple to connect with people gathering there in the dawn's light.

Suddenly, He heard a commotion—men shouting, the sound punctuated by the screams of a woman being manhandled up the rocky stairs and into the courtyard. Tears stained her face, and sheer terror distorted her features as she realized she was about to die at the hands of the angry mob.

Reaching Jesus, they hurled the woman down at His feet. The pain of her skinned hands and knees was nothing compared to the sentence she knew would be passed on her. As she cowered on the ground, Jesus began to write in the dirt. Finally, the Righteous Judge spoke:

> "He who is without sin among you, let him throw a stone at her first." And again He stooped down and wrote on the ground. (vv. 7–8)

No one knows with certainty just what it was that Jesus wrote on the ground. Could it have been only one simple word: Forgiven? Is that the word you would want Him to write for you?

FEBRUARY 9

She said, "No one, Lord."
And Jesus said to her,
"Neither do I condemn you;
go and sin no more."
(JOHN 8:11 NKJV)

NOW, THE LAW OF MOSES required that in order for a sentence to be carried out, there had to be two witnesses to bring the charges. The men who had plotted against the woman in order to trap Jesus had likely not counted the entire cost of their actions. It would be their duty to pick up stones and take the life of the person on the ground before them.

Quietly, the men began to slink away into the shadows. As the noise abated, the woman realized that something was happening. Raising her head slightly, she saw that she had been left alone with only the One they called Jesus:

> When Jesus had raised Himself up and saw no one but the woman, He said to her, "Woman, where are those accusers of yours? Has no one condemned you?" (vv. 10–11)

While the Mosaic Law could offer only condemnation and retaliation, she needed forgiveness of sin and abundant grace. At no time did Jesus belittle this young woman for her immorality; not once did He shout angrily at her. He offered only hope and renewal; Jesus provided exactly what she was lacking—life and peace, grace and forgiveness. He still provides that for you and me.

FEBRUARY 10

Husbands, love your wives,
just as Christ also loved the church
and gave Himself for her.
(EPHESIANS 5:25 NKJV)

THE LITTLE OLD TESTAMENT BOOK of Hosea doesn't just tell us of God's love for Israel; the prophet lived it out in a way that would be difficult, if not impossible, for many to do. Hosea was instructed to find a wife, and not just any wife; he was to marry a prostitute, the basest of women. Hosea was to love with a God-like love a woman who perhaps would not reciprocate his affections. Jehovah wanted Hosea to love the wife he would choose with the same love that He had for Israel. This was to be about Hosea's unconditional love for her.

Ready to fulfill God's instruction, Hosea set out to find God's choice. He settled on a woman named Gomer—not a name we hear a lot today. Oddly, it means "complete." Much to Hosea's surprise and chagrin, he fell deeply in love with this woman. They married and had three children together. But one day the ordinariness of being a wife and mother got the better of Gomer and she abandoned her family only to return to the life of prostitution. Hosea took up the reins of parenthood and raised the children alone.

Hosea would be stunned by Jehovah's next directive to him. It would be a test of his obedience. Has God ever prompted you to do something that was a challenge to obey?

FEBRUARY 11

If they obey and serve him,
they will spend the rest of their days in prosperity
and their years in contentment.
(JOB 36:11 NIV)

GOD ALLOWED separation for a time, but one day He instructed Hosea to go out and search for Gomer, who by then had been abandoned by her lover and had sold herself into slavery. Hosea searched all the back alleys and houses of ill-repute until he found his beloved wife—even though still an adulteress. How was it possible for Hosea to love Gomer that much—to love her desperately? We find the answer in Hosea 3:1 NIV, "Love your wife ... as the LORD loves." The account of Hosea and Gomer is a remarkable illustration of God's great and gracious love; an outstanding biblical example of sacrificial love.

Hosea had finally found Gomer—dirty, unkempt, ill, and wretched, a mere shadow of her former self, yet he still loved her. He offered far more than she might have been worth on the auction block—fifteen shekels of silver and thirteen bushels of barley. (See Hosea 3:2.) I like to picture Hosea wrapping her in his cloak to protect her from prying eyes and then leading her home.

Was it easy for Hosea to offer that kind of forgiveness to the one who had so betrayed him? Marriages are destroyed by far less than Hosea endured. But God had a lesson for Israel, and for you and me: He loves with an everlasting love. It is a mirror of God's constant love that reaches far beyond our sinfulness all the way to the Cross, where Love personified hung between heaven and earth.

FEBRUARY 12

*For in Him we live and move
and have our being.*
(ACTS 17:28 NKJV)

WHAT JOY! You and I are wholly loved by Jehovah. We are rooted and grounded, anchored—planted deeply in the bedrock of His love for us. We draw sustenance from our Father and His Word. It nurtures us; it is the divine food and living water that causes us to thrive.

In West Texas during the winter months, tumbleweeds abound, piling up against buildings, homes, or anywhere there is a barrier to impede their progress. Why? Because at certain times of the year, the plant detaches from the root system, dries up, and is completely at the mercy of the wind. So, is this what we become when we choose to separate ourselves from Christ? An old country preacher once said, "When we become separated from the Vine, we can wind up in a real pickle."

You and I can find our resources from the all-encompassing love of God, drawing our strength from Him. We become like the house built on a rock (see Matthew 7:25), able to withstand the storms of life, knowing how great is our Father's love for us.

FEBRUARY 13

May you experience the love of Christ,
though it is too great to understand fully.
Then you will be made complete with all
the fullness of life and power that comes from God.
(EPHESIANS 3:19 NLT)

THE WORD USED in Ephesians 3:19 is the Greek word *agape*. It is defined as "selfless, sacrificial, unconditional love." Agape love always involves sacrifice; it is the kind of unconditional love that drove Jesus to the cross for our sins. Agape love requires a decision on the part of the one who loves; it is a choice. God's kind of love means that you choose to love your unlovable mate, your wayward child, your unkind co-worker, your estranged parent. This kind of love is a charitable love, given not because it is deserved, but because God so loved us.

God's agape love for His children is not something we can earn; it is fully undeserved, but freely given. In 1 John 3:1, we read, "Behold what manner of love the Father has bestowed on us, that we should be called children of God."

The reason God sent His Son to Earth can be summarized in six words from John 3:16: "For God so loved the world." Jesus came to earth because of love—the Father's love for His fallen creation. His love for all mankind directly affects you and me. We can now be restored to a loving relationship with Jehovah-Yasha—the Lord my Savior—because of Jesus' death on the cross. Now we are no longer enemies, we are beloved friends!

FEBRUARY 14

Peace I leave with you:
My [own] peace I now give...to you.
Not as the world gives do I give to you.
Do not let your hearts be troubled,
neither let them be afraid.
(JOHN 17:27 AMP)

PEACE! It is a missing commodity in many lives today. Outside pressures and problems beset us. Headlines scream of terrorist attacks, rampant disease, and wars or rumors of wars around the world. Peace is in short supply.

When we arise in the morning, we might find ourselves fearful, irritated, and discouraged. Yet this is not the life God wants for us. Second Timothy 1:7 promises, "For God has not given us a spirit of fear, but of power and of love and of a sound mind." (NKJV)

Jesus has promised us a peace that passes all understanding, one utterly unlike anything the world offers. It is a peace that surrounds and sustains us even when our human reasoning screams, "Oh no! We're all going to die!" Fear will destroy us. Choose God's love, and live your life without fear.

FEBRUARY 15

You will keep him in perfect peace,
***Whose** mind **is** stayed on You, Because he trusts in You.*
(ISAIAH 26:3 NKJV)

IT WAS GOD'S PEACE that I experienced following my encounter with Jesus at the age of eleven. As a child, I was fearful because of my father's actions. I was shy and withdrawn. Anxiety, fear, worry, and hurt dogged my every step. I was ensnared by a spirit of rejection. I was unwanted and unloved—and I knew it. And then Jesus came to my rescue. When I embraced Him and dedicated my life to His service, I learned that the Jesus of whom I was taught in Sunday school was as real as the air I breathed, as close as the scarred skin, the result of my father's beatings. Jesus had called me "son," said He loved me and had a wonderful plan for my life. I knew firsthand how the woman in the Bible with the issue of blood must have felt when He called her "daughter." (See Mark 5.) What indescribable peace and joy to know that I was the beloved son of God!

When faced with adversity, you and I can do one of two things—we can accept it as our lot in life, or overcome it through the peace of God and His Word. The moment in my life that I realized the Enemy was out to destroy me and my ministry, I did what God had told me to do: I got up and went—all the way to Israel. Then I began to worship God, to praise, to exalt my Creator. Praise dispelled the darkness and allowed the light of God's love to shine in and His peace to flood my being.

I have learned that peace is not the absence of conflict; it is having the courage to *face* the conflict. This is true in my life; it is true in yours. Peace and worry cannot occupy the same space. One forces the other to vacate.

FEBRUARY 16

"For with God nothing will be impossible."
(Luke 1:37 nkjv)

SHIRA JOY, our second daughter, whose name in Hebrew means "Song of Joy," was born prematurely and weighed only three and a half pounds at birth. The doctor who delivered her told us she might not survive. After Carolyn was settled in her hospital room, I stumbled down the hall to the tiny chapel and fell on my face before God to intercede for our baby girl. As I prayed, a verse from Psalm 118 flooded my spirit. The psalmist, in verse 17, declares: "I shall not die, but live, and declare the works of the Lord."

Our precious baby girl survived but was left with some physical frailties. When she started school, Shira had difficulty keeping up with the other students. Noticing her frustration, I devised a plan to help her. Each night before she dropped off to sleep, I sat by her bedside and quoted scripture to her, reminding her that she was strong in the Lord. She began to memorize those verses, and soon was attempting physical challenges she had been afraid to even try. Before long, the entire family began to notice a remarkable difference in Shira's attitude as well as in her physical strength and endurance. The result? Shira grew into a strong, intelligent, capable young woman.

Bring whatever plagues you—mental or physical—and give it to the Lord as you pray. Then, expect your miracle!

FEBRUARY 17

The just shall live by faith.
(GALATIANS 3:11B NKJV)

MY DEAR FRIEND and mentor, the late David Wilkerson, wrote:

> God has decreed that all his promises are conveyed through the prayer of faith. God knows all—he knows what we need before we ask—and he has promised to do the impossible. Yet it all comes to pass through prayer.[9]

I grew up watching the old television series *Mission Impossible*. The show's opening sequence was identified by the head of the team receiving instructions via a recorded message. It always ended with, "Your mission, should you decide to accept it..." and then concluded with the mysterious tape self-destructing.[10]

There are times when each of us feels as if our life is an impossible undertaking. When sickness, broken relationships, joblessness, divorce, or death of a mate or family member comes our way, we encounter unbearable issues. At these times, we are often faced with questions and no answers; seemingly impossible situations. Author Elisabeth Elliott wrote: "Faith does not eliminate questions. But faith knows where to take them."[11]

FEBRUARY 18

O God, You are my God; early will I seek You;
my soul thirsts for You; my flesh longs for You
in a dry and thirsty land where there is no water.
(PSALM 63:1 NKJV)

AS BELIEVERS we all seek something, but is that which we seek God's will? David, the shepherd king, pursued God from an early age, watching over his father's sheep and crafting songs about God's love and provision. In doing so, he found enormous favor with God.

In Acts 13:22 God said of him, "I have found David the son of Jesse, a man after My own heart, who will do all My will." David had a heart that followed after God; he chose that path, and even though he oft-times struggled with sin, David never ceased to pursue Jehovah.

The future king of Judah was an obedient child who performed the tasks set before him, whether tending sheep or catering lunch to his brothers. His job in the hills was isolated, tedious, and difficult, but David's body of work in the Psalms is indicative of a mind that remained focused on Jehovah.

David enjoyed great acclaim for a time after defeating Goliath, but jealousy entered the heart of King Saul and he began a campaign designed to destroy David. The young man was stalked like a criminal, yet he rejected opportunities to slay Saul.

David refused to repay evil with evil; he repaid Saul's evil with good. Consider David's actions when you are confronted by adversity.

And everyone who was in distress,
and everyone who was in debt,
and everyone who was bitter in soul,
gathered to him.
And he became commander over them.
And there were with him about
four hundred men.

(1 SAMUEL 22:2 ESV)

AFTER YEARS of evading Saul, the jealousy-crazed king, a betrayed and embattled, lonely and weary David took refuge in the cave of Adullum where he was joined by a ragtag band of the discontented and dispossessed. (See 1 Samuel 22.)

David refused to become a victim of "cave mentality." He was surrounded by the distressed, debtors, and the discontent. Did he fall into self-pity? Not David! He turned the pursuit into an opportunity to gather those men around him and teach them how to pursue Jehovah in order to become mighty men of valor. David found himself in a cave, but the cave was not in him! David was content to wait for Jehovah to elevate him to a place of honor.

Have you ever found yourself in a pit of despair, hoping against hope that someone would come by and point you in the right direction? Step out of the darkness and into the brilliant light of God's Word! Abandon the pity party for a praise party. Begin to pursue a deeper relationship with God instead of surrendering to the pressure of pursuit.

For You do not desire sacrifice,
or else I would give it;
You do not delight in burnt offering.
The sacrifices of God are a broken spirit,
a broken and a contrite heart—these,
O God, You will not despise.

(PSALM 51:16–17 NKJV)

DAVID'S PASSION in life was to have favor with God, to prepare a dwelling place for Jehovah in his heart and in Jerusalem. This seed was planted when he was a young shepherd boy; it was watered by Samuel's anointing; and matured by Saul's pursuit. David developed a heart attitude that moved God to action and produced favor with the King of Kings. David pursued God even when he was homeless and in great distress.

Our quest should constantly be to seek His presence. How *do* we develop a desire to pursue God? It is through communication with Him. As you and I spend time in His presence, we position ourselves to receive His favor and His grace.

David, in Psalm 27:4, wrote, "One thing I have desired of the LORD, that will I seek: that I may dwell in the house of the LORD all the days of my life, to behold the beauty of the LORD, and to inquire in His temple." (NKJV)

FEBRUARY 21

The sacrifices of God are a broken spirit,
a broken and a contrite heart—these,
O God, You will not despise.
(PSALM 51:16 NKJV)

DAVID LONGED FOR the presence of God to surround him, and he craved the blessing of Jehovah on his life; he coveted the relationship he knew would come with spending time in God's presence, and valued the closeness he found there.

It is so easy in this life to get sidetracked by the pursuit of things that we fail to stop and spend time in the presence of God. King Solomon, said to be the wisest of all men, was perhaps also the greatest seeker of pleasure. He said in Ecclesiastes 2:3–10:

> I searched in my heart how to gratify my flesh with wine, while guiding my heart with wisdom, and how to lay hold on folly, till I might see what was good for the sons of men to do under heaven all the days of their lives. (NKJV)

What a waste—a life given to the pursuit of pleasure rather than the pursuit of God! David had learned the value of beholding the beauty of the Lord, of seeking Him. He knew that God wanted a man whose heart was submitted to Him. And with his life dedicated to pursuing God, David finally understood exactly what God wanted.

You and I can rest assured that God rewards those who diligently seek Him.

FEBRUARY 22

Because he has set his love upon Me,
therefore I will deliver him; I will set him on high,
because he has known My name.
He shall call upon Me, and I will answer him;
I will be with him in trouble;
I will deliver him and honor him.
With long life I will satisfy him, and show him
My salvation.
(PSALM 91:14–16 NKJV)

PSALM 34 gives us the perfect outline for pursuing God. There are several steps that the psalmist suggests we follow. In verses 1–3 he tells us that we are to applaud the majesty of Jehovah-Bara—God our Creator:

> I will bless the LORD at all times; His praise shall continually be in my mouth. My soul shall make its boast in the LORD; the humble shall hear of it and be glad. Oh, magnify the LORD with me, and let us exalt His name together. (NKJV)

David's worship was a conscious choice of his will. He was determined to worship, to bless the Lord—not just when he felt like it or when circumstances dictated. Just as love is an act of the will, so is praise. David made a deliberate decision with no thought of what others might or might not do. Just as Joshua before him said, "But as for me and my house, we will serve the LORD," so David chose, as should we, to worship, and not just sometimes—"at all times!"

FEBRUARY 23

I will remember the deeds of the LORD;
yes, I will remember your miracles of long ago.
(Psalm 7:11 NIV)

DAVID'S PRAISE was vocal and braggadocios, for he was confident in the One of whom he boasted! His God was omnipotent, omnipresent, and omniscient! David, like the apostle Paul, could assert:

> And I am convinced that nothing can ever separate us from God's love. Neither death nor life, neither angels nor demons, neither our fears for today nor our worries about tomorrow— not even the powers of hell can separate us from God's love. (Romans 8:38 NLT)

In Psalm 34:3, David invited others to join him in praise and worship in pursuit of the presence of God. As the voices of His children rose together in adoration for our God and who He is, His heart must have swelled with joy.

I believe God can't take His eyes of love off those who spend time in the passionate pursuit of Him. Every prayer catches His ear; every sigh touches His heart; every song of praise pleases Him. The crowd may pass by on the other side; your friends may forget you in the hustle of everyday life, but God *never* forgets!

FEBRUARY 24

The LORD reigns, He is clothed with majesty;
the LORD is clothed, He has girded Himself with strength.
(PSALM 93:1–2 NKJV)

IS YOUR HEART a place devoted only to God, or has He been crowded out by other things of this world? Too often, we begin our walk with Him filled with good intentions; we petition God wholeheartedly to occupy first place in our lives, but eventually the world begins to intrude. If our priorities are in order, our motivation will be about pleasing God, putting Him first and foremost in our life, and then He will add His blessings.

In Isaiah 6, the prophet was face-down in the Temple and exhausted from interceding for the children of Israel. As Isaiah's supplications filled the edifice, Jehovah responded with a vision for the prophet's eyes only. Isaiah was transported from the earthly Temple into the very throne room of God. There, his attention was not captured by the beauty of his surroundings, but was centered on the One whose presence was overwhelming. God was reassuring Isaiah that He, Judah's Supreme King, was on the throne for all time and eternity. Isaiah described God's appearance:

> In the year that King Uzziah died, I saw the Lord, high and exalted, seated on a throne; and the train of his robe filled the temple. (Isaiah 6:1–4 NIV)

As did Isaiah, you and I sometimes stand in awe of earthly authority; how much more should we stand in awe of the God of the universe!

FEBRUARY 25

*Jesus Christ is the same
yesterday, today, and forever.*
(HEBREWS 13:8 NKJV)

DAILY EVENTS portend change, yet God never changes. He is faithful and immovable. Have you heard the old saying, "When the going gets tough; the tough get going"? The reality is: "When the going gets tough, go to Jesus!" It is a move you will never regret; it is there that you will find the help you need. It is in His presence that you will find peace and protection.

Hebrews 4:16 reminds us that as Believers, because of our relationship with Christ, we can "come boldly to the throne of grace, that we may obtain mercy and find grace to help in time of need." (NKJV)

There are those who place great value in who they know—especially if those they know are considered to be the movers and shakers of the world. Those "in the know" will quickly recite a litany of "who's who" and "what's what" in order to impress others. But you and I should always be intimately acquainted with the only One who really matters—God the Father.

FEBRUARY 26

Now this is the confidence that we have in Him,
that if we ask anything according to His will, He hears us.
And if we know that He hears us, whatever we ask,
we know that we have the petitions
that we have asked of Him.

(1 JOHN 5:14-15 NKJV)

WE ARE HEIRS of God and joint heirs with Jesus Christ, and are sealed by the Holy Spirit. (See Ephesians 1:13–14.)

Because we have a close, personal relationship with the triune Godhead, we have the privilege of entering the throne room anytime we choose. Revelation 5:8 says that the prayers of the saints are "golden bowls full of incense."

Unlike those who may spend great sums of money to hobnob with the "A-listers," our entrée is a gift freely given; yet it cost Jesus everything. God's grace has made it possible for us to have access to the throne and to Him who sits upon it.

As obedient children, we know that we can approach His throne with the assurance that if we ask according to His will, Jehovah will hear and respond. That, my friend, is the most important relationship you and I can have—one of fellowship and favor *with* God!

FEBRUARY 27

My son, do not forget my teaching,
but keep my commands in your heart,
for they will prolong your life many years
and bring you peace and prosperity.

(PROVERBS 3:1 NIV)

AS BELIEVERS, you and I can rest in the truth that God loves us. The proof of that love is present in the Person of Jesus Christ. Thomas à Kempis wrote:

> Without the Way, there is no going,
>
> Without the Truth, there is no knowing,
>
> Without the Life, there is no living.[12]

God is our Father, and we are His beloved children. Ephesians 1:3–6 tells us:

> Blessed be the God and Father of our Lord Jesus Christ, who has blessed us with every spiritual blessing in the heavenly places in Christ, just as He chose us in Him before the foundation of the world, that we should be holy and without blame before Him in love, having predestined us to adoption as sons by Jesus Christ to Himself, according to the good pleasure of His will, to the praise of the glory of His grace, by which He made us accepted in the Beloved. (NKJV)

Because of that acceptance, we have favor with God and are free to enjoy His peace, protection, blessings, deliverance, grace, forgiveness, and love.

FEBRUARY 28

Fear not [there is nothing to fear], for I am with you;
do not look around you in terror and be dismayed,
for I am your God. I will strengthen and harden you to difficulties,
yes, I will help you; yes, I will hold you up and retain you
with My [victorious] right hand of rightness and justice.
(ISAIAH 41:10 AMPLIFIED)

WHY WOULD GOD assure us that we are to "fear not" if we live in His favor? It is because our Father knows that we will be faced with challenges and difficulties that will try our faith, but not rob us of our favor with Him.

Even through the trials that will surely come our way, God adds benefits daily that help us turn those adversities into victories.

Can you hear the Father and His angels leaning over the balcony of heaven shouting encouragement, urging you onward, reminding you that it *is* Who you know and Whose you are? My friend, don't hesitate to pray for God's favor—for yourself, your spouse, your children and grandchildren.

Then, as Jesus did, walk before the Father in integrity, in obedience, and in faith. Paul reminds us in 2 Corinthians 6:2 (NIV) of God's Word to His children: "In the time of my favor I heard you, and in the day of salvation I helped you."

FEBRUARY 29

For he says, "In the time of my favor I heard you,
and in the day of salvation I helped you."
I tell you, now is the time of God's favor,
now is the day of salvation.
(2 CORINTHIANS 6:2 NIV)

ON FEBRUARY 29, you awaken with an additional day to spend in any way you wish. What will you do with those seconds, minutes, and hours?

Spend them wisely. If you do not know Christ as your Lord and Savior, the most important thing you can do with this extra time is to commit your life to Him. Today is the day of salvation!

What if all the precious things you cherish came about only once every four years? Seeing your children, grandchildren, or parents? Smelling the roses, listening to a songbird, enjoying the rain?

When Leap Year comes around, use the extra time to contemplate how privileged you are to have *each* day to enjoy the blessings God has given you. Write a note, call a friend, kiss your children or mate, and thank God for His love and grace that you enjoy daily.

MARCH

MARCH 1

Remember ye not the former things,
neither consider the things of old.
Behold, I will do a new thing;
now it shall spring forth; shall ye not know it?
I will even make a way in the wilderness,
and rivers in the desert.
(ISAIAH 43:18–19 KJV)

IN 2012, I related some of my personal experiences in a book titled *Living in the FOG (Favor of God)*. It detailed how we, as Believers, can have God's favor at work in our lives. More recently, the question in the forefront of my thoughts has been: What is favor *with* God, and does that differ from the favor *of* God? That may best be explained by an example from my own life:

It was also in 2012, that I traveled to Jerusalem to seek a location for the planned Friends of Zion (FOZ) Museum in the Holy City. Through the museum, the accounts of Christians who played a crucial role in helping to promote, defend, support, and establish the modern state of Israel would be told, as would the stories of those men and women who fulfilled their moral duty to rescue Jewish people from the Holocaust.

Today, the evidence of God's grace and favor—the Friends of Zion Heritage Center and Museum—sits in the heart of Jerusalem at 20 and 22 Yosef Rivlin Street, a prominent location overlooking Independence Park and within walking distance to the Old City.

MARCH 2

He opened the rock, and water gushed out;
It ran in the dry places like a river.
(PSALM 105:41 NKJV)

MY HEART IS OVERFLOWING with gratitude to God as the fulfillment of a dream—the Friends of Zion Heritage Center. When the contract for the purchase of the building that now houses FOZ—just a short distance from the Temple Mount—was signed, I was reminded once again that every promise from God is certain and sure, no matter how long we have to wait for it. Not only has this "great and effective door...opened to me" (1 Corinthians 16:9), God has made it possible for us to purchase an adjacent building to use as a welcome center and coffee shop.

Abraham waited for the promised birth of Isaac for some twenty-five years, but in God's perfect timing, the son of promise was born. Likewise, when I first met with Prime Minister Menachem Begin more than thirty years ago and we agreed to work together to build a bridge between Christians and Jews, part of that dream was to have a permanent presence in the Holy City. Now we are moving forward with this beautiful facility to minister to the Jewish people and to you.

Over the years the favor *of* God has opened doors for me; favor *with* God has given me the grace and strength to walk through those doors to experience the full blessings of God in my life and ministry.

Remember: Every promise from God is certain and sure. Expect Him to fulfill His promises to you.

MARCH 3

My Presence will go with you,
and I will give you rest.
(EXODUS 33:14 NKJV)

JUDGES 6 relates the story of Gideon, a man who was basically a wimp! When we first meet Gideon in this chapter, he is hiding in fear from the Midianites in order to thresh wheat for his family. And yet when the angel of the Lord approached Gideon, his greeting in verse 12 was, "The LORD is with you, you mighty man of valor!" Gideon questioned God's choice of a deliverer:

> O my Lord, how can I save Israel? Indeed my clan is the weakest in Manasseh, and I am the least in my father's house. (Judges 6:15 NKJV)

Even in his own eyes, Gideon was not a "mighty man of valor." He was pretty sure God could not use him for anything, much less something that required boldness! He viewed his life as one without the power and presence of Jehovah God. Apparently he had not heard the totality of what the angel had said in verse 14, "Go in this might of yours, and you shall save Israel from the hand of the Midianites. Have I not sent you?"

Gideon was slow to warm up to the idea of being a mighty man of valor, to be the one chosen of God to engage the entire Midianite army in battle. He could not comprehend that God wanted *him* for the task at hand, but he had two things in his favor: God's power and presence.

Believe in and accept God's power and presence, and you, too, can become a mighty man or woman of valor!

"Be strong and of good courage, do not fear
nor be afraid of them; for the LORD your God,
*He **is** the One who goes with you.*
He will not leave you nor forsake you."
(DEUTERONOMY 31:6 NKJV)

WHEN GOD CALLED him to lead the Israelites to freedom, Gideon finally chose to obey, only because of God's assurance that he was the man for the job. He quietly issued a call for the people to gather and was astounded when 32,000 showed up! But God had a different plan, one that would further challenge Gideon's dependence on Him. Imagine his dismay when God told Gideon the army was too large and instructed that it be pared to a mere 300 troops.

The men were divided into three companies of one hundred each and spread around the perimeter of the Midianite camp. At the appointed time, they were to blow their trumpets, smash their lamps, and yell, "The sword of the LORD and of Gideon." (Judges 7:20b NKJV)

When the cacophony of noise awoke the Midianites, they were seized with panic and fled before the army of the Lord. Gideon pursued the enemy until it was vanquished. He could have walked away from God's plan at any time. However, Gideon chose to believe that the power and presence of Jehovah was greater than the multitude of Midianite militia.

That is the same assurance you and I have in God's promises and His word today.

MARCH 5

The eternal God is your refuge,
and underneath are the everlasting arms.
(DEUTERONOMY 33:27A)

STORMS MOST ASSUREDLY do come to us even though we would much prefer that God hold them at bay. However, "Sometimes God calms the storm; sometimes He lets the storm rage and calms His child."[13]

When Moses and the children of Israel departed Egypt, the people had experienced firsthand Jehovah's defense during plague after plague. Finally, they were on their way to the Promised Land. After six days on their journey, the Israelites faced yet another problem—a sea of water before them and an army of Egyptians in their rearview mirror. They were figuratively between the devil and the deep blue sea!

In abject fear they chided Moses for not leaving them in Egypt as slaves. Moses assured them that God would protect His children:

Do not be afraid. Stand still, and see the salvation of the LORD, which He will accomplish for you today. For the Egyptians whom you see today, you shall see again no more forever. The LORD will fight for you, and you shall hold your peace." (Exodus 14:13–14 NKJV)

MARCH 6

*The name of the LORD **is** a strong tower;*
The righteous run to it and are safe.
(PROVERBS 18:10 NKJV)

FROM THE TIME God led His people out of bondage He had guided and protected them with a cloud by day and a pillar of fire by night. As the multiplied hundreds of thousands of men, women, and children bedded down for the night, the cloud shifted from before them for direction to behind them for protection. It became a veil of darkness to the Egyptians and a huge night-light for the Israelites.

As sleep settled in over the multitudes, a strong east wind began to blow so that when morning dawned a thoroughfare of dry ground could be seen stretching from one side of the Red Sea to the other. As the call went out to move forward between the towering walls of water, the Israelites moved toward safety from the Egyptian army.

Soon, Pharaoh's troops realized what was happening—their slaves were escaping—and set out in pursuit. But God had another surprise in store for the mighty army as the walls of water closed over them. Just as Moses had had favor with God which came from walking and communing with his heavenly Father, so did Jesus. That favor was sharpened by relationship and fellowship.

All we must do is dwell securely in the "secret place of the Most High" and protection and favor with God will be ours as His beloved children.

MARCH 7

In the day of my trouble I shall call upon You,
For You will answer me.
(PSALM 86:7 NASB)

IN 1 SAMUEL 4, we read the account of one of the children of Israel's blackest hours. The nation had been overpowered by their archenemy, the Philistines. The priests in Israel, including Eli, the High Priest and his son, Phineas, had been put to death and the Ark of the Covenant had been taken by the adversary. When the news of the death of her husband and father-in-law reached the wife of Phineas, she went into labor and bore a son whom she named Icabod, meaning "the glory of God has departed."

Two noteworthy incidents took place in the period that led to Israel's downfall and the capture of the Ark: disobedience and loss of leadership. First it was said of Eli's sons, Hophni and Phineas that they made the Lord's people transgress. (See 1 Samuel 2:24.) The two men entertained prostitutes inside the Temple and profited from those who offered sacrifices at Shiloh. The two also failed to keep the lamps in the Temple full of oil so that their flame would not be extinguished.

Even before judgment was pronounced on Eli and his sons, God was preparing a child, one born to preach a message of redemption to Jehovah's wandering children, just as He prepared the One who would be sent for the redemption of all mankind.

MARCH 8

If My people who are called by My name
will humble themselves, and pray and seek My face,
and turn from their wicked ways,
then I will hear from heaven,
and will forgive their sin and heal their land.
(2 CHRONICLES 7:14 NKJV)

IN THE FIRST CHAPTER of 1 Samuel, a heartbroken and barren woman made her way to the Temple to offer a sacrifice and pray. She pleaded with God to grant her request for a child. Hannah covenanted with Jehovah to rear her son only until he was old enough to be weaned from her breast and then to present the child to the Lord for service in the Temple. Out of Hannah's despair, God raised up a righteous prophet—Samuel—to serve Him.

Just as God had not abandoned Hannah, just as He heard her prayer, so He also heard the prayer of the righteous that remained in Israel. Jehovah had a faultless strategy and flawless timing with which to raise up His people and restore righteousness in the land.

God desires that His people experience His glory; He wants you and me to trust in Him, and Him alone.

MARCH 9

*Now it shall come to pass, if you diligently obey the voice
of the LORD your God, to observe carefully all His commandments
which I command you today, that the LORD your God
will set you high above all nations of the earth.
And all these blessings shall come upon you and overtake you,
because you obey the voice of the LORD your God:*
(DEUTERONOMY 28:1–2 NKJV)

IN 1983, MY BELOVED WIFE, Carolyn, and I already had three beautiful daughters. One day she came to me in tears and said, "God spoke to me and told me that we would have a son who would be a mighty man of God." I took her statement very seriously, as she rarely said that God spoke to her. Several months later, she informed me that she was pregnant. "This is a boy," she announced.

During the pregnancy Carolyn had two sonograms and both times was told she was carrying a girl. She replied very strongly, "I am not; it's a boy!" On July 17, 1984, Michael was born. As I cut the umbilical cord, I lifted him above his mother's womb and dedicated him to the Lord.

Later when I walked down to the nursery to look through the window at our son, I saw that the name on the bassinet read "Michael David Evans II." I had no middle name." I went back to Carolyn's room and asked, "Honey, how can he be Michael David the second? I'm not Michael David the first."

Her response was, "God told me to name him that. Now it's your problem to resolve." I did that by legally changing my own name to mirror that of my son. Isaiah 43:1b is a constant reminder of God's promise: "I have called you by name, you are mine." (ESV)

MARCH 10

Blessed shall be the fruit of your womb
and the fruit of your ground and the fruit of your cattle,
the increase of your herds and the young of your flock.
(DEUTERONOMY 28:4 ESV)

IN DEUTERONOMY 28, Moses stood before the children of Israel and delivered a message of blessing from Jehovah to the assembly. He knew above all that future stability rested solely in their union with Yahweh. Moses could not bless them; the priests of Levi could not bless them; the most devout among their number could not bless them; that fell to God alone. Only God could infuse His blessing with action. Only He could exalt; only He could redeem His people, Israel.

The psalmist wrote in chapter 84, verses 11–12: "For the LORD God is a sun and shield; the LORD will give grace and glory; no good thing will He withhold from those who walk uprightly. O LORD of hosts, blessed *is* the man who trusts in You! (NKJV)

The apostle Paul knew that God is able to do all things if we but believe in Him for the blessing. Too often we find it easier to fall prey to the Enemy rather than fully trusting in the blessings of a benevolent, loving, patient, and righteous heavenly Father.

MARCH 11

I will call upon the LORD, who is worthy to be praised;
So shall I be saved from my enemies.
(PSALM 18:3 NKJV)

IN THE SECOND CHAPTER of Joshua we are told of another divine intervention and miraculous deliverance; it is the story of Rahab, a prostitute. Days before the march around the walls began, Joshua had sent two men to assess the situation inside the city.

As they stealthily slipped from shadow to shadow down the streets, an alarm was sounded and the men were forced to run for their lives. They took refuge in the home of Rahab, a prostitute. Taking them up to the roof of the house, she hid them among stalks of flax that had been drying in the hot desert sun.

The lookouts posted on the wall could see the vast army of the Israelites as they approached the city, whose inner protective wall was said to have been approximately forty-five feet tall and twelve feet thick. The might of the advancing throng was well-known.

One family inside the walls waited, however—not for Jehovah's destruction, but for His deliverance. After having saved the Israelite spies from the king's men who sought them, Rahab was given instruction for the salvation of her family.

You and I can be assured that, "God shows no partiality."(Acts 10:34b NKJV)

MARCH 12

"Now therefore, I beg you, swear to me by the LORD,
since I have shown you kindness, that you also
will show kindness to my father's house,
and give me a true token..."
(JOSHUA 2:12 NKJV)

RAHAB, THE HARLOT, and her family were delivered because of her faith and obedience. That is supported by her response in Joshua, chapter 2. She, along with the other inhabitants, had heard of the exploits of the God of Israel. They responded with fear; she responded with faith. Then she took steps to exhibit her confidence in Jehovah; she followed their instructions and met the conditions outlined by the two Israelites:

> A red cord hung from her window;
>
> Her entire family was gathered as had been instructed;
>
> She kept silent, not divulging what she had learned
> from the two spies.

After seven days of marching in complete silence, the priests blew ram's horns and the "wall fell down flat." (See Joshua 6:20.) Rahab and her family were miraculously spared from the destruction of Jericho.

Quite simply, deliverance means turning from unrighteousness to righteousness—making a 180-degree turn from sin to salvation. It is then and only then that you and I will find our deliverance and blessings from God.

MARCH 13

... nevertheless I am not ashamed,
for I know whom I have believed and am persuaded
that He is able to keep what I have committed
to Him until that Day.
(2 TIMOTHY 1:12B NKJV)

ALL TOO OFTEN, people blame God when bad things happen. Blessings might bring the response of "See what I've done," or "I reached my goal." Bad things, on the other hand, are frequently referred to as an "act of God."

Faced with an excruciating situation, Elijah turned to the God of the possible, and the result was restoration. The prophet refused to focus on the dead child of the Shunammite woman (see Acts 4); he turned to the One who with His very breath created man.

Rest assured: When an impossible situation arises, God is there, to comfort you when you mourn, to console you when you are distressed, to transform the ashes of your life into a beautiful song, and replace your heavy spirit with praise. (See Isaiah 62: 2-3.)

MARCH 14

You have turned for me my mourning into dancing;
You have put off my sackcloth and clothed me with gladness,
to the end that my glory may sing praise to You and not be silent.
O LORD my God, I will give thanks to You forever.

(PSALM 30:11–12 NKJV)

IN LUKE 7:11–17, Jesus and His disciples were traveling across Judea when they arrived at the village of Nain. As they entered the town, a crowd of mourners was leaving the city to bury the only son of a widow. The mother was inconsolable, and those surrounding her wailed because of her sad predicament: "When the Lord saw her, He had compassion on her and said to her, "Do not weep." (v. 13)

As at other times in His ministry, the crowd must have rolled their eyes in disbelief. Who was this stranger that dared tell a grieving mother not to weep? But then the very air became charged with hope as He approached the funeral platform and called, "Young man, I say to you, arise." (v. 14)

The mourners, those who remained after the young man sat up and took a deep breath, were most certainly speechless! Or perhaps someone in the crowd began to sing the above verses from Psalm 30.

God still does the impossible: He redeems us and calls us to new life in Him. That, my friend, is the greatest example of favor *with* God!

MARCH 15

For I have chosen him, that he may command his children and his household after him to keep the way of the LORD by doing righteousness and justice, so that the LORD may bring to Abraham what he has promised him.

(GENESIS 18:19 ESV)

HAVE YOU EVER WONDERED why God chose Mary and Joseph to parent His only begotten Son? Jehovah recognized the attributes Mary and Joseph would bring to parenthood.

One small verse almost hidden in Luke 2:52 is an open window on the early life of Christ: "And Jesus increased in wisdom and stature, and in favor with God and men." At the age of twelve, Jesus had found favor with the teachers in the Temple. At the conclusion of the Passover feast, the family gathered its belongings and joined the crowd returning to Nazareth.

After having traveled for a full day, His parents suddenly realized Jesus was not in the company of His friends. Apparently He was a trustworthy boy whose absence had not raised an alarm. Perhaps it was time for dinner when He was missed, and a frantic Mary and Joseph began the journey back to Jerusalem. After three days of fear and anguish, of searching and longing, the parents found Jesus in the Temple court.

Perhaps these words of the father of the prodigal son are appropriate: "For this my son was dead, and is alive again; he was lost, and is found." (Luke 15:24 ESV)

MARCH 16

And He said to them [Mary and Joseph],
"Why did you seek Me? Did you not know that
I must be about My Father's business?"
But they did not understand the statement
which He spoke to them.
(LUKE 2:49-50 NKJV)

IT IS LIKELY THAT JESUS had stayed behind in Jerusalem, not to cause pain to His parents, but from an insatiable desire for knowledge, and maybe for another reason altogether. Perhaps the reason Jesus flourished under the tutelage of Joseph was that He also grew in stature. Rather than proclaim to Joseph and Mary the importance of His ministry, Jesus humbled himself and went home to Nazareth. There, He worked alongside Joseph in the carpenter shop, sat beside him in the synagogue, and learned obedience.

The favor of man is not easy to obtain or retain. People are capricious; one moment adoring, the next ready to destroy the beloved. And yet, finding favor with man is important even for Christians as we try to traverse the rocky path before us.

This doesn't mean that we are to compromise our beliefs in order to gain that favor; it simply means that we should constantly seek to know what Jesus would do and follow His lead.

MARCH 17

"Nor is there salvation in any other, for there is no other name under heaven given among men by which we must be saved."

(ACTS 4:12 NKJV)

ACTS CHAPTER 16, relates the story of the apostle Paul and his missionary traveling companion, Silas. The two men arrived in the city of Philippi and discovered that there was no synagogue for them to attend. Before long, Satan had recognized his adversaries and set a demon-possessed young slave, a fortune-teller for her owners, on the trail of God's agents. She shadowed Paul and his colleague through the streets of the city derisively shouting, "These men are the servants of the Most High God, who proclaim to us the way of salvation."

Finally Paul became so annoyed that he turned and said to the spirit, "In the name of Jesus Christ I command you to come out of her!" At that moment a demonic spirit left the sorceress and her owners realized they had lost their effortless income from her soothsaying.

Paul and Silas were then dragged into the town square, and hauled before the magistrates. They were stripped of their outer garments and beaten before being taken to jail. The two were forced into the inner prison and shackled, suffering from the battering they received. "But at midnight Paul and Silas were praying and singing hymns to God, and the prisoners were listening to them." (v. 25)

David asked the question in Psalm 139:7: "Where can I go from Your Spirit? Or where can I flee from Your presence?" (NKJV) The answer: No matter where you or I might find ourselves, God is there!

Suddenly there was a great earthquake,
so that the foundations of the prison were shaken;
and immediately all the doors were opened
and everyone's chains were loosed.

(ACTS 16:26 NKJV)

AS PAUL AND SILAS were singing praises to God, an earthquake rolled through the jail. It was massive enough to throw open the doors of the cells, and break open the stocks that bound the two prisoners, ripping their chains out of the stone walls.

The other prisoners had been listening to Paul and Silas serenade them with praise-and-worship music from hearts filled with gratitude to their Heavenly Father. Suddenly, they were free. The terrified Philippian jailer rushed into the confines of the jail and, seeing no one, drew his sword with every intention of falling on it. He knew that had one prisoner escaped, he would have been held accountable and summarily executed.

Perhaps by the light of the torch the jailer carried, Paul saw what the guard was about to do and shouted at him, "Do yourself no harm, for we are all here." (v. 28) The jailer threw himself down at the feet of Paul and Silas and cried out, "Sirs, what must I do to be saved?" (v. 30)

Without hesitation, Paul answered simply and unhesitatingly, "Believe on the Lord Jesus Christ, and you will be saved, you and your household." (v. 31)

Salvation is available for you today, if you only believe in the One, and only One, who saves.

MARCH 19

The righteous man walks in his integrity;
his children are blessed after him.
(PROVERBS 20:7 NKJV)

IF YOU HAVE STUDIED the Bible, you know the story of Jacob—how he and his mother, Rebekah, deceived his twin brother, Esau; how he was sent away to live with his mother's brother, Laban. Soon after his arrival in Haran, Jacob fell deeply in love with his cousin Rachel. After pledging to work seven years for her hand in marriage, Jacob was, in turn, deceived by Laban, who replaced Rachel at the marriage ceremony with her veiled older sister Leah.

After Jacob had spent a week's honeymoon with Leah, Laban allowed him to marry Rachel and then serve an additional seven-year commitment. In seven days, Jacob went from being an enthralled young man enraptured by his beautiful younger cousin to being an overworked husband of not one, but two wives.

Over the ensuing years, Jacob was blessed with eleven sons and one daughter. Laban, too, was blessed because of Jacob and became a very wealthy man. At any time, Jacob could have stealthily gathered Rachel and her two sons, abandoned the covenant he had made based on Laban's deception with Leah, and run from his father-in-law's demands. Instead, Jacob ultimately chose the way of integrity.

Walking in the way of integrity is not always easy, but essential for the Believer.

MARCH 20

The integrity of the upright will guide them.

PROVERBS 11:3 NKJV)

PROVERBS 20:7 SAYS, "The godly walk with integrity; blessed are their children who follow them." (NLT) Jacob had made his peace with Jehovah, learned a very valuable lesson about deception, and made the determination to live a righteous life. He served with honor for seventeen long years before asking Laban to release him and allow him to return home.

Knowing that he was reaping the benefits of a righteous relative without having to pay for Jehovah's favor:

> Laban said to him, "Please stay, if I have found favor in your eyes, for I have learned by experience that the LORD has blessed me for your sake." Then he said, "Name me your wages, and I will give it." (Genesis 30:27–28 NKJV)

As a result of the agreement, Jacob became a very wealthy man despite Laban's repeated attempts to cheat him. (See Genesis 30:9–43.) Because of his uprightness, Jacob left the home of his father-in-law, not only with his wives and children but with God-given favor with man.

That is precisely how God works—what Satan means for evil, God turns to good. (See Genesis 50:20.) Never underestimate God's abundant blessings and man's favor bestowed on those who continue to live a righteousness life.

MARCH 21

But you [David] shall not cut off your kindness
from my house forever, no, not when the LORD has cut off
every one of the enemies of David from the face of the earth."
So Jonathan made a covenant with the house of David,
saying, "Let the LORD require it at the hand of David's enemies.

(1 SAMUEL 20:15–16)

INTENDING TO HONOR his promise to his friend, David called in one of his servants and asked, "Is there still anyone who is left of the house of Saul, that I may show him kindness for Jonathan's sake?" (See 2 Samuel 9:1.)

David dispatched servants to track down any remaining relatives of King Saul. Finally, Jonathan's crippled son (see 2 Samuel 4:4), Mephibosheth, was located—living in abject poverty in a far-flung and desolate corner of the land. He was summoned to the palace, where he shuffled in to the presence of the most powerful man in the kingdom—King David. I believe he anticipated the worst.

Imagine Mephibosheth's shock when he heard, "Fear not: for I will surely shew thee kindness for Jonathan thy father's sake, and will restore thee all the land of Saul thy father; and thou shalt eat bread at my table continually." (2 Samuel 9:7 KJV.)

What an act of generosity! David had extended grace to the son of his friend. Given his living conditions and his handicap, it may well have been years since this outcast had heard words of compassion and consideration.

Kindness can sometimes be misconstrued as weakness rather than a profound act of love. Be kind, anyway.

MARCH 22

Saul's son Jonathan had a son named Mephibosheth, who was
crippled as a child. He was five years old when the report came from
Jezreel that Saul and Jonathan had been killed in battle. When the
child's nurse heard the news, she picked him up and fled. But as she
hurried away, she dropped him, and he became crippled.
(2 SAMUEL 4:4 NLT)

DAVID SENT HIS SERVANTS to bring Jonathan's son to
the palace, and upon his arrival, Mephibosheth might have asked,
"Why me, Lord?" Have you ever asked that question when faced
with life's challenges; when the loss of a job, fear, abandonment,
illness, divorce, or a shattered relationship plagues you? God's
response to us is, "I want to open the windows of heaven and pour
you out a blessing that you cannot contain. (See Malachi 3:10.)

Mephibosheth's life had likely been one of hurtful words hurled
at breakneck speed, penetrating his very soul. Now, in one act
of kindness, this long-forgotten grandson of a king had been restored. He was granted a perpetual pension; he became family,
wrapped in the serenity of knowing someone cared. He moved
from the desert to the dining room of the king, from a dwelling
of desolation to a palace of plenty, from having been abandoned
to being adopted.

Imagine Mephibosheth's wonder as David presented him with
new clothes to replace the homespun garments of yesterday, and
with jewels befitting the favored son of a king! He was offered a
seat at the king's table.

You and I have that same privilege—a seat at the table of the
King of Kings!

MARCH 23

Anyone with ears to hear should listen and understand!
(MATTHEW 11:15 NLT)

THE CACOPHONY of the twenty-first century often forces those around us to listen very closely. It is essential that we develop the gift of careful listening—not only with our ears but with our eyes and with our hearts. Really hearing what another person has to say is not sitting on the edge of your seat eagerly planning your rebuttal, or interrupting to interject your own comment. It is waiting, sometimes while silence fills the room, giving your friend, spouse, or acquaintance time to marshal their thoughts and find the words to express their hurt, fear, anger, or hopelessness.

That was what Jesus did so lovingly during His encounter with the woman at the well in John 4. He knew her past, present, and future, yet He gave her space to bare her soul to the only One who could change her life.

You and I have the answer to the question, "Lord, to whom shall we go?" (See John 6:68.) You and I have been entrusted with the Good News—the gospel of Jesus Christ. In order to help others find that answer, we must cultivate the art of listening. Luke 8:18 (NIV) reads, "Therefore consider carefully how you listen."

Matthew 11:15 (NLT) admonishes: "Anyone with ears to hear should listen and understand!" Cultivate listening, and as you do, God will bless you with favor among those who desperately need to hear about the gift of salvation and the One who brought it to us.

Let the words of my mouth and the meditation of my heart
Be acceptable in Your sight, O LORD,
my strength and my Redeemer.
(PSALM 19:14 NKJV)

LISTENING has another dimension, according to James 1:19, "So then, my beloved brethren, let every man be swift to hear, slow to speak, slow to wrath." (NKJV)

In my book about relationships, *Turning Your Pain Into Gain*, I wrote:

> Closely monitor and guard what you think in your heart. The Scriptures reveal a vital, but often ignored, principle concerning the importance of our thoughts. Proverbs 23:7 declares that "As a man thinks in his heart, so is he." Thoughts shape the soul. We can use words and actions to conceal, counterfeit, and misrepresent, but all the time our thoughts are determining who we are and what we will become. We are either being built up or destroyed from within.

All too often, disagreements can be averted if we simply heed the words of Solomon who admonished, "A soft answer turns away wrath, but a harsh word stirs up anger." (Proverbs 15:1 NKJV)

Silence the nagging, negative voice within and replace it with a strengthening, encouraging winner's voice. Fill your heart and mind with the life-giving words of your heavenly Father.

MARCH 25

After two days he will revive us; on the third day
he will restore us, that we may live in his presence.
(HOSEA 6:2 NIV)

ENCOURAGEMENT: What precisely does that mean? The Merriam-Webster definition is, "to inspire with courage, spirit, or hope, hearten." We are human beings; God created us with the need for encouragement. Do you know someone who is pessimistic; who always seems to have a dark cloud hovering over them—who sees the glass as half empty, never half full? An unknown author said, "A pessimist's blood type is always B-negative."[14]

On the night before His crucifixion, Jesus invited the disciples to go with Him to the garden of Gethsemane to watch and pray. Totally God and totally man, Jesus needed the closeness and encouragement of His friends as He prepared to face His darkest hour. We, too, are surrounded by people who often need encouragement in their darkest hour.

It is important that we are ready and willing to offer reassurance when needed. When the world is screaming, "Oh, God, we're all going to die!" the Believer should be ready to share the hope that is within him. To do that, we must be sincerely concerned about others rather than plotting how those relationships can best benefit us. There is power in encouragement; it has the capacity to change lives when coupled with the message of hope and salvation.

MARCH 26

Bear one another's burdens,
and so fulfill the law of Christ.
(GALATIANS 6:2 NKJV)

IN HIS LETTER to the Romans, Paul admonishes us:

> Be kindly affectionate to one another with brotherly love, in honor giving preference to one another; not lagging in diligence, fervent in spirit, serving the Lord; rejoicing in hope, patient in tribulation, continuing steadfastly in prayer; distributing to the needs of the saints, given to hospitality.... Rejoice with those who rejoice, and weep with those who weep. (Romans 12:10–13, 15 NKJV)

Encouragement and optimism go a long way. Remember Jehovah's words to Joshua: "Have I not commanded you? Be strong and courageous. Do not be afraid; do not be discouraged, for the LORD your God will be with you wherever you go." (Joshua 1:9 NIV)

With God's blessings comes responsibility. Ask the Lord today what you can do to encourage someone—make a phone call, send an email, write a letter, invite a friend to lunch or for coffee. Oh, and don't forget to say, "I love you," to the people who mean the most to you, and treat all men with courtesy and appreciation.

MARCH 27

Do to others as you would like them to do to you.
(LUKE 6:31 NLT)

IN LUKE 6:35–36, Jesus expounded on His commandment to "do unto others" by saying:

> But love your enemies, do good, and lend, hoping for nothing in return; and your reward will be great, and you will be sons of the Most High. For He is kind to the unthankful and evil. Therefore be merciful, just as your Father also is merciful. (NIV)

How long has it been since you've invited a struggling office-mate for lunch or a round of golf? Or called a grieving friend to meet for coffee? Or slipped an envelope with a few dollars to someone you know who is struggling financially? Listen to the voice of the Holy Spirit and be ready to reach out as He directs. Consider: What would you want someone to do for you if you were in their situation? Or what has someone done for you in similar circumstances? Respond with agape love, mercy, and charity.

The greatest act of kindness you and I could ever do is to tell someone the story of God's love from John 3:16, "For God so loved the world that He gave His only begotten Son, that whoever believes in Him should not perish but have everlasting life."

MARCH 28

Owe no one anything except to love one another,
for he who loves another has fulfilled the law.
(ROMANS 13:8 NKJV)

TWO OF THE GREATEST NEEDS of mankind are forgiveness and love. God offered both through His Son, Jesus Christ. It has been said that a human being has a God-shaped hole in his heart, a place that can only be filled with a relationship with his Creator. Or, as Ecclesiastes 3:11 reminds us, "He has planted eternity in the human heart." (NLT)

It is a spiritual law written on a tablet of flesh. When we reach out in love with the message of the gospel, those with whom we come in contact can be pointed to the answer of how to fill that void. Can you hear Paul shout in 2 Corinthians 9:15: "Thanks be to God for His indescribable gift!"

You and I are not asked to "leap tall buildings in a single bound," or perform mighty miracles; we are simply called upon to reflect the love of God in our daily words and deeds. What is most important is the motivation with which we serve.

To love as Christ loves will bring favor with man—for that kind of love is not an emotion; it is a living reality.

MARCH 29

... and the peace of God, which surpasses all understanding,
will guard your hearts and minds through Christ Jesus.
(PHILIPPIANS 4:7 NKJV)

ONE OF THE THINGS I remember clearly about my encounter with Jesus at age eleven was the enormous sense of peace that flooded my spirit—the calmness He brought into my room that dark and dismal night of my near-death. It not only changed my life, it changed my countenance from one of cringing in fear to one of peace despite the circumstances.

Just as people are drawn to an attitude of joy, so they are drawn to a sense of peacefulness, like iron filings attracted to a magnet. In this turmoil-filled world, people crave the calm. Your countenance can produce a favor-filled life.

This is the kind of peace for which the world is looking and to which we will be drawn. Peace is yet another characteristic that should be exhibited by those to whom God has granted favor with man.

As a Believer, when we encounter people it is with a sense of the "peace which surpasses all understanding" (see Philippians 4:7) promised to us by our Lord.

*Blessed **be** the God and Father of our Lord Jesus Christ,
who has blessed us with every spiritual blessing
in the heavenly **places** in Christ...*
(EPHESIANS 1:3 NKJV)

GOD BESTOWS His blessings not just for us to prosper and reap the benefits, but so that we, too, may encourage, uplift, and introduce those in need to the Prince of Peace.

When the peace of God rests upon us, others see His handprint upon our lives, and our influence is felt in their lives. The words of Jesus lodged in the heart of the woman at the well and brought about a transformation.

First Samuel 3:19–20 gives us a picture of how the life of the prophet influenced those around him:

> So Samuel grew, and the LORD was with him and let none of his words fall to the ground. And all Israel from Dan to Beersheba knew that Samuel had been established as a prophet of the LORD. (NKJV)

The picture presented in this verse is one of water—historically a precious commodity in the Middle East—being poured out on rocky ground, or an arrow missing its target. Our ultimate aim should be that of living our lives in such a way that our words do not miss their mark.

MARCH 31

We also pray that you will be strengthened
with all his glorious power so you will have
all the endurance and patience you need.
(COLOSSIANS 1:11 NLT)

RICHARD WURMBRAND was a minister of the gospel who had been imprisoned for his stand against Communism. He suffered through years of incarceration and the most brutal of tortures before $7,000 was paid for his ransom. His family immigrated to the United States, where he and his wife, Sabina, devoted the remainder of their lives to aiding Christians persecuted for their beliefs.

Before his death in 2001, I was honored to share a meal with this devout man. As we talked that evening, I posed some questions about his experiences in the Communist prison camps. "Did you ever feel as if you were losing your mind?" I asked. He said that he had, but gave those feelings to Christ so he did not have to worry. He also said that when he suffered heartache for his family, he gave those emotions to Christ as well. Finally, he gave his body to Christ and no longer needed to worry about his health. Armed with complete death to his flesh, the Communist prison guards and interrogators no longer had the power to hurt him.

"The guard came for me one day and said, 'You must realize that I can break your arms, your legs, anything I want,'" Wurmbrand told me. "I answered him, 'If you break my arm, I will say, *God loves you* and if you break my leg I will say, *I love you too.*'" He said the stoic guard began to cry at his answer, and Wurmbrand was then able to lead him to Christ.

APRIL

APRIL 1

By your patience possess your souls.
(LUKE 21:19 NKJV)

PATIENCE IN TRIBULATION, the love of Christ, and the joy of the Lord that passes understanding enabled imprisoned Pastor Richard Wurmbrand to gain favor with a prison guard who was, perhaps unknowingly, searching for truth.

Longsuffering, or patience, are words too often unused in this modern, "get it now" generation. The inability to secure every want can produce irritation, bias, hypersensitivity, and rage—unfortunately, sometimes even among Believers. It is listed among the fruits of the Spirit in Galatians 5:22-23:

> But the fruit of the Spirit is love, joy, peace, longsuffering, kindness, goodness, faithfulness, gentleness, self-control. Against such there is no law. (NKJV)

Patience is one virtue that genuinely requires God's divine help. I'm reminded of the old cartoon character crying in desperation, "Give me patience, and give it to me NOW!" These characteristics of the Spirit-filled Believer adorn the child of God.

Does your "tree" bear the fruit of the Spirit?

For ye have need of patience, that,
after ye have done the will of God,
ye might receive the promise.
(HEBREWS 10:36 KJV)

ABRAHAM IS A CLASSIC example of longsuffering, of waiting on Jehovah to do the impossible in providing a son in his old age. God promised a Deliverer after Adam and Eve sinned and were driven from the Garden of Eden. Thousands of years passed before that promise was fulfilled in the person of Jesus Christ.

In some verses, the Greek word for longsuffering is *makrothumos*—*makro* meaning "long" and *thumos*, which translates as "temper—or long-tempered." Have you heard the expressions "short-tempered," "temperamental," "irritable"? Folks with those maladies tend to lose their cool more often than those who possess longsuffering. No one wants to spend time in the presence of someone who reaches the pinnacle of success by tearing others down. Those building blocks resemble the house built on sand that Jesus described in Matthew 7. It is a precarious structure, one where few want to spend time.

Are you that person who is impatient with clerks, other drivers, your children or spouse? Are you prone to overreact to the simplest situations? Are you tolerated instead of welcomed wholeheartedly? If the answer is yes to any one of these, check your patience quotient. In Romans 12:14, Paul tells us that we should bless rather than curse those who try our patience.

APRIL 3

With all lowliness and meekness,
with longsuffering, forbearing one another in love;
(Ephesians 4:2 kjv)

FIRST CORINTHIANS 13 has come to often be known as the "love chapter." It describes the characteristics of a man or woman who puts others first, and in so doing finds favor with man. It is not a calculated behavior, but is instead a love relationship. The apostle wrote in verses 4–7:

> Love suffers long and is kind; love does not envy; love does not parade itself, is not puffed up; does not behave rudely, does not seek its own, is not provoked, thinks no evil; does not rejoice in iniquity, but rejoices in the truth; bears all things, believes all things, hopes all things, endures all things. (nkjv)

What motivates you—love, longsuffering, kindness? Or are you driven by anger, scorn, bias, condescension? Are you more concerned with winning than you are with losing the respect of a colleague, or the opportunity to share the gospel with an unbeliever?

How even the most casual of relationships would change if our lives were governed by longsuffering!

APRIL 4

I have come to call not those
who think they are righteous,
but those who know they are sinners
and need to repent.

(LUKE 5:32 NLT)

ARE YOU A FRIEND of sinners? What? Of course not! Aren't Believers supposed to draw their robes around themselves to keep from being tainted by the world? No, Jesus knew how to interact with people where they lived, in the streets and alleys of Palestine. The men He called to be His disciples—His daily companions—were a broad cross-section. He chose fishermen, a warrior plotting to overthrow the Romans, a tax collector and a doctor. What a mismatched group, and yet He gave them favor with man, the ability to learn from Him and then spread the gospel after His ascension.

In Acts chapter 8, Luke tells the story of an obedient deacon, Philip, who did not fail when prompted by the Holy Spirit to take a detour through the desert. Off in the distance, Philip spots a chariot whose driver is engaged in the dangerous pastime of reading and driving. Philip's order from God was to ride along with the distracted Ethiopian eunuch. Immediately, the deacon recognizes the passage from which the man is reading; it is the book of Isaiah, chapter 53.

What joy for the eunuch—first to learn about the life, death, and resurrection of Jesus Christ, and then to learn that he was eligible to partake of the salvation offered!

Just as Philip listened to the still, small voice that sent him on a missionary journey, so must we.

APRIL 5

I myself am satisfied about you, my brothers,
that you yourselves are full of goodness,
filled with all knowledge and able to instruct one another.
(Romans 15:14 esv)

PROVERBS 31 gives the reader a picture of the worthy wife—a woman of goodness:

> Who can find a virtuous wife? For her worth is far above rubies. The heart of her husband safely trusts her; So he will have no lack of gain. She does him good and not evil all the days of her life. (Proverbs 31: 10-11 NKJV)

When my tour in the army ended, I felt what I can only describe as a force compelling me to Texas to prepare myself for the ministry. I was certain it was what God intended me to pursue. I was accepted into a Bible college near Fort Worth, Texas, and for the next two years spent most nights in the dormitory prayer room seeking to hear God's voice again.

It was there that I met my own Proverbs 31 woman and very special friend, Carolyn. She had the sweetest smile I'd ever seen. We became best friends and enjoyed that friendship for some time while she dated others. When Carolyn took me home to meet her parents, I was captivated. It was my first real glimpse of a Christian home filled with love and grace. I was also soon deeply in love with this special treasure whose name means "joy," and that is just what she brought into my life.

Do you thank God daily for your mate?

APRIL 6

Who can find a virtuous wife?
For her worth is far above rubies.
The heart of her husband safely trusts her;
So he will have no lack of gain.
She does him good and not evil
all the days of her life.
(PROVERBS 31: 10-11 NKJV)

THERE IS SUCH EVIL in the world today, it sounds a bit trite to talk of goodness. Yet the scripture in Proverbs, when given thoughtful consideration, is overpowering. It is descriptive of a person of great integrity and moral consistency. It is a picture of a woman who has the best interests of her husband, her family, and her household at heart. Her character is not based on what others think of her, but on what God sees on the inside. American writer and poet Dorothy Parker wrote satirically, "Beauty is only skin deep, but ugly goes clean to the bone."[15]

A godly woman's inner kindness and goodness comes not from her outer wrappings, but from her relationship with her heavenly Father. His love and grace and goodness shine through her as a beacon from a lighthouse guides ships to safe harbor. Peace emanates from within because she knows that she can trust in Jehovah.

APRIL 7

Every good gift and every perfect gift is from above,
and comes down from the Father of lights,
with whom there is no variation or shadow of turning.
(JAMES 1:17 NKJV)

THE GREEK WORD for "goodness," *agathosunes* is a deep-seated goodness that brings with it an inherent honesty and decency toward others. Sometimes that characteristic requires us to speak the truth in love. (See Ephesians 4:15.) As Christians, we are called upon to challenge someone about a sin that could destroy them. It's not a pleasant thing to do, but can be done with kindness and goodness.

Goodness can take the form of giving to aid the needy, helping a sick friend or neighbor, perhaps working at the food pantry, or the most difficult, to "pray for those who spitefully use you." (Luke 6:28) Just as we can't force a lemon tree to produce cherries, so we cannot force the development of the fruit of goodness in our own lives.

It is this fruit of the Spirit that endears us to others; they are drawn to goodness and kindness. It is a characteristic that will win us favor with man. It is often a simple expression of thanks that can leave the most lasting impression.

APRIL 8

"Salt is good for seasoning. But if it loses its flavor,
how do you make it salty again?
(Luke 14: 34 nlt)

AS BELIEVERS, we are called to be salt and light in a dark and decaying world. What does that mean? In the days before iceboxes and, later, refrigerators, salt was used as a preservative. Today we know it more as a flavor enhancer to improve the taste of food. If you are not aware of the value of salt, try eliminating it from your diet for a few days. The lack of the proper amount of sodium can soon result in an increased heart rate and dizziness.

By sharing the gospel of Jesus Christ with others, you and I become the salt that helps safeguard the world from evil, and through the help of the Holy Spirit, influence it for good. When conflict arises, we are to be mediators; when sorrow overwhelms, we are to be consolers. Where hatred abounds, we are to spread God's love.

One tiny light can dispel the darkness and bring a sense of security in the depths of darkness. Our testimony is severely hindered if we lack goodness. Goodness and kindness is the light of God that illuminates your life. People will then be drawn to you and to the God whom you serve.

APRIL 9

But the fruit of the Spirit is love, joy, peace,
longsuffering, kindness, goodness, faithfulness...
(GALATIANS 5:22 NKJV)

IN MY BOOK *Finding Favor With God*, I wrote of my trip to Beirut in 1983 and the opportunity to witness to American troops stationed near the airport in that city. The night before the attack on the US Marine barracks, my traveling companions and I spent the night on the beachhead beside the Mediterranean Sea. We were awakened the following morning by the sounds of the terrible blast and found out later that the explosions claimed the lives of 299 American and French soldiers.

My dear friend Dr. James Dobson wrote of that tragic day in his book *Children at Risk*:

> Marine Corps Commandant Paul X Kelly, visited some of the wounded survivors then in a Frankfurt, Germany, hospital. Among them was Corporal Jeffrey Lee Nashton, severely wounded in the incident....
>
> As Kelly neared him, Nashton, struggling to move and racked with pain, motioned for a piece of paper and a pen. He wrote a brief note and passed it back to the Commandant. On the slip of paper were but two words—"Semper Fi" the Latin motto of the Marines meaning "forever faithful."[16]

As Believers, we are called to be faithful—trustworthy—in all that has been committed to us, whether it is our relationship with Christ, our marriage, our children, or our employer. With the practice of faithfulness one must employ dependability, commitment, diligence, persistence, loyalty, and devotion.

But Ruth said, "Do not urge me to leave you
or to return from following you.
For where you go I will go,
and where you lodge I will lodge.
Your people shall be my people,
and your God my God.
(RUTH 1:16 ESV)

ONE WOMAN who exemplifies faithfulness is a Bible character of whom I've written several times—Ruth. This sweet-natured lady was not afraid of hard work. Ruth would rise from her bed while it was yet night to provide food for Naomi, her mother-in-law. Her faithfulness won favor with Boaz, led to their marriage, and gained Ruth a place in the genealogy of Jesus.

This was not a coincidence, but the powerful hand of a loving Jehovah-Jireh who made provision for Ruth. It was the Holy Spirit who whispered into the ear of Boaz, *"See that lovely and diligent young woman. Provide for her."* His obedience had kingdom consequences for the young woman who was just going about the business of taking care of a loved one.

Like Ruth, you and I are not meant to see the completed tapestry, but we can make a difference by being faithful to the work of God. What does that involve?

For a loving father, it is rising and going to work to provide for his household.

For a gentle mother, it is wiping runny noses and mopping up spilled milk.

For a pastor, it is serving his congregation in untold ways.

APRIL 11

"The Spirit of the Lord GOD is upon Me,
Because the LORD has anointed Me
To preach good tidings to the poor;
He has sent Me to heal the brokenhearted...

(ISAIAH 61:1A NKJV)

GOD PROVIDES RELIEF for His children in many ways:

For the brokenhearted, it is hope. For the suffering, it is reaching out to the One who can bind your wounds. For the sinner, it is grace.

Every act of faithfulness, no matter how small, has the capacity to touch the life of someone. Faithfulness equals obedience; simply doing what God's Word and the Holy Spirit instruct us to do. It is, again, listening to that still, small voice and responding. It is time spent in the Word and in prayer. The old adage "Practice makes perfect" is valid. The more time we spend with Jesus, the better able we are to recognize His voice and respond to Him.

Just as faithfulness is a characteristic of a Believer, so are there other attributes to being faithful. Proverbs 27:6 (NLT) says, "Wounds from a sincere friend are better than many kisses from an enemy." Friends sometimes choose to speak the truth lovingly for our greater good. The colleague who can honestly and kindly offer constructive criticism is a friend, indeed.

God has called us to faithfulness and that includes trusting Him absolutely, even when conditions might indicate otherwise.

APRIL 12

Don't think you are better than you really are.
Be honest in your evaluation of yourselves,
measuring yourselves by the faith God has given us.
(ROMANS 12:3 NLT)

TOO OFTEN we associate meekness with weakness, and nothing could be further from the truth. While our Lord was said to be gentle, He exhibited great strength. Meekness is not weakness, but rather great power under control. There is a blessing to be found in the life of the truly meek Believer, for "The meek will he guide in judgment: and the meek will he teach his way." (Psalm 25:9 KJV)

Pastor and author John Piper wrote, "Meekness is the power to absorb adversity and criticism without lashing back."[17] The world deals daily with those who lash out when mistreated in some way. The truly meek Christian has the ability not to retaliate when wronged.

Meekness and a self-inflated ego cannot march hand-in-hand to the beat of God's drum. In the Sermon on the Mount, Jesus preceded "blessed are the meek" with "blessed are the poor in spirit," which indicates that we are to approach God with a deep sense of contrition and a tender conscience. (See 2 Corinthians 7:10.) This produces Believers who are saved, sanctified, and freed from the penalty of sin.

It is in this state that God can develop the true sense of meekness in His child.

But the meek shall inherit the earth,
And shall delight themselves in the abundance of peace.
(PSALM 37:11 NKJV)

MEEKNESS IS a God-infused quality that will produce favor with man, but a characteristic that is often sadly lacking. In today's ego-fed, self-centered world, meekness is a trait too often lost. Temperamental people rage uncontrollably while others are trodden underfoot. Few people want to be known as being meek. Meekness is a lost art among some Believers. This, despite the fact that in Matthew 11:29 (KJV), Jesus said, "Take my yoke upon you, and learn of me; for I am meek and lowly in heart..."

When was the last time you told someone you were meek, even though it is a fruit of the Spirit? Meekness should be a much-sought-after character trait, especially if we want to be true disciples of Christ. Why is it not?

Check a Thesaurus for synonyms of *meek*. You will find words such as *timid, submissive, docile, weak, cowed, fearful, compliant,* and *mild*. These are not descriptive words with which today's macho society wants to be linked. But can you honestly say that these words are descriptive of Jesus, or Moses, or Elijah, or Paul—each of whom was unafraid to confront evil? It is this God-imparted meekness that is a characteristic to be sought after and much valued.

APRIL 14

A man without self-control is like a city
broken into and left without walls.
(Proverbs 25:28 esv)

AT HIS BIRTH, Samson was dedicated to Jehovah and as a young man took his Nazarite vows seriously; one of which was that a razor would not touch his head.

The power of God rested upon him to the point that at one time he killed a young lion with nothing but his bare hands. (See Judges 14:5–6.) Samson was no ordinary man, but despite his great strength, he failed to exhibit self-control.

In Judges 16, we read the story of Samson's downfall at the hands of Delilah. She agreed to entice him to reveal the secret of his strength, and seems to have been induced by monetary gain.

Delilah preened and pouted her way into Samson's confidence, until he divulged that he had taken a vow never to cut his hair.

Luring Samson into taking a nap on her lap, Delilah called for her Philistine collaborators, who rushed in, bound the strongman, blinded him, and shaved off his locks. Weakened, Samson was taken captive. But something began to happen inside him even as his hair grew. Samson asked to be placed between the two main supports of the Dagan's Temple. As he began to press against the two columns, they shifted and the temple collapsed. Three thousand people were killed.

Samson is one of countless individuals then and now who have suffered because of the lack of self-control. Just as this lack ultimately cost Samson his life, so it can happen to the most unassuming man or woman.

APRIL 15

Good understanding produces favor,
But the way of the treacherous is hard.
(PROVERBS 13:15 NASB)

ONLY TWICE in the Bible do we read of individuals gaining favor with both God and man—Samuel and Jesus. Yet the Bible is replete with instances of men—and women—finding God-given favor with man: Ruth, Hannah, Nehemiah, Esther, Daniel, Joseph, David, and many others.

Teacher and writer Dr. Lance Wallnau has said, "Favor is like being dipped in the honey of God's presence so that all the blessings He has sent start to stick to you!"[18]

When God pours out His favor, it clings like honey and sweetens our actions and interactions with others. It enhances our ability to wait patiently, to smile when things go wrong, and to remain calm when everyone around you is in panic mode. Others are drawn to you because God has given you favor with man.

APRIL 16

But the fruit of the Spirit is love, joy, peace,
longsuffering, kindness, goodness, faithfulness, gentleness,
self-control. Against such there is no law.
(GALATIANS 5:22-23 NKJV)

IF WE ALLOW GOD to develop the fruit of the Spirit in our lives, we will attract favor with man. That is because what they see will be such a vast departure from the norm. If you sow kindness, you will reap kindness. The same is true of love, joy, peace, and the other godly attributes Jehovah is developing in your life. *God-given* success and favor is dependent on Him alone—not on your talents, skills, good looks, witty tongue, or weighty wallet.

A discerning heart begets favor with man. People around us desire to be understood, to be validated by someone. The question becomes, "Do you really see me as a person? Am I just a fixture in your daily routine—a waitress, a clerk, a secretary, a co-worker—or does what I do and say mean something to you? If I were lying wounded on the side of the road, would you stop and offer assistance, or would you simply pass by on the other side?" (See Luke 10:25–37.)

Take time to reach out to someone today in love—with a smile, a sincere compliment, or a few extra dollars as a gratuity for a job well done. When God blesses you with favor with man, use the opportunity to make a significant difference in that person's life.

APRIL 17

*"But seek first the kingdom of God and His righteousness,
and all these things shall be added to you."*
(MATTHEW 6:33 NKJV)

FAVOR IS UNMERITED GRACE; regard shown by another, especially a superior; an act of kindness; a token of love; effort on one's behalf. Because you are His child, God, in an act of kindness and as a token of His love, extends unmerited grace, and works tirelessly on your behalf. Not only does He bestow favor on you, He blesses you with favor and affirmation from those around you.

Living in God's favor will help you reach the place in life where you will turn the head of God, touch the heart of God, and move the hand of God; a place where you can gain affirmation from the Father and His Word rather than from those around you. You can learn to refuse to allow people and problems to define you.

The Bible says we were created in God's image. What does that mean? God speaks, hears, sees, and feels; He has personality. He created you for friendship, relationship. Knowing that, how can you live in His image? First, surrender your life to Him.

*But those who wait on the LORD Shall renew **their** strength;*
They shall mount up with wings like eagles,
They shall run and not be weary, They shall walk and not faint.
(ISAIAH 40:31 NKJV)

THE FAVOR OF GOD means that He will give you the resources you need to develop His image in your life, to do what He has called you to do—whether it is to be a missionary or an evangelist, a pastor or teacher, a salesman or chief executive officer, a doctor or a stay-at-home parent ministering to your family. Whatever your need, He will supply it, and all because of His favor.

There is a wonderful Greek word, *sphragizō,* which means "sealed, hidden, or kept in secret." God has placed within you hidden treasures, and has sealed you "for the day of redemption." (Ephesians 4:30, NKJV) These "hidden treasures" are four absolute principles that have been the cornerstone of my ministry for decades. They are: obedience, humility, forgiveness, and generosity.

Psalm 27:14 admonishes us: "Wait on the LORD; Be of good courage, And He shall strengthen your heart; Wait, I say, on the LORD!" (NKJV)

Wait for Him to speak His Word into your life, and don't allow anyone to talk you out of your blessing, your favor.

APRIL 19

The Lord said to Samuel,
"How long will you grieve over Saul, since
I have rejected him from being king over Israel?
Fill your horn with oil, and go"
(1 SAMUEL 16:1 ESV)

DAVID WAS Jesse's youngest son, the runt of the litter, the sheepherder. Samuel was the high priest in Jesse's day. It was a rare thing for the man who held that position to be out in the field searching for a candidate to be king. Saul had been king, and yet God had rejected him because of disobedience. Now He had sent Samuel on a mission to find the man who would be king.

God sent Samuel to the house of Jesse to anoint one of his sons. As each stood before the high priest, God rejected him for the role of king. He did not reject the man; each was loved by God. It was simply that Jesse's older sons were not God's choice to rule over Israel.

Disappointed, Samuel turned to Jesse and asked, "Is that all?" Jesse thought of his youngest son who was out in the field keeping the sheep. Jesse was certain he had known which of his sons would be best to be king, but there was no one left—except the youngster.

These words of Timothy are as timeless today as they were for him, and certainly for David:

Let no one despise your youth, but be an example to the believers in word, in conduct, in love, in spirit, in faith, in purity. (1 Timothy 4:12 NKJV)

APRIL 20

O God, You have taught me from my youth;
*And to this **day** I declare Your wondrous works.*
(PSALM 71:17 NKJV)

JESSE, WHEN ASKED by Samuel to produce his youngest son, David, must have thought: *He's just a kid. He lives alone—well, just him and the sheep. How in the world could he be God's choice? Surely Samuel doesn't intend to anoint David! He's just my harp-playing, psalm-singing son, occupied with sticks and stones and a slingshot.* But Jesse obeyed Samuel and sent someone to fetch David. Samuel was determined that the gathering would not eat until the last son had stood before him and God.

David was stunned when someone showed up to take his place in the sheepfold. The moment Samuel saw this handsome young man with the beautiful eyes, he said, "He is the one! I will anoint him." God had chosen David. He had equipped His choice in the Judean foothills; He had seen the heart of a servant in David; and He had watched as the young shepherd developed the skills to protect his father's flocks that had been entrusted to him.

When David was called home from his duties as a shepherd, he was obedient to his father, to his king, and to his God. Obedience placed David in the forefront of Jewish history, and on the same throne that would one day be occupied by the Messiah.

When God calls, do you answer promptly? Or, do you spend valuable time trying to escape doing God's will?

APRIL 21

So Samuel took the horn of oil and anointed him in the presence
of his brothers, and from that day on the Spirit of the LORD came
powerfully upon David. Samuel then went to Ramah.

(1 SAMUEL 16:13 NIV)

DAVID SPENT YEARS of his life running from King Saul, the
man he was anointed to replace. He was rejected by the one whom
he served as armor bearer. He was ridiculed by his brothers, and
in Psalm 27, David says, "[Even] my father and mother forsake
me." (Psalm 27:10 NIV)

David was humble. He willingly served his father as a shepherd. It had not been his lot to be the eldest with the greatest
inheritance, or the warrior who served under the king. It was
his place to submit to the will of his father, Jesse; to follow his instructions, even if it meant being the laughingstock of his siblings.

After David's anointing by Samuel there came a morning when
Jesse ordered his youngest son to take supplies to his brothers
who were battling the Philistines in the Valley of Elah. Upon
his arrival, David saw the imposing figure of Goliath and heard
the challenge being hurled across the valley to his quaking audience on the other side. David was incensed that no one in Saul's
army had the courage to face the giant. They all stood on the
sidelines, intimidated by the ferocity of the huge warrior. David
then marched before Saul and offered to fight the giant.

You and I can be bold while fighting the giants in our lives
when we know that God stands with us.

Moreover David said, "The LORD, who delivered me
from the paw of the lion and from the paw of the bear,
He will deliver me from the hand of this Philistine."
And Saul said to David, "Go, and the LORD be with you!"
(1 SAMUEL 17:37 NKJV)

DAVID BOLDLY assured Saul that God would stand with the man who dared go forth in His name; that God would give him the victory. In humility, David offered himself to be an instrument in his Father's hands.

King Saul offered David his personal armor for the battle with Goliath. After having tried it on, the young man realized that the covering made by mortal hands was insufficient for the task. David had learned that lesson as a shepherd. God had miraculously provided protection for him and for his flock. When he faced the giant, he was prepared. Crossing the brook, David selected five smooth stones and dropped them into his shepherd's bag. As he approached the valley of Elah, Goliath began to fling insults at David: "Am I a dog, that you come at me with sticks?" (1 Samuel 17:43 NIV)

In the end, Goliath lay dead on the ground—a stone embedded deeply in his forehead. David used the giant's own weapon to lop off his head and give Israel the victory—not by might, nor by power, but by the Spirit of the Lord of hosts.[19] David had long known that with God on his side, he was in the majority.

From David you can learn that operating in humility does not mean you renounce your own self-esteem. While some would view a humble man or woman as a submissive doormat, the truth is that through God the individual possesses power—controlled by strength and self-control.

APRIL 23

The king was overcome with emotion.
He went up to the room over the gateway and burst into tears.
And as he went, he cried, "O my son Absalom!
My son, my son Absalom! If only I had died instead of you!
O Absalom, my son, my son."

(1 SAMUEL 18:33 NLT)

THE SHEPHERD BOY who became king also was forgiving. When his brothers belittled him in front of the entire army of Israel, David forgave them. When his father didn't think him worthy to be introduced to Samuel, David forgave him. David spent his early years running and hiding from Saul. He was stalked like a criminal because of Saul's jealousy. In the end, David forgave the man that God had chosen to be the first king over Israel.

David later forgave his son Absalom, who tried to wrest the kingdom of Judah from his father. Filled with pride and egotism, blinded by his own good looks, proud of his long, luxuriant mane of hair, besotted with power, this son of David and Maacah decided he was above the law.

In 2 Samuel 19, David was finally able to return to Jerusalem after Absalom's death. Betrayed by his son, banished from the throne, expelled from Jerusalem, still David mourned the betrayal of his son. When his troops gathered in battle against the army of Absalom, David waited anxiously for word of his son's safety. A messenger arrived from the battlefront to inform the exiled king that Absalom had been hacked to death by his pursuers. David was heartbroken and fell into deep and bitter mourning, but in his grief, he forgave.

God calls on us to forgive those who have wrongfully used us.

APRIL 24

To obey is better than sacrifice...
(1 Samuel 15:22 niv)

OBEDIENCE can be defined as "the act or practice of obeying; dutiful or submissive compliance." One of the earliest examples of obedience to God's command was that of Abel, the second son of Adam and Eve. Cain, the older brother, was a tiller of the ground—a farmer; Abel was a keeper of sheep.

Both worshipped God and brought their sacrifices to present to Him, but each brought a different offering. Abel brought a lamb as ordained by Jehovah, and Genesis 4:3 says that "Cain brought the fruit of the ground." Cain's wrathful response when God rejected his offering was indicative of his character:

> But he did not accept Cain and his gift. This made Cain very angry, and he looked dejected. "Why are you so angry?" the Lord asked Cain. "Why do you look so dejected?" (Genesis 4:5-6 NLT)

The two brothers walked away from the altar with totally different countenances. Abel's was radiant with God's love and approval; Cain's was dark, his face infused with rage, his heart filled with jealousy. He was so resentful that he lured Abel into the field and murdered him.

When you live in obedience, you are doing well, for it is the highest level of devotion you can present to God. You live under the blessings of God when you overcome sin through obedience.

APRIL 25

"By faith Noah...in reverence prepared an ark for the salvation of his household."
(HEBREWS 11:7 NASB)

SIMPLY STATED, Noah believed God, and it was "counted it to him for righteousness." (Genesis 15:6 KJV) Because of his faith and obedience, Noah received a rich reward from the Creator. He enjoyed intimacy with Jehovah. They walked and talked together. God laid out the plan for the ark and Noah followed it to the letter. Faith coupled with obedience cannot be undervalued. These are qualities that must infuse the spiritual life of a Christian.

Noah and his sons labored one hundred years building the ark. He obeyed when God warned him of "things not yet seen." God hadn't given Noah a preview of what "rain" was. Noah hadn't seen anything that remotely resembled a flood.

When God gave the blueprint for the ark, it contained only one door set in the structure. It hung open, ready and waiting to receive any who desired to enter in and be saved from God's judgment. The ark was another foreshadow of Jesus.

God's covenant was a covenant of hope. It was a covenant of love. When He remembered the estate of sinful Man, God sent His Son to redeem Mankind.

APRIL 26

I am the door. If anyone enters by Me, he will be saved,
and will go in and out and find pasture.
(JOHN 10:9 NKJV)

THE DOOR TO THE ARK was left open until the last possible moment. After 120 years of Noah's preaching, of warning people of the judgment of God upon all the earth, of obedience in building the boat, not one person chose to board the ark! Then Noah and his family members entered in...and GOD SHUT THE DOOR!

Why was it important that God shut the door? It was symbolic of His authority, and of man's accountability. As the sound of the door being slammed shut echoed throughout the surrounding area, the first drops of rain began to fall. Now it was too late—no one else was allowed to enter the ark. Judgment was falling from the cloud-laden sky. Lightning flashed and thunder rattled as torrents of water poured down. From beneath the earth, underground waters erupted and raced across the landscape. The ark began to rock and then rise to float on the flood waters. Noah and his sons had faithfully and obediently executed God's command to construct the ark and to enter it, and thus they were spared.

From a rainbow in the clouds to a covenant written in blood, God's love for His Creation is evident. When we accept His invitation, He showers us with blessings.

Then [God] said, "Take now your son,
your only son Isaac,
whom you love, and go to the land of Moriah,
and offer him there as a burnt offering
on one of the mountains of which I shall tell you."
(GENESIS 22:2 NKJV)

WE OFTEN UNDERESTIMATE just how outrageous this must have seemed to Abraham. It is impossible to believe that he didn't question God's directive, but the narrative doesn't suggest that. You and I have read the rest of the story and know the outcome—Abraham knew only what God had demanded of him. Verse 3 says:

> So Abraham rose early in the morning and saddled his donkey, and took two of his young men with him, and Isaac his son; and he split the wood for the burnt offering, and arose and went to the place of which God had told him.(Genesis 22:3 NKJV)

Abraham immediately made arrangements for the three-day journey to Mount Moriah. When they arrived, Abraham asked the servants to wait while, "the lad and I will go yonder and worship." Then he added what might well be a hint regarding the strength of his faith, "and we will come back to you." Genesis 22:5 NKJV)

Each time you and I accept God's will above our own, we prepare an altar of sacrifice. Each time you and I surrender to His will, we exercise our faith. Is it easy? No, but it is essential.

APRIL 28

Abraham said, "God will provide for
Himself the lamb for the burnt offering, my son."
So the two of them walked on together.
(Genesis 22:8 nasb)

WHEN THEY ARRIVED at their destination, Abraham and his son, Isaac, set about gathering stones to erect an altar to Jehovah. Abraham laid the wood and knelt before his son. He gently bound Isaac's hands and feet, and laid him on the altar.

Consider: Just as Abraham raises the knife to plunge it into Isaac's heart, an angel of the Lord cries, "Do not lay your hand on the lad, or do anything to him; for now I know that you fear God, since you have not withheld your son, your only son, from Me." (Genesis 22:12 nkjv)

Obedience and faith go hand in hand. One cannot exist without the other. Strong faith touches the heart of God, moves the hand of God, and releases the blessings of God. This extraordinary happening took place about two thousand years before Christ was born, and yet it's a perfect picture of God's offering of a substitute for our sins. He would offer up His own son for our redemption.

God was faithful to Abraham; He committed to be faithful to His children today. He lovingly gives us just what we need—not what we want. In so doing, He fulfills His will in our lives—to redeem us unto Himself.

APRIL 29

Now when Daniel knew that the writing was signed,
he went home. And in his upper room,
with his windows open toward Jerusalem,
he knelt down on his knees three times that day,
and prayed and gave thanks before his God,
as was his custom since early days.

(DANIEL 6:10 NKJV)

ONE THING IS CLEAR throughout Daniel chapter 6: God rules! That should give us great hope as we see Daniel standing exactly where God had placed him. We will also see that God is unfettered by Man's pronouncements. Darius, the new leader, was a man of power and organization; he had great skill and intellect. He held no loyalty to the God of Israel, and yet as we read in the sixth chapter, we find that he has knowledge of Daniel's Jehovah.

It might surprise you to know that Daniel was no longer a young man. It is likely that he was nearing ninety years of age. Through all the intervening years, he had remained faithful to God and was a committed witness. Far from being "on the shelf," his experience was utilized both by Darius and by God. Daniel was a man of wisdom, a dynamic leader, and a capable administrator. Added to those traits was a close relationship with Jehovah, which afforded him the ability to interpret dreams and visions.

Daniel was God's man for that time and in that place. Are you in a situation today where you might be God's man—or woman—for this time and place? He will give you exactly what you need, to do what He has called you to do.

APRIL 30

So at last the king gave orders for Daniel to be arrested
and thrown into the den of lions. The king said to him,
"May your God, whom you serve so faithfully, rescue you."
(DANIEL 6:16 NLT)

OFTEN WHEN BELIEVERS are set in a place of authority, it is not long before the Enemy raises his ugly head, determined to target the faithful—and Daniel was no exception. His accusers could find no fault in Daniel; in fact his life was exemplary. They had to resort to subterfuge in order to trap their rival.

Daniel was known abroad for his custom of praying three times each day with his face toward Jerusalem. The pattern had been established. So his adversaries took advantage of Daniel's routine and approached King Darius, presenting a document demanding that prayer be offered only to the king.

Obviously, the king succumbed to temptation and signed the decree. When Daniel heard of the new edict that had been imposed, he went home, opened his window toward Jerusalem, and again prayed to Jehovah as was his custom. Fear did not reign in Daniel's life.

God had been faithful to him and to his friends. Either he would be preserved in the lion's den, or he would not, but he was committed to doing the will of God.

Have you refused to compromise your beliefs to gain the favor of the world?

MAY

MAY 1

Daniel, servant of the living God,
has your God, whom you serve continually,
been able to rescue you from the lions?
(DANIEL 6:20B NKJV)

THE MEN WHO had lain in wait for Daniel to make a misstep were overjoyed. When he was seen kneeling in his window with his face toward the Holy City, they gleefully ran to the king, and shouted, "That Hebrew, that foreigner, refused to obey the king! Now you *must* obey the decree you have signed and toss him to the lions."

Daniel was summarily arrested and led to the lair where the lions were penned. He was cast inside and a stone was brought to close the mouth of the den. King Darius then sealed it with his signet ring and returned to the palace. So distressed was the king that he spent the night silently fasting. The Bible says, "And he could not sleep." The king arose early in the morning and hurried to the lions' den to check on Daniel.

There is no record that Daniel offered any argument to the king before he was led away to the lion's den; only after God had vindicated him and saved him from the jaws of the ferocious beasts did he offer any defense. He knew he had been innocent of anything other than obedience to Jehovah, the Lord who was present in the lion's den. Daniel had sought the kingdom of God and had been rewarded.

Obedience brings favor for the children of the King of Kings.

MAY 2

*"We came to your brother Esau, and he also is coming
to meet you, and four hundred men are with him."
So Jacob was greatly afraid and distressed.*
(GENESIS 32:6-7 NKJV)

AFTER WRESTING HIS BROTHER Esau's birthright
through trickery, Jacob fled Canaan to the land of his mother's
brother, Laban where he stayed for years. The day finally came
when Jacob was so homesick he gathered his family and flocks,
folded his tents, and set out for Canaan. As they neared the land,
Jacob sent word to his brother, Esau, only to learn that Esau and
400 men were coming to meet him. Four hundred men—were they
coming to greet him, or to kill him and his family?

Alone in the camp Jacob fell on his face before Jehovah God
in prayer and supplication. He was attacked, and wrestled for
his very life. As the light of dawn peeked over the horizon, Jacob
realized that this was no ordinary foe; he was wrestling with an
angel of God. In order to end the combat, his opponent touched
Jacob's hip socket and dislocated it. After his wrestling match,
Jacob could no longer fight Esau in hand-to-hand combat. He was
now totally dependent on God's mercy and Esau's grace.

Forgiving someone who has wronged you is one of the great
challenges of life. Those who refuse to forgive overflow with rage
and resentment. Unforgiveness defiles the one who bears it. Conversely, forgiveness secures the exceedingly abundant blessings
of God.

MAY 3

Then He said: "A certain man had two sons.
And the younger of them said to his father,
'Father, give me the portion of goods that falls to me.'
So he divided to them his livelihood.
(LUKE 15:11-12, NKJV)

IN LUKE CHAPTER 15, Jesus first told the story of the lost sheep, then the lost coin. He ended the chapter with the parable of the prodigal, or lost, son. We read of a father who had two sons. The eldest was the practical plodder. He lived at home, labored in his father's business, and was sensible and levelheaded.

The younger son was the playboy. He sought pleasure, wanted to party, and catered to his friends. He shirked his responsibilities for a life of self-indulgence. He longed to answer to no one. He saw gaining his inheritance as the answer to all his problems in life.

Heartlessly, the younger son went to his father and said, (paraphrased), "Old man, it's taking you way too long to die. I don't want to wait until you're in the ground to get my inheritance. Give it to me now."

The father's heartbreak was palpable, but he was determined to be guided by love and to offer grace to his wayward child. Prayer became his constant companion as his son turned and walked away.

If you have a child who has turned his/her back on God, seek Him continually. It is the only answer.

MAY 4

But the father said to his servants,
'Bring quickly the best robe, and put it on him,
and put a ring on his hand, and shoes on his feet.
(LUKE 15:22 ESV)

THE HEARTBROKEN FATHER of the prodigal had agreed to the request of his beloved son, and presented an inheritance to his demanding child. All went well initially, but when he had spent his last farthing, he found himself without a friend in the world. There was nothing left for the son to do but wrap himself in sackcloth and find a way to survive.

Bowed and broken, he made his way to the local pig merchant and pled for any menial task available. He was soon put to work doing the most demeaning task any Jew could have been given—working in a pigsty among the unclean animals! He was so hungry that even the husks he fed the swine looked like a feast, but no one offered him a bite.

Meanwhile, the desolate father was watching for and praying for his wayward child, while the faithful elder son was taking care of the family business. As the father paced the rooftop each evening, he longingly peered down the road hoping to catch a glimpse of his beloved younger son.

The love of the father was exceeded only by the love of his Heavenly Father. The lure of the far country swiftly loses its attraction, but God's love never fails. He stands with arms open wide to receive the repentant child. Turn toward Him today and receive His grace and abundant favor.

MAY 5

I will arise and go to my father, and will say to him,
"Father, I have sinned against heaven and before you...
(LUKE 15:17 NKJV)

THE VIGILANT FATHER, keeping watch for his long-lost son
from the rooftop, spotted someone in the distance. The father
dropped everything, and tucking up his robe to make running
easier, he raced down the road toward the lonely traveler.

The returning son barely stammered out his prepared speech,
when the overjoyed father grabbed his son and embraced him
tightly. He called for the servants to bring the best robe—likely
one of the father's own. It was a sign of worth and of devotion. The
servants were told to bring a ring for the long-lost son's hand—a
sign of influence and relationship. Sandals were placed on his feet
as an indication that he was not to be a servant but a son, and a
fatted calf was ordered.

The son thought lost to the father had been found. The son
would long remember the grace—the unmerited favor and mercy—
shown to him by his loving father.

Jesus used the parable of the prodigal son to impress on His
followers the depth of His heavenly Father's love and the all-
encompassing power of forgiveness.

If you have, as an act of the will, separated from your heavenly
Father, turn and run toward home. Avail yourself of the salvation
that is so freely offered.

MAY 6

So he [Paul], trembling and astonished, said,
"Lord, what do You want me to do?"
*Then the Lord **said** to him, "Arise and go into the city,*
and you will be told what you must do."
(ACTS 9:6 NKJV)

IN THE 1980S I was invited to the White House during Ronald Reagan's presidency. In the Oval Office, we walked to his magnificent desk that had been a gift to President Rutherford B. Hayes from Queen Victoria. Sitting on the desk was a plaque that read: "A man can become too big in his own eyes to be used by God, but never too small."

The apostle Paul proved the truth of that statement. He was one who, after his conversion, humbly served Christ. Before he met the Savior on the road to Damascus, his character was quite different. American football player and legendary sportscaster Pat Summerall said of humility:

> When someone saves your life and gives you life, there's gratitude, humility; there's a time you've been so blessed you realize you've been given another chance at life that maybe you did or didn't deserve.[20]

Does gratitude and humility rule your life as it did Paul's? His humility was based on obedience to Christ. Walk humbly before Him today.

MAY 7

I became a servant of this gospel by the gift of God's grace
given me through the working of his power.
Although I am less than the least of all the Lord's people,
this grace was given me: to preach to the Gentiles
the boundless riches of Christ.
(EPHESIANS 3:7-8 NIV)

IN PAUL'S DAY, before his conversion and name change, there was no word for "humility" in either the language of the Greeks or the Romans. The very idea of a man being humble was totally alien.

Paul's fervent opposition reached the stage of fanaticism as he traveled from city to city hunting for followers of Christ. Paul went to the high priest:

> He requested letters addressed to the synagogues in Damascus, asking for their cooperation in the arrest of any followers of the Way he found there. He wanted to bring them—both men and women—back to Jerusalem in chains. (Acts 9:2 NLT)

Before his conversion, Paul was radical, fanatical, egotistical, determined, uncompromising, and arrogant; the exact opposite of the humble servant of Christ. What a change was wrought in Saul as he stalked toward Damascus on his mission! He lost Self in the light of God's love and grace, and his entire character was transformed.

You and I are changed when we meet Jesus and allow Him to control our life. Turn to Jesus today and let Him transform *your* life.

MAY 8

Arise, go to Zarephath, which belongs to Sidon,
and dwell there. Behold,
I have commanded a widow there to feed you.
(1 Kings 17:9 esv)

NEAR THE TOP of any list of men in the Bible who were humble would be the name of the prophet Elijah. His life is a prototype of Christ before His journey to the cross. The comparisons are many: Both were humble, tender, kind, and patient. Yet upon occasion, both uttered scorching words of judgment and retribution. Both enjoyed the unending Favor of God during their journey on earth.

Elijah was schooled in humility during a devastating famine in the land, and Jehovah ordered him to depend on a poor widow for his sustenance.

Is there a famine in your land today? Perhaps it is a financial famine, and the job that provided food and drink has dried up. How are you thinking about your circumstances? Is your famine found in a crumbling relationship that you thought would endure "until death do us part"? Consider that God is your source—He is the One who can meet your every need. He knows what you need and how to provide for you, His child.

As you meditate on the life of Elijah and his walk of faith, look heavenward to the Author and Finisher of your faith for the grace to walk humbly before Him!

MAY 9

And my God shall supply all your need
according to His riches in glory by Christ Jesus.
(PHILIPPIANS 4:19 NKJV)

CORRIE TEN BOOM, long esteemed by evangelical Christians as the ideal of Christian faith in action, had been confined to the Ravensbrück concentration camp with her sister, Betsie who suffered from pernicious anemia (a chronic blood disease). Before being transported to the camp, a friend had given Corrie a bottle of liquid vitamins. As the desperate days mounted, Corrie found that she was more often forced to share her hoard of the life-giving liquid rather than save it solely for Betsie.

Corrie was stunned when she realized that though she often administered the precious drops to as many as twenty-five women in a day, the contents never ran dry. She was reminded of the woman in the Old Testament, the widow of Zarephath, whose cruise of oil held a perpetual supply as long as there was need of it—all because she willingly gave all that she had to the prophet Elijah.

One day one of the nurses from the infirmary smuggled a bottle of the precious liquid to Corrie. She rejoiced to be able to refill her small bottle. God's provision was truly confirmed that night as she held her bottle upside down to drain the last drop. No matter how long Corrie held it or how many times she tapped the bottom, the bottle refused to give up another single drop. As God provided the new, the old ran dry.

Trust Him for every need in your life.

MAY 10

Woe to me! ... I am ruined! For I am a man of unclean lips,
and I live among a people of unclean lips,
and my eyes have seen the King, the Lord Almighty.
(ISAIAH 6:5 NIV)

IN ISAIAH chapter 6, the prophet had entered the presence of God and had come away with a renewed conviction of the holiness of the Master. It was not to be trivialized or marginalized. God is love! God is holy! God is righteous! That doesn't mean God meets the standard for those qualities; God *is* the standard by which all else is measured. Isaiah had entered into the presence of the epitome of holiness—Jehovah God.

The prophet was in the presence of holiness, and with great humility, realized his position. He had been concerned with the sinfulness of Judah; now he was concerned with his own impurity when seen under the microscope of God. Isaiah realized he was ruined. He had no place to hide.

To come to Christ, you must recognize that you are a sinner in desperate need of a Savior. That realization then requires the humility to lay aside your own pride and ego and figuratively lie prostrate at the foot of the cross of Christ.

This means acknowledging that no matter how you might have failed, God is greater than your sin.

MAY 11

Then one of the seraphim flew to me with a live coal
in his hand, which he had taken with tongs from the altar.
With it he touched my mouth and said, "See, this has touched
your lips; your guilt is taken away and your sin atoned for."
(ISAIAH 66:6-7 NIV)

AS ISAIAH lay on his face before the Lord God Almighty, he became more and more aware of how holy his God is and how sinful *he* was. He was struck by his own guilt in the presence of utter Holiness, and realized the entire nation was equally guilty.

Isaiah prostrated himself in the awesome presence of the Most High God. In the midst of the smoke, Isaiah was called to a new pursuit and responded to the summons:

Then I heard the voice of the Lord saying, "Whom shall I send? And who will go for us?" And I said, "Here am I. Send me!" (Isaiah 6:8 NIV)

An encounter with God always brings inevitable change. Either your commitment to Him grows deeper and you become more like your heavenly Father, or you harden your heart and die spiritually.

God calls the humble to fulfill His mission. His power is made perfect in your weakness. Only with the realization that you can do nothing without Jehovah are you then ready to be used by Him. Only then can you humbly say as did Isaiah, "Send me."

MAY 12

He is without father or mother or genealogy,
having neither beginning of days nor end of life,
but resembling the Son of God he continues
a priest forever.
(HEBREWS 7:3 ESV)

THE FIRST WAR recorded in the Bible is found in Genesis chapter 14. Chedorlaomer, the king of Elam, had joined forces with five other kings in the region. They attacked the kings of Sodom and Gomorrah and after having put them to flight, sacked the cities and carried off the inhabitants. Among the captives were Abraham's nephew, Lot, and his family. Abraham quickly summoned 318 of his trained servants and set out to liberate his family members.

After rescuing Lot and his family, Abraham returned home, and on the way was met by Melchizedek, who some say was the pre-incarnate Christ. Whether he was God or simply a type, it is apparent that he was truly representative of a heavenly visitation with Abraham. The tired leader needed to be strengthened, comforted, and inspired. Often when you, child of God, have been wearied by the battle, strength comes through His Word or the tender ministries of a servant of God.

Abraham, a type of Christ, pursued his nephew, Lot, rescuing him from a life of bondage. Lot could not free himself; he was held captive by an evil king.

Jesus Christ pursues you, who were dead in your trespasses and sin and rescued you, not with troops and arms, but by His precious blood and through His unmerited grace. You were set free through the shedding of His blood and restored to the Kingdom of God.

MAY 13

Give, and it will be given to you.
They will pour into your lap a good measure—
pressed down, shaken together, and running over.
For by your standard of measure
it will be measured to you in return.
(LUKE 6:38 NASB)

TO THE WORLD, being radically generous is a senseless act: "What? Give abundant offerings? How am I going to pay my bills?" Let me encourage you today. Giving opens the windows of heaven and brings God's blessings. They may not just be monetary blessings...bargains come your way, unexpected gifts, or perhaps a better job.

It is not mere coincidence that the word *give* is found 880 times in scripture. The farmer sows extravagantly so that he can harvest abundantly. When he deposits one seed into the ground, he expects a plentiful return. When you practice generosity, you reap God's unmerited favor. When you return to God a portion of your material blessings, you will recognize that "it is he who gives you the ability to produce wealth, and so confirms his covenant." (Deuteronomy 9:18 NIV)

The spirit of giving releases a flood of blessing and you can, in turn, give of your time and your abilities. You can actually alter the effects of adversity by releasing a spirit of generous giving in every area of your life.

MAY 14

Then a despised Samaritan came along,
and when he saw the man, he felt compassion for him.
(LUKE 10:33 NLT)

IN LUKE 10, Jesus introduced the hero of a parable—a lowly Samaritan, a half-breed. Riding on his donkey, he traversed the barren places alone until he spotted a bloody and naked man on the roadside. His heart seized with compassion, and I can picture him running forward and dropping to the ground to offer help. This religious outcast didn't hesitate; he saw the need and he acted. He was not concerned with fulfilling the letter of the law, as had been the priest and Levite.

No, he immediately went to work. He took oil and wine from his pouch. The two, stirred together, were used as both a cleanser and a salve. After cleaning the man's injuries, he took garments from his supply and tore them into strips to bandage the cuts and abrasions.

The Samaritan didn't stop there; he didn't abandon the victim to the elements. He placed the unfortunate traveler on the back of his donkey and supported him until they came to an inn. He left the equivalent of two days' wages for a worker to take care of any needs the man might have. He assured the business owner that when he returned, he would gladly reimburse him for any additional charges.

Compassion can be costly. Loving one's neighbor as oneself can be more involved than a casual wave when paths cross. As Christians, the motivation must be one of love, mercy, and kindness.

MAY 15

I can do nothing on my own.
As I hear, I judge, and my judgment is just,
because I seek not my own will
but the will of him who sent me.
(JOHN 5:30 ESV)

OBEDIENCE is not always easy, as we learn from Jesus when He was in the Garden of Gethsemane. When He walked away from His disciples, it was to wrestle in solitude about that which was to come. He fell on His face before the Father and in torment, agony, and desolation, He began to petition for his release: "Abba, Father, all things are possible for you. Remove this cup from me."

And yet He ended the cry in the same verse with a plea for an obedient spirit: "Yet not what I will, but what you will." (Mark 14:36 NIV)

This is the prayer that never fails. Words fail and grief overwhelms. That was the place where Jesus found himself in the garden—grief-stricken, facing the horrors of an unspeakable death, so heartbroken that He sweat drops of blood—but He uttered the words that He knew would capture the ear of the Father: "Thy will be done." He surrendered in absolute compliance with the Father's will.

Jesus left heaven in order to become the Lamb of God, the perfect sacrifice for the sins of all. He was obedient to the Father's commands, to His call, and to His will.

Our Lord's ordeal from arrest to death demonstrated obedience. He was the ultimate example of an obedient Servant, and thus lived, and died, to provide pardon for you and me.

MAY 16

And whosoever will be chief among you,
let him be your servant...
(MATTHEW 20:27 KJV)

JESUS WAS TO GIVE His disciples a powerful lesson on the role of a servant as He neared the end of His earthly ministry: The scene is the upper room; the occasion is Passover; the meal was at an end. Jesus, the Son of God, Messiah, the Savior of the World, rose from the table and laid aside His robe. He took a towel, and, girding it about His waist, picked up a basin and a pitcher of water, and began to make His way around the room. As He did so, He knelt on the floor in front of each disciple and gently washed and dried their feet.

It was a dirty task relegated to the lowest of servants. Those feet had followed in the steps of goats and sheep, of cattle and horses. The sandals on their feet provided little in the way of protection from the filth. What a picture of humility! The Creator ministering to the creation! Gently He reminded them:

> For I have given you an example, that you should do as I have done to you. Most assuredly, I say to you, a servant is not greater than his master; nor is he who is sent greater than he who sent him." (John 13:15-16 NKJV)

By His act of humility, Jesus made it very obvious that the role of His followers was one of service, not of infighting to determine who was the greatest. He performed the lowliest of tasks as an example for us to follow. Christ's Radical Humility was the ultimate lesson in how to gain the Favor of God.

MAY 17

And every creature which is in Heaven and on the earth
and under the earth and such as are in the sea,
and all that are in them, I heard saying:
"Blessing and honor and glory and power be to Him
who sits on the throne, and to the Lamb, forever and ever!"
(REVELATION 5:13 NKJV)

IN ISAIAH CHAPTER 6, we read of the prophet's vision of heaven's throne room and the majesty of He who sits on the throne. In Revelation, John describes how what we consider costly goods on earth become building materials in heaven. Jewels become supplies for gates, and gold paves the streets. Despite the magnificence of heaven, Jesus Christ laid aside all of that to become a living sacrifice.

Since before the beginning of time, Jesus sat at the right hand of the Father, active in creation, ruling over everything—stars, planets, galaxies, all He surveyed. The angels adored Him. All heaven bowed before Him.

He gave it all up in order to become mortal Man! The Lamb of God, Bread of Life, the Holy One of God, the Prince of Peace, the King of Kings laid aside His glory, His robes and scepter, clothed Himself in flesh, took on the frailties of mankind and became the sacrifice for sin. It is incomprehensible; a profound truth.

Even more overwhelming...He died for you and me so that we might someday enjoy the glorious beauty of heaven.

MAY 18

For you know the grace of our Lord Jesus Christ,
that though he was rich, yet for your sake he became poor,
so that you by his poverty might become rich.

(2 CORINTHIANS 9:9 ESV)

CHRIST RELINQUISHED His rights to all that heaven held for Him as God's Son. He surrendered His omniscience, His omnipotence, and His omnipresence. He became dependent on His earthly mother for food and clothing. He was no longer arrayed in splendor but rather in homespun cloth. His feet walked not on streets of gold but on the rocky and dusty roads of Palestine. He was subject to the authority of His parents, Mary and Joseph. He worked alongside His earthly father and studied in the synagogue with other children His age.

Jesus gave us access to God the Father. When He uttered the words, "It is finished," and breathed His last on the cross, the veil in the Temple was torn from the top to the bottom. It became possible for Man, covered by the blood of Christ, to enter into the Holy of Holies and offer his prayers and petitions directly to God. What a magnificent gift! No longer was it necessary to wait for a specific day or festival to present an offering.

Because of Christ's sacrifice, you can now have all that the Father offers through His beloved Son.

MAY 19

"Test me in this," says the Lord Almighty,
*"and see if I will not throw open the floodgates of heaven
and pour out so much blessing that you will not have
room enough for it.*
(MALACHI 3:10 NIV)

JESUS GAVE US ACCESS to God the Father, and because of His sacrifice, you can now offer *your* body as a living sacrifice, holy and acceptable to God.

Do you want God's blessings on your life? When you practice unparalleled generosity from a heart filled with love and compassion, God responds—financially, physically, spiritually.

God acts in good measure and great abundance. Have you ever tried to fill a bag with fall leaves or grass clippings? When the bag looks full, you shake it down, and stand on the contents of the bag so you can perhaps cram in another armload or two.

That is what God says He will do for you—He will pour your bag full of blessings, shake it down, then compress it just so He can stuff in another armload. But He doesn't stop there, He adds even more—so that it's full and running over.

Jesus brought us salvation and crowned His work with the promise of eternal life.

MAY 20

For a day in Your courts is better than a thousand.
I would rather be a doorkeeper in the house of my God
Than dwell in the tents of wickedness.

(PSALM 84:10 NKJV)

MERRIAM-WEBSTER defines favor as "regard shown toward another especially by gracious kindness; a special privilege or right granted."[21] As children of God, we receive forgiveness and favor—His gracious kindness. His favor comes as a result of our obedience, our willingness to forgive others, our humility and our open-hearted and open-handed generosity.

Jesus *humbled* Himself in *obedience* to the Father. He *gave* His life so that you and I could experience *forgiveness* for sin. God's favor rests upon Him, and is released abundantly in our lives when we follow in Jesus' footsteps. One important lesson to be learned: God bestows His favor so that you may be transformed and produce the fruits of His blessing. When that happens, God is glorified and you are blessed beyond measure.

When you, as a child of God grasp this essential principle, you become more assured as follower of Christ. As you are released to walk in the blessings of God—you are then free to bless others.

MAY 21

Heal the sick, raise the dead, cleanse the lepers,
cast out demons: freely ye received, freely give.
(MATTHEW 10:8 ASV)

OBEDIENCE CAN BE ACHIEVED even when being submissive to God's Word seems illogical. It means acquiescing to God's plan when your own strategy seems more logical. It defies conformity and marches on, regardless of what others may think. It means stepping outside your comfort zone to fulfill God's call.

Humility mandates that you do what God has called you to do even when those on the sidelines laugh and point fingers in derision. It will destroy your ego and turn you into a genuine follower of Jesus Christ. Someone wrote a book about the kingdom of Self[22] and how it robs us of a close relationship with God. Like little kids, we defiantly yell, "I can do it myself." Then we wonder why we can't get anything done. God won't go around us or over us; He will work *through* us—but only if we allow Him.

Forgiving others simply means relinquishing your right to retaliate. It doesn't lessen the price the one who has harmed you must pay. There are consequences to the choices people make. Forgiveness, however, sets you free to move forward, to live your life in God's grace and peace.

Generosity is fostered by an intimate relationship with a profoundly giving heavenly Father. His love for us becomes the benchmark by which we invest in the lives of others. Just as Jesus poured out Himself to provide salvation and rescued us from sin and death, so generosity prompts us to reach out to better the lives both of those close to us and those far removed.

MAY 22

But as it is written: "Eye has not seen, nor ear heard,
nor have entered into the heart of man the things which God
has prepared for those who love Him."
(ISAIAH 64:4 NKJV)

THE BEST OF GOD'S FAVOR is yet to come! And how we
live our lives *here* has a direct relationship to what we will find
awaiting us in heaven. Artists who have tried to paint the splendor
of heaven have come up short simply because it is impossible for
the human mind to conceive the grandeur of God's house.

Paul was lifted all the way up to the third heaven, but failed to
write a book that would give us a true picture of the tree of life,
those gates of pearl, streets of gold, and walls of jasper. John the
Revelator wrote of heaven, but gave us only a scant description
of its beauty. One reason is that it may be impossible to do justice
to the majesty of a place totally overshadowed by the presence of
God Almighty.

When you have lived a life of obedience, forgiveness, humility,
and generosity, you will be greeted with the words:

Well done, good and faithful servant; you were faithful over a
few things, I will make you ruler over many things. Enter into
the joy of your lord. (Matthew 25:21 NKJV)

MAY 23

Behold, how good and how pleasant it is
for brethren to dwell together in unity!
It is like the precious ointment upon the head,
that ran down upon the beard, even Aaron's beard:
that went down to the skirts of his garments...
(PSALM 133, KJV)

UNITY AND HARMONY were non-existent in my childhood home. Neither my parents nor my siblings dwelt "together in unity." Not until I later began to study the Word of God did I realize just how important these words are.

In Psalm 133, the writer paints a beautiful picture of unity in the anointing of Aaron, the high priest, brother of Moses. He pictures oil being poured over Aaron's head, flowing sweetly and smoothly, fragrantly down his face, through his beard, all the way to the hem of his priestly garments. Unity is the glue that holds a family, a Church, a nation together.

The result of such harmony is a place where God's people are refreshed and strengthened by His Spirit—just as the dew nourishes the dry ground! It is the place where God *commands* blessing and where His anointing flows! And it is the place where *zoe*—Hebrew for life, the eternal, God-kind of life—flows freely!

The Hebrew word for unity denotes a people drawn together for one purpose—to follow Jehovah, fulfill His plan and purpose, and to dwell together under the umbrella of His blessings. Live under that umbrella today and enjoy God's best for you.

MAY 24

This day I call the heavens and the earth as witnesses against you
that I have set before you life and death, blessings and curses.
Now choose life, so that you and your children may live.
(DEUTERONOMY 30:19, NIV)

JEHOVAH GOD'S BLESSINGS cannot be separated from obedience to His Word. This is never more obvious than in Deuteronomy 28: 1, 2, 15, KJV:

> ...if thou shalt hearken diligently unto the voice of the LORD thy God, to observe and to do all his commandments..., ...all these blessings shall come on thee, and overtake thee.

Moses delivered this bountiful promise of Yahweh's blessings on His children if they would but obey God's commands. If they rebelled, He likewise swore the people would be cursed—cruelly cursed. Moses declared that life and blessing was in obedience to God's Word; death and destruction resided in disobedience.

How then, can you discover the blessings of God for your life? As Moses warned the Children of Israel in Deuteronomy 28:1(NIV), obedience is the key that unlocks the door to Yahweh's abundant blessings.

A loving, active, vibrant relationship with God is vital. As you live and walk daily with Him, blessings and benefits follow.

MAY 25

Then Moses lifted his hand and struck the rock twice
with his rod; and water came out abundantly,
and the congregation and their animals drank.
(NUMBERS 20:11-12 NKJV)

DURING FORTY YEARS of wandering through the desert,
Moses was obedient to the Divine instructions given him. He
displayed extraordinary patience as he led a company of people
that continually grumbled, complained, and mutinied. It was not
surprising that eventually Moses' patience reached its breaking
point, and in anger, he failed to follow God's instructions. (See
Numbers 20.) He disobeyed God at that one crucial juncture and
his punishment was that he was not allowed to enter into the
Promised Land. That honor would belong to his successor, Joshua.

However, God *did* take Moses to the top of the mountain and
allow him to see the other side—the land that flowed with milk
and honey. Then Moses died and the Lord buried him.

Despite missteps, Moses' life was characterized by obedience.
He led that nation of rebellious, dissatisfied, disobedient, quarrel-
some people through the wilderness to the banks of the Jordan
River.

Moses was able to defeat the forces of the enemy because he
was submissive to God's will, and so can you. He delivered his
people from the chains of darkness and degradation. He complied
with Jehovah's instructions and won the unfailing commanded
blessing of God, as can you!

MAY 26

For the law of the Spirit of life has set you free
in Christ Jesus from the law of sin and death.
(ROMANS 8:2 ESV)

FORGIVING SOMEONE who has wronged you is one of the great challenges of life. Those who harbor unforgiveness are burdened with misery and guilt. Those who refuse to forgive overflow with rage and resentment. Their hostility is a wall that encloses them, and no one can scale that wall. Unforgiveness may go unnoticed by the individual to whom it is directed, but it defiles the one who bears it. It can, and sometimes does, literally destroy the body and the soul of the one bearing the ill-will, and it certainly blocks the flow of God's blessings into that life.

Releasing unforgiveness is not something one does easily. The normal reaction is to either retaliate or hold on to resentment. Forgiveness flies in the face of every natural instinct. The sad truth is that when you harbor unforgiveness—against a spouse, parent, co-worker, or anyone who wronged you—it separates you from God and His bounty, and that person controls your life.

God has called you to forgive, which sets you free from sin and death.

MAY 27

"Don't be ridiculous!" Saul replied.
"There's no way you can fight this Philistine and possibly win!
You're only a boy, and he's been a man of war
since his youth."
(1 SAMUEL 17:33 NLT)

AFTER DAVID WAS ANOINTED by Samuel, there came a morning when his father ordered his youngest son to take supplies to his brothers who were battling the Philistines in the Valley of Elah. Upon his arrival, David saw the imposing figure of Goliath and heard the challenge being hurled across the valley to his quaking audience on the other side. He asked those around him what would be the reward for the one who slayed the enemy. David's brothers were angered by his question and began to ridicule him. He then marched before King Saul and offered to fight the giant.

Saul offered David his personal armor for the battle with Goliath. After having tried it on, the young man realized that the covering made by mortal hands was insufficient for the task.

In this modern-day "me first" society, instead of doing it God's way, we've done it our way. James 1:17 (NKJV) says, "Every good gift and every perfect gift is from above, and comes down from the Father of lights..."

We need to acknowledge God's provision and offer the praise due Him. He is the Source of every good thing—life, health, opportunity, talent, and blessing. God is Jehovah-Jireh, our Provider.

MAY 28

Submit yourselves therefore to God.
(JAMES 4:7A KJV)

WHILE SOME WOULD VIEW a humble man or woman as a submissive doormat, the truth is, through God that individual possesses power—controlled by strength and self-control.

David's brothers belittled him in front of the entire army of Israel; he forgave them. His father thought him unworthy to be introduced to Samuel; David forgave him. David spent his early years running and hiding from King Saul being stalked like a criminal because of Saul's jealousy.

The future king had become the hunted outlaw with a price on his head. Day and night for years Saul dogged David, just waiting for the moment when he would become vulnerable.

Jealousy turns giants into jerks! Saul had a golden opportunity to demonstrate greatness when the Israelites sang, "Saul has slain his thousands, and David his ten thousands." (1 Samuel 18:7, NKJV) Saul could have taken a bow for sending David into battle.

Success sometimes causes people to turn on you with a jealous rage. When that happens, know this: What God has told you in secret will keep you from giving up in the greatest battles of your life. Get your eyes off what you're going through...and get them on what you are going *to*—God's deliverance!

MAY 29

"Give, and it will be given to you:
good measure, pressed down, shaken together,
and running over will be put into your bosom."
(LUKE 6:38 NKJV)

EXPERIENCING A LIFE of God's favor and abundance is similar to opening a combination lock. Without using the correct key or code the lock simply won't open for you. The first three steps for releasing God's favor: forgiveness in abundance, unquestioned obedience to our Heavenly Father, and sincere humility—but you still need the fourth and final ingredient: limitless generosity.

It's impossible to experience God's abundant, overflowing favor without practicing abundant generosity. The Bible tells us, "He who sows sparingly will also reap sparingly, and he who sows bountifully will also reap bountifully." (2 Corinthians 9:6 NKJV)

God will multiply the seed you have sown—but you first must give Him something with which to work.

Take a look at the seeds you possess—your time, talents, and treasure. Then step out in faith to release God's favor by generously sowing into His kingdom and the lives of others.

MAY 30

*Cast all your anxiety on him
because he cares for you.*
(1 PETER 5:7 NIV)

YOU AND I *need* Jesus. We sing about how much we need Him. We pray, "Jesus help me; I need You." We've felt His presence, and knew that we had been with Jesus. We've experienced the salvation, grace, forgiveness and mercy of Jesus. Sometimes we've seen His miracles, or experienced His life surging through our own.

Despite our feelings, the miracles we've heard reported, the success we've seen on the mission fields, today a growing number of Christians intensely yearn to be with Jesus.

I've experienced what I can only describe as the "kiss of God" in my life—events that were so spectacular I could never understand why they happened to me... until now. They always came when my self-confidence was at its lowest. In fact, that's exactly what needed to happen so I would learn to trust Him.

At these times, you and I are completely dependent upon God, knowing we can do nothing in our own strength. The cry of a desperate heart is the fertile soil in which the glory of God can be manifested. When we move out, Jesus can move in and meet our needs.

MAY 31

*There is therefore now no condemnation
for those who are in Christ Jesus.*
(ROMANS 8:1 ESV)

WHEN WE ACKNOWLEDGE our sins and come before the
Lord, He is faithful to forgive us and cleanse us. Isaiah 1:18 says,
"Though your sins are like scarlet, they shall be as white as snow;
though they are red like crimson, they shall be as wool."

Once we receive God's forgiveness, we must not continue to
wallow in defeat or condemnation. We have to pick ourselves up
and get going again. But one of the big lies of the Devil is to tell
us we've done such bad things that God will not forgive us. Never
believe that lie!

There is nothing you or I can ever do to separate us from the
love of God (Romans 8:35-39). There is nothing, *nothing* we can
ever do that's so bad that God will refuse to forgive us when we
ask Him.

Thank God for his grace and mercy in forgiving you!

JUNE

JUNE 1

To Him who is able to do exceedingly abundantly
above all that we ask or think...to Him be glory.
(Ephesians 3:20-21 NIV)

WITHOUT AN UNDERSTANDING of God's character, you won't understand His favor. As children, many people learned the prayer, "God is great, God is good..." In order to receive more of the Lord's favor in your life, you must grasp this great declaration of two of His wonderful traits.

First, you need to remember that God is good. He's not some cosmic being far out in the universe, disengaged from the cares and concerns of your life. He loves you. He cares about you. And He can be as close to you as the air you breathe.

Second, you must understand that God is great. He not only makes great promises to us, He also is big enough and strong enough to fulfill those promises!

He can heal your body...provide the money for your bills...restore your broken relationships...and give you peace of mind when everything is crazy all around you. Jeremiah 32:27 tells us that nothing is too difficult for Him!

JUNE 2

Sanctify them by Your truth. Your word is truth."
(JOHN 17:17 NKJV)

ARE YOU EXPERIENCING confusion or uncertainty in your life today? God's favor can help you cut to the heart of the issues you face, enable you to discern the source of your battles and discover the Lord's prescription for victory.

This favor comes when you commit yourself to studying and obeying God's Word. Hebrews 4:12 declares:

> The word of God is living and powerful, and sharper than any two-edged sword, piercing even to the division of soul and spirit, and of joints and marrow, and is a discerner of the thoughts and intents of the heart. (NKJV)

If you're going through a battle with your health, family, finances, or emotions, you need a powerful sword to combat the lies of the Enemy—"the sword of the Spirit, which is the word of God." (Ephesians 6:17 NKJV)

Let God's Word expose Satan's lies with the light of truth. Use it as a mighty sword to wage war for God's promised favor in your life.

JUNE 3

Let us therefore come boldly to the throne of grace,
that we may obtain mercy and find grace to help
in time of need.

(HEBREWS 4:16 NKJV)

WHEN WE DISOBEY God's Word and do things we shouldn't,
His arms are wide open to us nevertheless. Like the prodigal son
in Luke 15, we simply must get up from our pigpen and return
home. We must ask the Lord to forgive us and help us do better
next time. It is that simple and that easy. God will welcome you
with open arms.

God forgives us, not because of any good works on our part, but
because of the blood of Jesus shed for us on the cross. The Bible
says we've been justified—just as if we've never sinned—and because of this we can experience God's amazing peace: "Therefore,
having been justified by faith, we have peace with God through
our Lord Jesus Christ." (Romans 5:1 NKJV)

Take time today to thank God for His forgiveness, favor, and
peace. If you've been a prodigal son or daughter, you *can* come
home to your loving Heavenly Father!

JUNE 4

Little children, keep yourselves from idols.
(1 JOHN 5:21 NKJV)

IF YOU ALLOW IDOLS in your life, they will sap your spiritual vitality and undermine God's favor. When Moses delivered the Ten Commandments to the children of Israel, the second one dealt with this issue directly:

> You shall not make for yourself a carved image—any likeness of anything that is in heaven above, or that is in the earth beneath, or that is in the water under the earth; you shall not bow down to them nor serve them. For I, the Lord your God, am a jealous God.... (Exodus 20:4-5 NKJV)

Take a moment to examine your heart in God's presence today. Ask Him to show you anything you've treasured more than Him. This could be money, some material possession, a relationship, a hobby, an area of pride or disobedience, or any "image" that comes before HIS image.

Repent of allowing *anything* to come between you and the Lord. When you do, expect a new outburst of His amazing favor in your life!

JUNE 5

Anyone who belongs to Christ has become a new person.
The old life is gone; a new life has begun!
(2 CORINTHIANS 5:17 NLT)

WHEN YOU ARE BORN again by God's Spirit, you receive His spiritual DNA. John 1:12 explains:

> As many as received Him, to them He gave the right to become children of God, to those who believe in His name: who were born, not of blood, nor of the will of the flesh, nor of the will of man, but of God. (NKJV)

The letters DNA stand for deoxyribonucleic acid; God's supernatural DNA can be defined as "Divine Nature Acquired." Jesus perfectly modeled the Father's DNA.

In addition to radically forgiving us, our Savior was radically obedient, humble, and generous. When you follow in His steps and exhibit these four traits, you express His DNA and manifest God's image. Then, and only then, can you live in God's favor and activate the promises of His Word.

As Believers, we have the great privilege of being "partakers of the divine nature." (2 Peter 1:4) So, go ahead and partake—it will change your life!

JUNE 6

O Lord of Heaven's Armies,
what joy for those who trust in you.
(PSALM 84:12 NLT)

GOD IS SOVEREIGN, and the Bible teaches that He is the One who determines the number of our days. The Lord holds us in the palm of His hand; we never need to see ourselves as helpless victims. In John 10:29 Jesus affirms the wonderful truth that no one is able to snatch us out of the hands of our Heavenly Father.

Deuteronomy 33:27 says, "The eternal God is your refuge and underneath are the everlasting arms." (NKJV) In John 10:29, Jesus affirms the wonderful truth that no one is able to snatch us out of the hands of our Heavenly Father.

Do you see what good news this is? When you give your life to Jesus Christ, you can be secure in the knowledge that He is your Protector and Provider. No one can snatch you out of His hands or separate you from His love. (Romans 8:35-39)

Living in God's favor is not a matter of striving and struggling, but rather a matter of resting securely in the Lord's amazing love and goodness. Trust Him!

JUNE 7

So the LORD said, "I will blot out man
whom I have created from the face of the land,
man and animals and creeping things
and birds of the heavens, for I am sorry
that I have made them."
(GENESIS 6:7 ESV)

GENESIS 6 SAYS wickedness and violence filled the earth during Noah's time. God "was grieved in His heart," (v. 6) and He decided to destroy most inhabitants of the earth and start over with a clean slate.

During this time of lawlessness and corruption, we read that "Noah found grace in the eyes of the Lord." (v. 8 KJV) Other translations say, "Noah found favor in the eyes of the Lord." And The Message renders this, "But Noah was different. God liked what he saw in Noah."

What made Noah stand out? How did he find God's grace and favor, when most of humankind was marked for judgment and destruction? Noah was a righteous man among the unrighteous, and he was committed to Jehovah.

Take time to search your heart today. Are you just trying to "fit in" with the people around you? Or are you willing to take a stand and do what is pleasing to the Lord?

JUNE 8

For by grace you have been saved through faith.
And this is not your own doing; it is the gift of God ...
(EPHESIANS 2:8 ESV)

REVEREND GREG PRATT made a list entitled "All I Will Ever Need to Know I Learned from Noah." One of his points was this: "Plan ahead. It wasn't raining when Noah built the ark."

This principle of planning ahead is found throughout the Bible. Solomon writes:

> Take a lesson from the ants, you lazybones. Learn from their ways and become wise! Though they have no prince or governor or ruler to make them work, they labor hard all summer, gathering food for the winter. (Proverbs 6:6-8 NLT)

It's important that you be wise enough to work hard and plan ahead. Genuine faith is followed by good works. When it's harvest time in your life, you should have the foresight to gather food for the winter season.

Take a few minutes today to pause and ask God to help you prepare for the days ahead. Listen for His instructions, be willing to work hard, and do what He says!

JUNE 9

Just as the body is dead without breath,
so also faith is dead without good works.
(JAMES 2:26 NLT)

THE BIBLE IS FILLED with promises that God desires to shower favor and blessings upon His children. Yet people throughout history have debated the keys to experiencing "a blessed life."

Jesus spoke to this issue after eating the Passover meal with His disciples and washing their feet. Encouraging them to follow His example of humility and servanthood, He made a stunning promise: "If you understand what I'm telling you, act like it—and live a blessed life." (John 13:17 MSG)

In essence, Jesus said, "I WANT you to live 'a blessed life,' and here's HOW you can." Other translations illustrate that's it's not enough just to know the principles of living in God's favor. We also must put them into practice: "If you know these things, blessed are you if you DO them." (NKJV)

Take a few minutes to review the principles in John 13. Then start putting them into practice, and get ready to be blessed!

JUNE 10

By faith Abraham, when he was tested,
offered up Isaac, and he who had received the promises
offered up his only begotten son...
(Hebrews 11:17 NKJV)

WHEN GOD TOLD Abraham to leave his homeland, his relatives, and the idolatrous culture behind, He also gave him wonderful "I will" promises of how he would be rewarded for obeying:

> I will make you into a great nation, and I will bless you; I will make your name great, and you will be a blessing. I will bless those who bless you, and whoever curses you I will curse; and all peoples on earth will be blessed through you. (Genesis 12:2-3 NIV)

Take a few minutes to quiet your heart before the Lord, and ask Him to show you His next steps for your life. What is He calling you to do? If you are obedient, as Abraham was, are there promises He has made for the outcome?

When God gives you instructions, He often gives you promises as well. Trust Him to bring more of His favor into your life! He says, "I will!"

JUNE 11

The plans of the Lord stand firm forever.
(PSALM 33:11 NKJV)

DESPERATE TO OFFER her husband an heir, Sarah offered her handmaiden Hagar to Abraham as a surrogate. In her misery, she had turned from faith in God's promises to dependence on self. Hagar represents human works—taking matters into our own hands instead of believing God.

Of course, Abraham could have said no to his wife and continued to hold on to the promises of God. But instead, he went along with Sarah's ill-advised plan.

When someone proposes a plan, make sure to check with God before you say yes. Terrible consequences resulted when Abraham agreed to follow Sarah's plan. And the entire human race has paid a horrible price for Adam's foolish willingness to follow Eve in eating the forbidden fruit. (See Genesis 3:6.)

In contrast to the unwise human plans we may be tempted to follow, the Bible tells us to trust in the Lord and follow HIS plan for our life. (See Proverbs 3:5-7.)

JUNE 12

And I will bless her and also give you a son by her;
*then I will bless her, and she shall be **a mother of** nations;*
kings of peoples shall be from her.
(GENESIS 17:16 NKJV)

DO YOU EVER have second thoughts about a bad decision you made? By the time Hagar was heavy with child, Sarah was consumed with jealousy, and Abram was forced to endure the contentious atmosphere he had helped create. Not a happy situation. Yet the Lord still had a plan for Sarah and Abraham—and He has a plan for you.

Instead of scolding Abraham and Sarah for their foolish actions, God reaffirmed His love for them and His plan for their lives. He changed Abram's name to Abraham (father of a multitude) and Sarai's name to Sarah (noblewoman). And He reminded them of His promise that Sarah would yet bear the son of promise.

You don't have to be perfect to be a child of God. When you've made mistakes, humble yourself before the Lord, receive His forgiveness, and let Him reaffirm His promises and His plan.

JUNE 13

*So Noah did everything exactly as God
had commanded him.*
(Genesis 6:22 nlt)

NOAH LABORED over 100 years constructing the ark, obeying God's warnings even of things he had never experienced before. Yet we read: "By faith Noah, being divinely warned of things not yet seen, moved with godly fear, prepared an ark for the saving of his household." (Hebrews 11:7 nkjv)

When the Bible says Noah was "moved with godly fear," you might get the wrong impression. "Aha, that's why he did it," you might say. "God held a big stick over him and said, 'You'd better do this, or I'll let you have it!'" But that wasn't it at all. Noah simply reverenced God enough to obey His instructions.

Do you trust the Lord enough to obey Him, even when it's impossible to see into the future? Trusting Him regarding "things not yet seen" is a key to living in His favor.

JUNE 14

Abraham believed God!
(JAMES 2:23 KJV)

DESPITE GOD'S PROMISE to give them a son, Abraham reached the age of 99 and Sarah was 89, both well past normal childbearing age. Yet we're told that Abraham continued to believe God, and this was the key to his breakthrough:

> When everything was hopeless, Abraham believed anyway, deciding to live not on the basis of what he saw he couldn't do but on what God said he would do. (Romans 4:18 MSG)

The day came when Sarah awoke to find that she was indeed pregnant in her old age. She who had laughed at the pronouncement that she would bear a child—she who had intervened and proposed her own plan for an heir—Sarah was now carrying Isaac, the son of promise. God had taken away her barrenness and provided the strength to carry the child to term—just as He had promised.

No matter what your circumstances may be, continue to believe God for a demonstration of His favor in your life!

JUNE 15

My purpose is to give them
a rich and satisfying life.
(JOHN 10:10 NLT)

THE MESSAGE offers this paraphrase of Romans 12:1-2:

So here's what I want you to do, God helping you: Take your everyday, ordinary life—your sleeping, eating, going-to-work, and walking-around life—and place it before God as an offering.

Embracing what God does for you is the best thing you can do for Him. Don't become so well-adjusted to today's culture that you fit into it without even thinking. Instead, fix your attention on God. You'll be changed from the inside out. Readily recognize what He wants from you, and quickly respond to it.

Take a few minutes to meditate on these words, and let them sink deeply into your heart. Make sure to place your life before God as an offering and embrace what He does for you. Fix your attention on Him, allow Him to change you from the inside out, and readily recognize what He wants from you, then quickly respond to it.

JUNE 16

Lord, You have heard the desire of the humble;
You will prepare their heart.
(PSALM 10:17 NKJV)

MOSES WAS REARED in luxury in the household of Pharaoh, but nothing else is recorded of his life until he was a young man. Moses was out walking one day when he saw an Egyptian taskmaster beating a Jewish slave. Moses was so incensed that he killed the Egyptian.

After hearing that Pharaoh had placed a price on his head because of this deed, Moses packed his knapsack and headed for the backside of the desert, where he found himself taking care of sheep for a living.

Even though this seemed at that time like a major detour in Moses' life, it turned out to be an additional part of God's training and preparation. Forty years later, Moses would be in the wilderness caring for sheep of another kind—God's people.

Be alert to how God is preparing you today for your assignment tomorrow.

JUNE 17

A sinner's wealth is stored up for the righteous.
(PROVERBS 13:22 NIV)

SOLOMON WRITES in Proverbs 16:7 that "when a man's ways please the Lord, He makes even his enemies to be at peace with him." (NKJV)

The story of Moses and the Israelites provides an even more fantastic principle for those who please God: We can receive favor and blessings even from our enemies!

God promised Moses, "I will give this people favor in the sight of the Egyptians; and it shall be, when you go, that you shall not go empty-handed." (Exodus 3:21 NKJV) Think of it: Not only would the Israelites be delivered from the Egyptians, but they would be given silver, gold, and clothing to leave: "So you shall plunder the Egyptians," (v. 22)

Do you need to be delivered from a difficult situation? Like the Israelites discovered, God can do miracles to make that happen. But He also wants to bless you in unimaginable ways—so that you don't leave empty-handed!

JUNE 18

This is the way, walk in it.
(ISAIAH 30:21 NKJV)

EPHESIANS 2:10 TEACHES that we are God's workmanship (NKJV), masterpiece (NLT), and handiwork (NIV). If that weren't enough, it says He has gone before us to prepare a path of incredible favor and blessings for us.

God had this same plan to lead the Israelites: "And the LORD went before them by day in a pillar of cloud to lead the way, and by night in a pillar of fire to give them light, so as to go by day and night." (Exodus 13:21 NKJV)

Pause for a few moments to close your eyes and picture the Lord going before you to clear a path. It's a good path—a path of blessing and abundance. And the good news is that you don't have to create this path for yourself—you just need to walk in it. Listen to His voice today. He is beckoning you to a new life, more blessed than you can dream or imagine.

JUNE 19

It is God who arms me with strength
and keeps my way secure.
(PSALM 18:32 NIV)

AFTER THE ISRAELITES escaped from Egypt, they were chased by Pharaoh and his army. The people second-guessed their decision to leave Egypt, as they so often did in the years that followed. And they complained to God and to Moses for bringing them on such a perilous journey.

Moses told them to stay calm, for "the Lord himself will fight for you." (Exodus 14:14 NLT)

When Moses raised his shepherd's rod over the Red Sea the waters parted and "the Lord opened up a path through the water." (v. 21) As a result, "the people of Israel walked through the middle of the sea on dry ground." (v. 22)

God had opened a pathway for the Israelites; even making sure the ground was dry for them! He will do the same for you when you learn to obey Him and walk in His favor. He will make a way, even when there seems to be no way!

JUNE 20

Satisfy the hunger of your treasured ones.
May their children have plenty.
(PSALM 17:14 NLT)

FOR HUNDREDS OF YEARS, the Israelites had been slaves in Egypt. It must have been difficult to grasp that God was giving them a whole new identity and purpose. Yet God declared, "You shall be to Me a kingdom of priests and a holy nation." (Exodus 19:6 NKJV) Instead of being slaves, they now were to be kings and priests—just as we are meant to be today. (See Revelation 1:6.)

Do you see the difference God's favor can make in your life? You're no longer a slave...a victim...an outcast. The Lord has set you FREE and called you to be part of His "holy nation."

Referring back to this scene at Mount Sinai, Peter says Believers are "a chosen generation, a royal priesthood, a holy nation, His own special people, that you may proclaim the praises of Him who called you out of darkness into His marvelous light." (1 Peter 2:9 NKJV)

Rejoice in your new identity in Christ!

JUNE 21

Draw near to God and He will draw near to you.
(JAMES 4:8 NKJV)

MOSES KNEW his obedience to the Creator wasn't meant to end with the crossing of the Red Sea and the defeat of Pharaoh's army. He had been assigned the responsibility of leading the Israelites to the Promised Land, and God had equipped him for the task.

In Exodus chapters 19 and 20, Moses was called by God to the heights of Mount Sinai to personally receive the Ten Commandments—the only man to have seen God's glory and lived. Although the Lord was inviting all the Israelites to be priests able to come into His presence (19:6), the people "trembled and stood afar off" when they witnessed the thunder, lightning flashes, and smoke surrounding the mountain. Only Moses went up the mountain and drew near to God.

Will you accept God's invitation to draw near to Him today? His favor is found in His presence, and He beckons you to come.

JUNE 22

When everything and everyone is finally
under God's rule...God's rule is
absolutely comprehensive—a perfect ending!
(1 CORINTHIANS 15:28 MSG)

ESTHER'S STORY would compare with a modern fairytale: A beautiful young Jewish girl torn from her homeland and taken captive to Persia; a tyrannical ruler who banished his queen from her royal position and initiated a search for her successor; and of course, an evil villain, Haman, who desired to perpetrate genocide against the Jews.

Perhaps your life seems much less dramatic than Queen Esther's—but it is significant in God's sight nevertheless. Just as the Lord sovereignly orchestrated the circumstances to prepare Esther "for such a time as this" (Esther 4:14), so too He is weaving together the strands of your life into a beautiful tapestry to reflect His glory.

Even when some things don't seem to make sense at the time, God has a plan for your victory and success. (Jeremiah 29:11) He has a happy ending in mind for *your* story, just as He accomplished for Esther!

JUNE 23

And the king loved Esther more than
any of the other young women.
He was so delighted with her
that he set the royal crown on her head
and declared her queen instead of Vashti.

(ESTHER 2:17 NLT)

IF GOD PRESENTED YOU with an unexpected opportunity today, would you be prepared to make the most of it? Esther was.

Her life began to take an unexpected turn when Persia's King Ahasuerus (also known as Xerxes) got upset with his beautiful queen, Vashti, and banished her from his presence. The king's advisors decided Ahasuerus needed something to take his mind off Vashti, and a decree was issued: "Let beautiful young virgins be sought for the king." (Esther 2:2 NKJV)

Just as a decree was sent out from King Ahasuerus in search of someone like Esther, King Jesus is searching for someone like YOU today! Can you hear His call? Are you spiritually fit and ready to respond?

Take a few moments to thank the Lord for the unexpected opportunities He is preparing for you. Then listen—really listen—for any instructions He has for you to obey on the road to your next assignment!

JUNE 24

*Let them no longer fool themselves
by trusting in empty riches,
for emptiness will be their only reward.*

(JOB 15:31 NLT)

JESUS DID NOT OWE US forgiveness or salvation. He gave His life freely for all. Instead of having to earn His love, we only have to accept His free gift. Just as the old song says, "He paid a debt He did not owe; I owed a debt I could not pay."[23]

We cannot activate the Word of God or live in His favor while wallowing in discouragement and defeat. But without a revelation of God's love for us, we will waste time seeking approval from other sources. People often look for affirmation and fulfillment from their careers, their spouses, their possessions, or their friends.

However, there is a God-sized vacuum in everyone's spirit, and nothing can fill it except the Creator. Take a few minutes to allow the Spirit of God to search your heart. Have you been trying to seek approval and fill your God-sized vacuum with other things?

JUNE 25

Love your enemies,
do good to those who hate you,
bless those who curse you,
pray for those who mistreat you.
(LUKE 6:27-28 NIV)

ONLY THROUGH THE WORD and the Spirit can you receive this incredible revelation: God is crazy about you! Your Heavenly Father can give you all the affirmation you will ever need. However, without receiving that affirmation from Him, you're likely to compromise your integrity, lie, cheat, steal, or lower your standards.

You and I live in a less than perfect world. Rest assured, you will be offended from time to time, and you must learn to greet the offense with love and forgiveness.

Remember: Forgiveness begins with God. He is the supreme Pardoner. It's impossible to forgive radically without Him working in your heart. Who do YOU need to forgive today?

JUNE 26

If you forgive those who sin against you,
your heavenly Father will forgive you.
(MATTHEW 6:14 NLT)

THE MESSAGE paraphrase of 1 Corinthians 13:4-8 reminds us that love "doesn't fly off the handle" and "doesn't keep score of the sins of others." It "trusts God always" and "always looks for the best."

Take a few minutes to ask God to search your heart. Have you tended to be irritable or fly off the handle lately? Have you been keeping score of all the ways people have wronged you and offended you?

Now ask God to fill your heart with His Holy Spirit, manifesting love, joy, peace, and the other aspects of the fruit of the Spirit in your life. (Galatians 5:22-23) And then you must make a conscious decision to let go of any offenses.

How often must you forgive a person? When Peter asked this, he suggested that seven times might be often enough. But Jesus replied, "Not seven times, but seventy times seven." (Matthew 18:21-22 NLT) In other words, it's time to quit keeping score!

JUNE 27

I learned God-worship
when my pride was shattered.
(PSALM 51:16-17 MSG)

WHAT IS THE OPPOSITE of humility? It is arrogance, conceit, self-importance, and pride. This kind of cocky attitude may seem perfectly fine to us, but God deals with pride quite severely: "All of you, clothe yourselves with humility toward one another, because, 'God opposes the proud but shows favor to the humble'". (1 Peter 5:5 NIV)

Notice that God actively resists—fights, confronts, and disregards—those who are proud. He takes a dim view of those who have an exaggerated view of their own importance. He opposes those who attribute their successes to their own labors and fail to admit that everything they possess comes directly from the benevolent hand of a loving Heavenly Father.

We can summarize God's message on humility in five little words: "I'm God and you're not!" But look at the wonderful converse of this: He "shows favor to the humble."

JUNE 28

Walk with the wise and become wise;
associate with fools and get in trouble.

(PROVERBS 13:20 NLT)

MOSES' EXTRAORDINARY POWER stemmed from the fact that he trusted God. He recognized how small he was and how big his God was. He acknowledged that his reputation and integrity must be based not on his own efforts, but on God's love and mercy.

Moses exhibited three of the most important characteristics of humility: 1) He accepted wise counsel; 2) He placed himself under God's authority, and 3) He was teachable.

Humble people don't think it beneath them to seek wise counsel from others. Solomon wrote in Proverbs: "Plans fail for lack of counsel, but with many advisers they succeed." (Proverbs 15:22 NIV)

Take a few minutes to consider whether your life reflects the traits of true humility. Do you accept wise counsel? Are you submitting to God's authority? Are you teachable? The level of God's favor in your life will be largely shaped by your answers to these questions.

JUNE 29

Fools are headstrong and do what they like;
wise people take advice.
(PROVERBS 12:15 MSG)

NONE OF US enters this world with the wisdom of Solomon. We need to grow in wisdom and understanding, and this comes from being mentored by wise parents, counselors, pastors, teachers, and friends. However, in order for this process to work effectively, we need to be humble enough to acknowledge our need for God's wisdom.

We also need to be careful of where we look for our source of wisdom. Not every self-help author, talk show host, or media pundit truly has the wisdom of God. They may be spouting worldly wisdom or political correctness rather than the truth based on God's Word.

The apostle Paul warned: "Don't let anyone capture you with empty philosophies and high-sounding nonsense that come from human thinking and from the spiritual powers of this world, rather than from Christ." (Colossians 2:8 NLT) Be careful where you get your wisdom!

JUNE 30

All glory to God, who is able,
through his mighty power at work within us,
to accomplish infinitely more than
we might ask or think.
(EPHESIANS 3:20 NLT)

SOMETIMES IT IS EASY to get the wrong idea about biblical heroes like Elijah. Awestruck by their mighty acts of faith, we can assume they are akin to comic book superheroes—people who are nothing at all like us.

However, James 5:17-18 points out that Elijah was just an ordinary man who knew how to pray to an extraordinary God:

The prayer of a person living right with God is something powerful to be reckoned with. Elijah, for instance, human just like us, prayed hard that it wouldn't rain, and it didn't—not a drop for three and a half years. Then he prayed that it would rain, and it did. The showers came and everything started growing again. (MSG)

Have you limited what God might be able to do in your life? Or have you accepted the challenge modeled by Elijah—learning to pray to a big God?

JULY

JULY 1

If you keep My commandments,
you will abide in My love,
just as I have kept My Father's commandments
and abide in His love.
(JOHN 15:10 NKJV)

IF YOU HAD a difficult childhood, you may think of "obedience" in harsh or abusive terms. But Jesus modeled and taught an entirely different kind of obedience—pleasing our Heavenly Father based on a love relationship with Him.

He explained that His own obedience was motivated by love rather than fear or obligation: "So the world might know how thoroughly I love the Father, I am carrying out my Father's instructions right down to the last detail." (John 14:31 MSG)

Likewise, Jesus said His followers would be motivated to obey because of this same kind of love: "Whoever has my commands and keeps them is the one who loves me...Anyone who loves me will obey my teaching." (John 14:21, 14:23 NIV)

Remember: You'll never receive God's blessings in full measure unless you are abiding in His love. Your obedience will flow from your love relationship with the Lover of your soul.

JULY 2

Your word I have hidden in my heart,
that I might not sin against You.
(PSALM 119:11 NKJV)

FOR MANY PEOPLE, obedience to God takes a backseat to their human cravings: power, praise, wealth, gluttony, sexual exploits, or addictions. The Bible teaches that even Jesus "faced all of the same testings we do, yet he did not sin." (Hebrews 4:15 NLT) Christ was victorious over temptation from the Enemy, because He relied on the power of the Word. (Luke 4:1-3)

Before Jesus' ministry had even begun, He was led into the wilderness for 40 days of temptation by the devil. While each of the devil's temptations included the word "IF...," each of Jesus' replies was based on Scripture: "It is written..."

How well do you know the Word of God? Do you take time to read it...study it...meditate on it...and then do what it says? God has given you this powerful weapon so that you can defeat Satan's lies and live in victory. There's no other way to continually abide in His favor.

JULY 3

"Even the Son of Man did not come to be served,
but to serve, and to give his life as a ransom for many."
(MARK 10:45 NIV)

HUMILITY WAS PERHAPS one of the most difficult traits Jesus had to teach His disciples. One day the Twelve engaged in a heated debate about which of them was the "greatest," and Jesus later used this as a teachable moment: "Anyone who wants to be first must be the very last, and the servant of all." (Mark 9:35 NIV)

In the next chapter of Mark's gospel, the subject came up again when James and John asked if they could sit on His right and left hand—the seats of honor—when Jesus came into His glory. (See Mark 10:35-45.) The other disciples were upset by the audacity of the two brothers in asking this, prompting Jesus to challenge all of them again: "Whoever wants to become great among you must be your servant, and whoever wants to be first must be slave of all". (vs. 43-44)

This is the surprising pathway to true greatness and favor—the path modeled by Jesus.

JULY 4

You will have complete and free access to God's kingdom,
keys to open any and every door:
no more barriers between heaven and earth.

(MATTHEW 16:9 MSG)

YOU'VE PROBABLY HEARD stories of people who crave access to political leaders, such as Presidents, Prime Ministers, and other powerful dignitaries. But Jesus Christ gave us something far greater than that: access to God the Father, ruler of the universe!

When Jesus uttered the words, "It is finished" (John 19:30), and breathed His last breath on the cross, the veil in the Temple was torn from the top to the bottom (Mark 15:38). Through the blood of Christ, it became possible to enter into the Holy of Holies—the very presence of God—and offer prayers and petitions directly to Him.

What a magnificent gift! No longer was it necessary to be a high priest and then wait for a specific day or festival to enter God's presence. Because of Jesus, every Believer has been given the gift of unlimited access to the throne room of Almighty God!

JULY 5

They will call him Immanuel,
which means "God is with us."
(MATTHEW 1:23 NLT)

AFTER JESUS' RESURRECTION, two of His followers were walking to the village of Emmaus. In the midst of their deep conversation, Jesus came and walked along with them, "but they were not able to recognize who he was." (Luke 24:13-32 MSG)

When Jesus inquired about what they were discussing, the men stood there, downcast for they had lost their dearest friend and beloved companion. Then they described to Him how Jesus the Nazarene had been a mighty, miracle-working prophet, and that He was loved both by God and His fellow man. Sadly, though, they related that Jesus had been crucified, and their hopes crushed. They were sure He would deliver Israel from the heavy yoke of the Romans. All the while, the risen Christ was standing right by their side!

Perhaps you're like these men traveling to Emmaus; struggling with some trial or loss that seems devastating. Remember: Even when you don't yet recognize Him, Jesus is right there with you!

JULY 6

Will you not revive us again,
that your people may rejoice in you?
(PSALM 85:6 ESV)

REVIVAL IS WITHIN US, waiting to be stirred up as it was in the disciples on the Day of Pentecost! Revival is not merely a church service with big crowds, enthusiasm, repentance or great worship.

If we define "revival" as simply a state of being revived, quickened or filled with God's presence, and not split hairs over the word, we can say that Christ lived on earth in perpetual revival. *He was filled with the presence of the Father.* That's why when He saw a widow's grief (see Luke 7) at the loss of her only son, Jesus reached out and touched the dead boy, who instantly sprang to life. *That's revival!*

Revival is something that happens to Believers when they get "fed up" with being fed up, get hungry and thirsty for God, and won't settle for anything but Him.

God has decreed an end-time manifestation of His power and glory that will shake the world and take us beyond Pentecost, beyond mere "revivals."

God will take us beyond these, because He will take us beyond ourselves.

JULY 7

That I may know him,
and the power of his resurrection,
and the fellowship of his sufferings,
being made conformable unto his death...
(PHILIPPIANS 3:10 KJV)

AT THE AGE OF 32, everything I'd worked so hard to achieve came crashing down. I was working nonstop, 16-hours-a-day, seven-days-a-week, thinking I had to "keep up the pace for Jesus."

As I soon discovered, my problem wasn't physical, it was spiritual. I had tried to live my Christian life in my own strength, and found that I couldn't. No one told me that a minister could be afraid or have insecurities, so I had hidden mine. But they were not hidden from God, and they eventually overcame me.

What I didn't understand was that having the fellowship and suffering of Christ in my life meant being willing to admit everything that I wasn't. I was afraid to admit this, for fear of rejection. But then Christ revealed to me who *He* was.

The fellowship of His sufferings is acknowledging what we are not. God doesn't leave us there. He takes what we are not and infuses us with what He *is*—Lord and Redeemer, Savior and Deliverer, Rescuer and Provider!

JULY 8

We know that, when He [Jesus] shall appear,
we shall be like Him;
for we shall see Him as He is.
(1 JOHN 3:2 NIV)

THE EYES OF GOD and the spotlight of Heaven, continually search for hungry hearts willing to surrender to the Person of Jesus Christ and thirst to be with Him.

Christ has determined that we will rule and reign with Him. It's His mission, and not just when we get to Heaven, but on this present earth.

Satan's two greatest goals are (1) to convince you to live the Christian life yourself, in your own strength, and (2) to make you believe that you must be "worthy" and "righteous."

Trust today in the One who can quench all the fiery darts of the Enemy, no matter the circumstances—our Lord, Jesus Christ. Satan has no power over us when we allow the Person of Jesus Christ to live through us.

JULY 9

*For he will order his angels
to protect you wherever you go.*
(Psalm 91:11 NLT)

ELIJAH THE PROPHET was with his servant, a young man who was training under him. This young prophet awoke one morning and went outside to discover hundreds and thousands of Syrians surrounding him and his master, and he was afraid for his life. When he informed Elijah of the dire situation, the prophet walked out and said, "Those who are for us are greater than those against us." (See 2 Kings 5.)

How was that possible? One man said, "Look around the mountain, there are 100,000 horses and men who are going to kill us." But Elijah said, "Lord, open his eyes that he can see."

What did Elijah see? He saw angels in chariots of fire, tens of thousands of them circling the entire mountain of Syria. Elijah simply spoke the word, and every one of those Syrians was struck blind. He led them as a massive, powerless army right into the king's capitol!

Remember: Psalm 34:7 says, "The angel of the Lord encamps all around those who fear him, and delivers them." (Psalm 34:7 NIV) You and I have not been left defenseless and unprotected.

JULY 10

For people will love only themselves and their money.
They will be boastful and proud, scoffing at God,
disobedient to their parents, and ungrateful.
They will consider nothing sacred.

(2 TIMOTHY 3:11 NLT)

SECOND TIMOTHY accurately describes the days in which we live. It says that people *would not* be grateful. A lack of gratitude in their hearts would make them critical, rebellious, pretentious, proud, self-righteous, seeking after their own lusts, and loving pleasure more than they loved God.

How can you and I combat all the bad news that comes at us from every quarter? Philippians 4:4 provides the answer: Rejoice in the Lord always. Again I will say, rejoice!" (NKJV)

Did you know that rejoicing is an act of your will? We *can* and we *must* choose to rejoice. Why? There are three reasons:

- ✧ **God is on the throne.** When God is your source, your problems become His problems, and you cease to worry.

- ✧ **Problems are not permanent.** In Jesus, there are no permanent problems.

- ✧ **If the Devil can steal your joy, he can ransack your whole house.** When you choose joy, you open the floodgates of heaven and allow God to fill you with His blessings.

JULY 11

But let all who take refuge in you be glad; let them
ever sing for joy. Spread your protection over them,
that those who love your name may rejoice in you.

(PSALM 5:11 NIV)

HOW CAN YOU LEARN to create a joyful attitude in your life day by day?

⟡ **Learn not to take yourself too seriously.** If you're able to realize that God is on the throne, then your problems are not permanent.

⟡ **Relax.** The Bible says that no temptation comes against you except what is common to man. God is on the throne.

⟡ **Hold fast to joy so fear cannot take root.** When you lose your *joy*, fear will move in.

⟡ **Remain fully aware of the glorious liberty that is yours in Christ.** The Bible says, "Now the Lord is the Spirit; and where the Spirit of the Lord is, there is liberty." (2 Corinthians 3:17)

These are very important principles. Life is not always easy, but God is always good. Living for Christ is not easy, but God has promised to make a way for us. He is the Guiding Light that leads us.

Whatever the price, it will be worth it! The joy of the Lord is your strength.

JULY 12

The fear of man brings a snare,
But whoever trusts
in the LORD shall be safe.
(PROVERBS 29:25 NKJV)

YOU MUSTN'T MAKE man your source. Neither should you try to be your own source. You didn't cause other peoples' problems, and you can't solve them. You can't control their decisions. In your own strength, you can't cure the diseases of a sick and dying world. Proverbs 3:5 reminds that you are to "lean not on your own understanding." (NKJV)

When you realize that our Lord is in control, and you surrender the leadership of your life as a servant, you go forth in His power. It works! Consider this story:

> A man fell into a pit and couldn't get himself out.
>
> A subjective person came along and said:
> "I feel for you, down there."
>
> An objective person came along and said:" It's logical that someone would fall, down there."...
>
> A Pharisee said: "Only bad people fall into a pit."...
>
> A Fundamentalist said: "You deserve your pit."...
>
> An optimist said: "Things *could* be worse."
>
> A pessimist said: "Things *will* get worse!"

Jesus, seeing the man, took him by the hand and lifted him out of the pit.[24]

Are you in a pit of despair today? Reach up; Jesus has His hand extended to you.

JULY 13

My son, give attention to my words;
incline your ear to my sayings.
Do not let them depart from your eyes;
keep them in the midst of your heart.

(PROVERBS 4:20-21 NASB)

BEFORE HIS EXPERIENCE on the road to Damascus, the apostle Paul had the mentality of a murderer. He was consumed with hatred and unbelief. But then he met Jesus, and was changed.

Perhaps pastor and songwriter Mosie Lister was thinking of Paul when he wrote:

> For all things were changed, when He found me.
>
> A new day broke through all around me.
>
> For I met the Master, now I belong to Him.[25]

There is nothing impossible for the man or woman who grasps the principle that Jehovah is our source. We must keep our eyes on, and place our trust in Him.

Do you walk in fear and defeat, or in righteousness, the Word, and His fellowship? The choice is yours.

JULY 14

O our God, will You not judge them?
For we have no power against this
great multitude that is coming against us;
nor do we know what to do,
*but our eyes **are** upon You.*
(2 CHRONICLES 20:12 NKJV)

HAVE YOU RECENTLY felt like giving up? We all do at some time in our lives. In this day and time, there is no way we can escape stress and pressure. Everything we do seems riddled with problems. When we watch the news, we usually see only the bad news.

King Jehoshaphat had a crisis of integrity. He was the king of Israel, doing the will of God. He was faithful to God. He was obedient—a covenant man—yet he was faced with adversity. Vast armies, coming from three different directions, were about to attack him.

The people said: "Jehoshaphat, what kind of program do you have to deliver us? What committees are appointed to help solve this problem? Where are the bright, glorious banners and the trumpet under which we will march?" He said: "None—no programs, committees or banners."

"Jehoshaphat, you are the king!" they cried. "What are we going to do?" He said: "I don't know. I just don't know, but *my eyes are upon the Lord.*"

When you feel like giving up—be certain your eyes are upon the Lord.

JULY 15

I will be glad and rejoice in your love,
for you saw my affliction
and knew the anguish of my soul.
(PSALM 31:7 NIV)

BAD NEWS! The headlines are daily filled with it. Do you ever wonder just how much bad news a person can take and still retain an attitude of gratitude and a spirit of joyfulness and faith?

It is apparent that we live in a dangerous day. A restless spirit prowls about, and people everywhere are full of ingratitude and discontent.

The apostle Paul didn't complain in the midst of bad news, not to mention persecution. He said in Philippians 2:14, 15: "Do all things without complaining and disputing, that you may become blameless and harmless, children of God without fault in the midst of a crooked and perverse generation, among whom you shine as lights in the world." (NKJV)

If we can develop an attitude of gratitude in the midst of this crooked and perverse generation, we will shine as lights to the world. What a marvelous thought in the face of seemingly insurmountable obstacles and pressures!

JULY 16

Be honest in your evaluation of yourselves,
measuring yourselves by the faith God has given us.
(ROMANS 12:3B NLT)

THE OPINIONS of others are not as important as God's. That means you must have a pure heart. Sitting on the side of a mountain, teaching those spread out below Him, Jesus said, "Blessed *are* the pure in heart, For they shall see God." (Matthew 5:8 NKJV)

Don't allow past guilt to drain your hopes for the future. Make a firm decision to deal with the past on a daily basis. When your past invades your present, if it is negative, reject it. Paul wrote to the Philippians in chapter 3, verses 13-14:

> No, dear brothers and sisters, I have not achieved it, but I focus on this one thing: Forgetting the past and looking forward to what lies ahead, I press on to reach the end of the race and receive the heavenly prize for which God, through Christ Jesus, is calling us. (NLT)

You have not been born to lose—you have been born to choose. Walking with God is a choice. Happiness is a choice. No one can make you unhappy. Choose today who you will serve; join forces with Joshua who said, "As for me and my house, we will serve the Lord." (Joshua 24:15 KJV)

JULY 17

*And after eight days His disciples were again inside,
and Thomas with them. Jesus came, the doors being shut,
and stood in the midst, and said, 'Peace to you!'"*
(JOHN 20:26 NJKV)

MANY PEOPLE LIVE in a world where they never rise above their defeats. They continually compare themselves with others, and are then discouraged and defeated. These folks listen to gossip and make excuses for why they are going round and round on the carousel of life. Their destination? Nowhere!

You and I need to accept that Jesus Christ is risen and that He thinks highly of us. If we can ever get that truth inside us, we will not live in defeat and disgrace. We must be willing to admit our needs. We need to recognize that we are guilty and the only way out of this life of sin is through Jesus' forgiveness.

If you let defeat go, you will rise to live in God's potential. Many people think they are born to lose, but God created you to choose life, joy, grace, and God's mercy. Your success is determined by listening to those who edify rather than crucify!

JULY 18

For He made Him who knew no sin to be sin for us,
that we might become the righteousness of God in Him.
(2 CORINTHIANS 5:21 NKJV)

ARE YOU EXPERIENCING a Friday in your life right now? On Friday, the disciples were discouraged, defeated, and desperate. They had lost all hope, forgotten what Jesus had tried to instill in them. One had even betrayed Him. It was as if Jesus looked in His wallet and pulled out a picture of Peter. You might say, "Jesus, you can't be proud of him; he quit on you." But Jesus replied, "Yes, he quit on Friday, but Sunday is coming!"

Jesus knew that once He approached the throne room, brought His precious blood, and sprinkled it in the Holy of Holies, a man or woman would never again need to say they were unforgiven. They could hear the words, "Forgiven. Not guilty!" when they accepted Him as their personal Savior.

Jesus' work on Earth is finished. The tomb will always be empty. We serve a risen Lord whose power is stronger than your past or present.

God loves you. You may say you are not perfect, and that you cannot see the glory of God or the power of His resurrection. God knows about all of your discouragements, about your Fridays, but get ready—Sunday is coming!

JULY 19

But now I come to You,
and these things I speak in the world,
that they may have My joy
fulfilled in themselves.
I have given them Your word;
and the world has hated them
because they are not of the world,
just as I am not of the world.

(JOHN 17:13-14 NKJV)

HOW DO YOU REACT when your worth as a man or woman is assaulted? What will you do when you are being falsely accused at work or in school? Will you retaliate when someone speaks unkind words about you?

What will you do when your husband says or does something cruel? Will you defend yourself? Will you give someone a piece of your mind? Will you hurt them before they hurt you? What will your response be to injustice?

Remember what Jesus said about His adversaries when He hung on the cross? He asked the Father to forgive them. What will you do with this powerful example of love? Rather than retaliate against those who hurt you, allow the power of God's love and His grace transform you. You are what His Word says you are! Redeemed and forgiven!

JULY 20

You are the salt of the earth,
but if salt has lost its taste,
how shall its saltiness be restored?
It is no longer good for anything
except to be thrown out and
trampled under people's feet.

(MATTHEW 5:13 ESV)

GOD'S WORD SAYS that His glorious Church is to be a bride. No church building existed until 265 AD, yet the greatest revival of all time shook the world as it had never been shaken. When did this dynamic move stop? It came to a halt in the third century when Constantine legalized Christianity and made it a state religion.

People also began to look at the structure—in this day that would be the musical instruments, praise team, air conditioning, sound system, and preacher. Sadly, they took their eyes off Jesus, the true Source.

Today, God wants to make the Church glorious again. The Church is to be salt, able to preserve. You are the salt of the earth. God is saying: "Be my bride. Salt this world that is decaying and bring it back to me." But you won't build a church or develop maturity through advertising or marketing techniques.

If you want God to birth His Church, you have to say, "God, help me to apply these New Testament principals until I become salt and light."

JULY 21

Now faith is the substance of things hoped for,
the evidence of things not seen.
(HEBREWS 11:1 KJV)

IN ACTS 10, we see the incredible story of Cornelius. He went through an experience similar to many ethnic minorities—discrimination.

Cornelius was a Gentile. Many of those in the great revival didn't believe that the gospel was for the Gentiles. They were pagans and simply not good enough!

So what did Cornelius do? Protest; give them a piece of his mind? No! Do you know what he did? Acts 10:30 says he prayed and fasted. He didn't complain that he had gotten a raw deal. He sought God.

Cornelius didn't allow bitterness to take root in his heart. After he had fasted and prayed, by faith, an angel appeared to him and said: "Cornelius, your prayer has been heard. As a matter of fact, Peter at this time is having a vision. Send someone to bring him to your house." The result was revival in the house of Cornelius, and rejoicing when the Church council in Jerusalem heard the news.

Faith wrought miracles in the life of Cornelius. Your attitude, not your aptitude, determines your altitude. Our attitude does not move the hand of God—faith does.

JULY 22

For the love of money is a root of all kinds of evil:
which some reaching after have been led astray from the faith,
and have pierced themselves through with many sorrows.
(1 TIMOTHY 6:10 ASV)

MONEY ITSELF is not evil. But it will bring a snare if it is loved. Money is necessary for daily needs. Prosperity is the result of divine love working in your behalf for the finances you need to carry out your hopes and dreams.

If you give money the #1 place in your life, it is like trying to harvest corn before the kernels are planted in the soil. Meet the needs of others, and money follows as the rainbow follows the rain.

Satan is aware that the Believer will give from the abundance of the heart. He knows that when finances are given to the cause of Christ by prosperous saints, then the work of God moves quickly. He also recognizes that if money is withheld from godly endeavors, the Lord's work moves slowly.

When money is given its proper place, all else will follow. Psalm 1:3 says, "And whatever he does shall prosper." (NKJV) God believes in prosperity; do you?

JULY 23

In the world you will have tribulation;
but be of good cheer, I have overcome the world.
(JOHN 16:33 NKJV)

DIFFICULT PEOPLE and situations will teach you diplomacy; to respond with wisdom, and how to make sharp decisions. You really learn the most when dealing with a difficult problem. You learn your own weaknesses and strong points in a problematic situation. The pressure from difficult people will only define you if you let it.

When you look for the best in everyone and in every situation, you will find it. You see that for which you are looking. You receive what you expect. The Bible tells us not to be surprised or alarmed when trouble comes. (James 1:2–3) Use it to give glory to God.

Expect to be delivered from tribulation or hindrances. Tribulation means you are locked in and there is no way out. God always finds a way out for those who will believe. The greater the hindrance, the greater is the deliverance. The bigger the battle, the bigger is the opportunity for great success.

JULY 24

*Be still, and know that I **am** God;*
I will be exalted among the nations,
I will be exalted in the earth!
(PSALM 46:10 NKJV)

THE BIBLE has much to say about the attitude and disposition of solitude. The psalmist wrote, "He who dwells in the secret place of the Most High shall abide under the shadow of the Almighty... He makes me to lie down in green pastures; He leads me beside the still waters." (Psalm 91:1; 23:2 NKJV)

God called Abraham to a life of separation. He spent valuable time alone with God. That solitude produced the seed of faith in Abraham. Moses was forty days and forty nights receiving the Ten Commandments. Jesus spent days on end in the solitude of prayer. Paul spent three years in the Arabian Desert in solitude and reflection.

Solitude and silence bring with them the realization of who you are and Whom you serve. If you are never alone with yourself, you will never know yourself.

Times of silence and solitude provided Moses an opportunity to hear directly from God. When you are beset by spiritual and emotional exhaustion, carve out time to spend with Him. Surrender the chaos that surrounds you, and invite God to help you sort through all the issues of your life.

JULY 25

You will keep him in perfect peace,
whose mind is stayed on You.
(ISAIAH 26:3 NKJV)

A CALM AND SERENE MIND is the mark of maturity in the Believer. The untroubled mind is a mind under God's control. You and I are not called to control the world—only ourselves.

The person who has learned to direct his thoughts away from the worry and aggravation of his surroundings is a person functioning with Christ at the center of his being. When your mind is stayed, or focused, on Him, the result is perfect peace.

The disturbed mind is a distrusting mind, its fears so great that any shadow is threatening. Life is out of focus when the heart is out of harmony. But the calm, serene heart produces the fruit of the Spirit—love, joy, peace, gentleness, goodness, faith, meekness and self-control. How? In 1 Corinthians 2:12, the apostle Paul provides the answer:

What we have received is not the spirit of the world, but the Spirit who is from God, so that we may understand what God has freely given us. (NIV)

JULY 26

Behold, I give you the authority
to trample on serpents and scorpions,
and over all the power of the enemy,
and nothing shall by any means hurt you.
(LUKE 10:19 NKJV)

NO ONE CAN PRAY effectively out of a disturbed and troubled heart. If the heart fails because of fear, our world seems to fall apart as well. The effective life is a life under God's control and in submission to His will. A peaceful heart enables us to walk with God through difficult situations. It is learning to use all things for good. (See Romans 8:28.)

People and organizations are searching for a calm and serene heart. There is a strength, assurance and confidence that stems from serenity. Most people are looking for someone on whom they can lean in times of distress. Only the serene can bear the burdens of others.

Jesus walked on troubled waters and called out to His disturbed disciples, "Peace, be still." Walk in peace and serenity with Christ, and you will be able to support others who are in need.

JULY 27

Don't you realize that in a race
everyone runs,
but only one person gets the prize?
So run to win!
(1 Corinthians 9:24 nlt)

IF THERE IS NO RACE, there can be no winner. If there is no battle, there can be no victory. Winners are the people who have entered the conflict and run to win the prize. The joy of crossing the finish line begins at the starting line.

Strength grows from weakness. Your greatest opportunities lie in the midst of your most severe trials. Welcome the problems. They come to make you wise. Salute the hills; the climb only makes you stronger. Look to Him, the author and finisher of our faith. (See Hebrews 12:2.)

Paul cried, "When I am weak, then am I strong." He had learned the most vital lesson in life. He knew that through his weaknesses he gained the strength he needed to achieve the victory. Opposition became his opportunity; his hindrances only made him stronger.

There is a way through your darkness, for Jesus is the light. Move toward Him.

JULY 28

And those who know your name
put their trust in you,
for you, O LORD,
have not forsaken those who seek you.
(PSALM 9:10 ESV)

IN *UP FROM SLAVERY: An Autobiography* Booker T. Washington wrote, "I have learned that success is to be measured not so much by the position that one has reached in life as by the obstacles that he has overcome while trying to succeed."[26]

Who knows what will happen if, by God's grace and help, you are able to overcome the hindrances imposed in your life. The more that is required of you, the stronger you will become in Him.

When people fail, it is usually from the inside out. Overcoming obstacles occurs when you place your trust in the One who knows your heart like no other. The power to go up and over is the power of Christ in you! You may be surprised to find that He has given you the ability to rise to every occasion.

No job, position, or responsibility is too overwhelming when, by your prayers and efforts, you reach it. Who knows what in you is yet to be developed for even greater positions of leadership! It is God who makes you and me mighty men and women of faith.

JULY 29

Fight the good fight for the true faith.
Hold tightly to the eternal life
to which God has called you,
which you have confessed so well
before many witnesses.
(1 TIMOTHY 6:12 NKJV)

BEING A CHRISTIAN does not mean you are problem free. Even though you are a child of God, you will still have to deal with difficult situations throughout your life.

As children, many of us sang this song in Sunday school or Vacation Bible School:

> I may never march in the infantry
>
> Ride in the cavalry
>
> Shoot the artillery
>
> I may never fly o'er the enemy
>
> But I'm in the Lord's army!
>
> Yes Sir![27]

Battles will come. Persecution will come. You will have to fight deception, guard yourself against occasional unforgiveness and bitterness, and struggle against unbelief. You will have to dislodge fear before it disarms you and makes you vulnerable to further assaults.

You have been drafted into the army of God, so be prepared to fight the good fight of faith!

JULY 30

Thus says the LORD to you:
"Do not be afraid nor dismayed
because of this great multitude,
*for the battle **is** not yours,*
but God's."

(2 CHRONICLES 20:15B NKJV)

WHEN DECEPTION, unforgiveness, bitterness, or unbelief knocks at the door of your heart, you must allow faith to answer. When fear knocks, faith must respond.

The difference between a citizen of God's kingdom and a defeated Christian is clear: When a Kingdom man is engaged in a battle, it doesn't make him bitter; it makes him better. The battle may be long and hard, but he is a *persistent* man of faith. He sees beyond the immediate skirmish to greater victory ahead. He learns what it means to walk in submission to the King, and to walk in authority over the Enemy.

Spiritual warfare can make you more sensitive to the Holy Spirit. By relying on Him when times are at their toughest, you learn to love others more. You begin to see people through His eyes, and you respond with a heart of faith and generosity.

Depend on His direction when you are in the heat of battle.

JULY 31

As a result, both of Lot's daughters
became pregnant by their own father. [37]
When the older daughter gave birth to a son,
she named him Moab. He became the ancestor
of the nation now known as the Moabites.

(GENESIS 29:36-37 NLT)

LOT AND HIS DAUGHTERS miraculously escaped the destruction of Sodom, but apparently carried the essence of that ungodly city with them.

Moab, born out of an incestuous relationship between Lot and his daughter grew up to be an unsavory character. His was an attitude birthed in Sodom and Gomorrah: "Go ahead, whatever you do is permissible. No one will hold you accountable." This is a destructive mindset.

God sets limits for you because He loves you. Those boundaries are for your protection. God cares about you! He cares so much He allowed His only Son to die for your sin. If you have strayed from Him, turn, repent, and find grace.

AUGUST

AUGUST 1

Then Joshua said to Achan,
"My son, give glory to the LORD,
the God of Israel, and honor him.
Tell me what you have done;
do not hide it from me."
(JOSHUA 7:19 NIV)

ONE DAY many years ago, I was out raking leaves in my yard. When I completed the job, I looked around with great satisfaction. The yard was beautiful, the grass lush and green. Everything was perfect. Putting my rake back in the garage, I stepped back outside for one more prideful look. As I walked across the lawn, I slipped on an acorn, fell, and nearly broke my back. One little acorn was my downfall.

Achan's "acorn" was greed. Stealing a forbidden object and then hiding it in his tent, he thought, "It is just one sin. No one will notice." But God knew his heart and his actions.

Do you try to hide things from God? Do you say: "It's just a small infraction. I can keep it a secret. I'm not really hurting anyone." Allow God to search your heart, cleanse it, and fill it with His Spirit. Forgiveness is always just a prayer away.

AUGUST 2

The LORD gave this message to Jonah son of Amittai:
"Get up and go to the great city of Nineveh.
Announce my judgment against it
because I have seen how wicked its people are."
But Jonah got up and went in the opposite
direction to get away from the LORD.

(JONAH 1:1-3A NLT)

THE PROPHET JONAH reacted badly to God's command. He turned his back and began a downward slide that ended in the belly of a "great fish." His every action took him farther and farther from the Father.

Jonah's was a sorry, half-hearted commitment. God told him to go to Nineveh and preach repentance, but Jonah didn't quite make it. He said, "I started to go. At least, I made the attempt."

Many Christians today are like Jonah—committed in word but not in deed. What about you? When God tells you to do something, do you run away? Or do you answer a resounding "Yes!" and move ahead with a heart full of faith?

AUGUST 3

*...being confident of this very thing,
that He who has begun a good work in you
will complete it until the day of Jesus Christ.*
(PHILIPPIANS 1:6 NKJV)

MANY PEOPLE BELIEVE they have been disqualified as Christian because they have been experiencing a period of barrenness. Perhaps this describes you. You have lost your joy. You can't seem to motivate yourself to pray or read the Word. God seems remote, and you feel utterly defeated. If this is your life right now, be encouraged! Barrenness does not have to be permanent! God is not angry with you! He is not finished with you!

Barrenness is a time of vulnerability. It is when the Enemy tries to torment you and lure you away from God. He will heap condemnation and confusion on you. He will bring fear and doubt and worry. That is when you must *stand* on the Word and *believe* that God is still at work in your life.

Jesus asked His disciples if they would leave Him, and Peter answered with words that should resonate through our lives today: "Lord, to whom shall we go? You have the words of eternal life." (John 6:68 NKJV)

God is committed to finishing what He started in you. If you are in a season of barrenness, don't despair. God is refining your faith. He is honing your patience. He is giving you an opportunity to reach out and touch His heart.

AUGUST 4

Give us this day our daily bread.
(MATTHEW 6:11 KJV)

FOR A DEVOUT JEW, sharing a meal is more than an act of hospitality. If you eat with someone, you are *one* with that person—you are not just filling your stomach. That's why the children of Israel spent so much time in fellowship with one another, particularly around the table—it was a symbol of forgiveness.

Peter experienced forgiveness, too. When the soldiers arrested Jesus in the Garden of Gethsemane, Peter followed. He wanted to know what was happening to his Master. But when someone identified him and questioned his relationship with Jesus, three times Peter denied ever knowing Him.

It was a terrible moment for Peter. His desolation drove him back to his fishing boat and onto the Sea of Galilee. But from somewhere on the beach, a familiar voice encouraged the men to cast their nets on the other side of the boat.

Peter recognized the voice of Jesus, jumped into the water and swam to the shore. As soon as Jesus saw him, He invited Peter to come have breakfast. Peter had been forgiven!

Through the atonement, God is calling us back to Him. He is calling *you* to rest in Him and His finished work on the cross.

AUGUST 5

More than that, we also rejoice in God
through our Lord Jesus Christ,
through whom we have now received reconciliation
[or the atonement].
(ROMANS 5:11 ESV)

THE WORD *atonement* is used in sixty-nine verses in the Old Testament, but only once in the New Testament, in Romans. When seeing or hearing the root word atone, I think of being "at-one." The act of atonement, or in some Bible translations, reconciliation, makes us one with God.

Jesus died so your broken relationship with the Father could be restored, and the basis for your restoration is rest. You are invited to be reconciled to Jesus and rest in His finished work.

As Hebrews 4:9 records, "There remains therefore a rest for the people of God." (NKJV) When you are "at one" with the Father, you are at rest.

AUGUST 6

Finally, brethren, whatever things are true,
whatever things are noble, whatever things are just,
whatever things are pure, whatever things are lovely,
whatever things are of good report, if there is any virtue
and if there is anything praiseworthy—
meditate on these things.
(PHILIPPIANS 4:8 NKJV)

IN ONE OF THE PRISONS where the apostle Paul was incarcerated was a dark hole, with barely enough room for the forty-two prisoners crowded inside. Those in the black chasm who had received the death sentence knew they would be crucified, strangled, skinned alive, or beheaded.

Imagine the apostle Paul, shackled in a rat-infested cell, having food dumped down on him. He is surrounded by sin and death and fear. But in Philippians 4:4 (NKJV), he says: "Rejoice in the Lord always. Again I will say, rejoice!"

Paul had mentally entered into God's rest. Can you imagine what the other prisoners may have thought when they heard him say this? They were about to be brutally slain. But for Paul, Jesus had stripped away the power of sin, death, hell, and the grave when He rose from the dead! He disarmed fear with His precious blood, and He also set you free from its grip.

Now you can enter into His rest by accepting the reality of the atonement.

AUGUST 7

The stone which the builders rejected has become the chief cornerstone. This was the Lord's doing; it is marvelous in our eyes. This is the day the Lord has made; we will rejoice and be glad in it.

(PSALM 118:22-24 NKJV)

GLADNESS IS A CHOICE. Notice, the scripture says: "We *will* be glad." As one of my daughters sometimes reminds me, "You need to notify your face that Jesus is Lord!"

You may feel you have reasons *not* to be glad. I had a reason one morning when I woke up very tired from a late night of work. In my haste, I grabbed what I thought was spray gargle, but I squirted deodorant into my mouth instead!

When things like this—or much worse—happen, choose to say, "I will be glad in the Lord." You *can* develop a spirit of gladness and joy!

AUGUST 8

But let all who take refuge in you be glad;
let them ever sing for joy.
Spread your protection over them,
that those who love your name may rejoice in you.

(PSALM 5:11 NIV)

PERHAPS YOU MAY RELATE to the story of the county extension agent from Texas who went out to visit an old farmer. The agent held out his hand and said, "I have a card here that gives me the authority to go through your farm and check everything. If your place doesn't match up to our codes, I can shut you down. That's right; this card gives me the power to do whatever I want."

The old man just looked at him and said, "Go on and exercise your rights, then. Take a look around." The agent walked over a large red barn and asked, "What's in there? Open the barn doors, now!"

As it so happened, the farmer had a big, ornery prize bull in that barn. When the man opened the doors, the bull bolted through it and headed straight for the agent, who cried. "Help me! Stop him!" The old farmer just smiled, "Show him the card, son. Show him the card!"

You may be a "card-carrying" member of the body of Christ, but does it mean you are experiencing His joy? His grace, blessings, and authority are yours for the asking. So is His joy—and you don't need a *card* to receive it!

AUGUST 9

May my meditation be sweet to Him;
I will be glad in the Lord.
(PSALM 104:34 NKJV)

THE BIBLE SAYS you need to *meditate* on scripture. Why? Because God's Word is true and it never fails. It is full of wisdom and will instruct you in the way you should go, the choices you should make.

It will reveal the Father's heart and help you understand His will for your life. It will cause your love for Jesus to grow, and bring peace even when your heart is filled with fear and turmoil. It will help you remember that God is still in control, and He is working everything out to your benefit.

Meditating on the Word will bring rest to your weary soul and body. Try this: Before you close your eyes at night, read one or two Bible verses. Let your mind *dwell* on them for fifteen minutes or so—and see if your sleep isn't sweet!

God is still on His throne! His Word is true! Hebrews 4:12 (NKJV) says it is "living and powerful, and sharper than any two-edged sword, piercing even to the division of soul and spirit, and of joints and marrow, and is a discerner of the thoughts and intents of the heart."

When the pressures of life weigh you down, meditate on the Word! When you are worried and fearful, meditate on the Word!

AUGUST 10

"If you faint in the day of adversity,
your strength is small.
(PROVERBS 24:10 NKJV)

FOCUSING on your problems can make you forget that gladness, joy, and laughter bring release and deliverance. But meditating on the Word of God puts everything into perspective. What a wonderful way to refresh your spirit and revitalize your joy!

Proverbs 24:10 says: "If you faint in the day of adversity, your strength is small." You are living in a day of tremendous pressure and adversity—are you going to faint?

The temptation to harbor an offense is greatest when you have pressures in your life. If you allow stress to determine your actions, you will be stumbling along in darkness. That kind of darkness will blind you to the truth and keep you from responding as you should. That's why you have to renew your mind.

God wants you to look and act like Jesus! Sometimes He allows pressures to build as a way of refining your patience and faith. The stress and pressures are temporary.

Jesus died so you could have abundant life. He didn't die for issues or causes—He died for *you*. He also rose again, making you a conqueror in Him. You will overcome the pressures of life when you recognize His love and care for you and submit to His lordship.

AUGUST 11

*It was about this time that King Herod
arrested some who belonged to the church,
intending to persecute them.*

(ACTS 1:3 NIV)

IN ACTS 12:1–17, we read that King Herod Agrippa, who was persecuting the Church, had already killed James, the brother of John with the sword. He then had Peter arrested and thrown in jail.

It was a dark time for God's people. They were being hunted by brutal Roman soldiers, and one by one, either killed or imprisoned. To their credit, the disciples sought the Lord for Peter's deliverance. Verse 5 says: "Prayer was offered to God for him by the church."

God miraculously released Peter, but when he knocked at the gate of the house where they were meeting, the disciples didn't believe he was really there!

Rhoda, the servant girl, was so excited to hear Peter's voice she didn't stop to let him in. She just ran back and told the others. "Guess what? Peter's here!" They didn't believe her.

When you pray, be ready to receive God's answer. Expect a miracle! Trust His Word, and allow Him to be God. He knows what you need, and He knows the best way to meet your needs. Remember, He is a good God!

AUGUST 12

For your Father knows the things
you have need of before you ask Him.
(MATHEW 6:8B NKJV)

DO YOU KNOW what is bothering you? Identify the root and you will be able to move to a place where God can supply your needs. Then you can go forward into the destiny God has planned for you.

Here's how to identify what's bothering you:

⟡ **Make a God-connection.** The apostle Paul said God's people are bound together by a band of constraining love. When you truly realize this bond with God and with fellow Christians, peace and harmony result.

⟡ **Identify your strength-stealers.** These can be worry, fear, stress, rejection, anger, confusion. Don't meditate on the lies of the Enemy.

⟡ **When the Devil assaults your mind, resist him!** Understand that you are in a war. Don't entertain the lies of the Enemy when God Almighty paid such a great price for your redemption.

Nothing can rob you of your hold on grace and your confidence in God—without your permission. The grace of God is too great. The love and mercy of God are too strong. The compassion and peace of God are too powerful.

You must believe God's Word. Never release your grip on the covenant Christ made for you. The Bible teaches that you are to walk by faith, not by sight.

AUGUST 13

Behold what manner of love the Father
has bestowed on us,
that we should be called children of God!
(1 JOHN 3:1a NKJV)

GOD LOVES YOU as much as He loves everyone in His kingdom. You are no less important to Him than your pastor or any other leader in the church. St. Augustine said, "God loves each of us as if there were only one of us." [28]

God loves you so much that He has called *you* to do great things in Jesus' name, but you won't fulfill that calling unless you are walking in faith, not fear. Living in fear is like living near a poisoned stream. You can take a drink from it and perhaps satiate your thirst for a moment, but the end result is sickness or death.

Some think fear is an effective motivator, but fear doesn't motivate anyone to grow, spiritually or otherwise; it only leads to deeper deception and greater bondage. Throughout your life, you will deal constantly with faith and fear. With faith comes power; with fear, paralysis. The Bible describes many individuals who were conquerors in life: Noah, Moses, Daniel, and many others.

What do the words of your mouth reveal about you? Do they reflect your faith in God, or do they indicate your bondage to fear?

AUGUST 14

The Lord is my light and my salvation;
whom shall I fear?
(PSALM 27:1 NKJV)

EVEN AS A YOUNG MAN, David knew how to speak the Word and disarm fear. When confronted by the menacing giant Goliath, David knew that his help came from Jehovah.

Like David, you are confronted by giants in your own life. They may not be physical adversaries, but they can be just as menacing. When one of those giants threatens you, remember David.

The Bible tells us that David *hid in a cave* as war raged about him and his foes pursued him relentlessly. But David used God's words as weapons to conquer his fear! He overcame both his fear and his foes, and God *blessed* his faith!

Have you ever read one of those self-help books written to build confidence? I have read many, but they did me no good. I couldn't relate to those authors. They talked about developing self-confidence, but confidence in *self* is not what I needed. Proverbs 14:26 reminds us that, "In the fear of the LORD one has strong confidence, and his children will have a refuge. (ESV)

The Bible doesn't talk about *self*-confidence—it says you should put your confidence in God!

AUGUST 15

Little children, you are from God
and have overcome them,
for he who is in you is greater
than he who is in the world.
(1 JOHN 4:4 ESV)

HOW DO YOU RESPOND to the dark times in your life? Do you face the darkness as a soldier in God's victorious army, as an overcomer? Do you face the darkness with a tender and repentant heart? Or do you retreat from the darkness? Does the pressure expose your anger and unbelief?

When darkness threatens to overtake you, do you lash out at God and others? Do dark moments make you want to compromise your faith?

How do you respond to the dark times in your life? Do you face the darkness as a soldier in God's victorious army, as an overcomer? Do you face the darkness with a tender and repentant heart? Or do you retreat from the darkness? Does the pressure expose your anger and unbelief?

When darkness threatens to overtake you, do you lash out at God and others? Do dark moments make you want to compromise your faith?

God has given you the strength and power to overcome the Enemy. Put on the whole armor of God, and when you have done all to stand; stand therefore, secure in Him.

AUGUST 16

So the LORD God banished him
from the Garden of Eden
to work the ground from which
he had been taken.
(GENESIS 3:23 NIV)

WHEN ADAM AND EVE were driven from the garden, a prayer has not been recorded for them. Surely they bent their faces to the earth and wailed, or perhaps they were simply rendered speechless when God proclaimed:

> The ground is cursed because of you. You will eat from it by means of painful labor all the days of your life. (Genesis 3:17b CSB)

Even though God had promised a way of restoration in His pronouncement (see Genesis 3:15), Adam must have been despondent when God drove the two from Eden and then "stationed the cherubim and the flaming, whirling sword east of the garden of Eden to guard the way to the tree of life." (verse 24)

Everything that has transpired in my life has been because of prayer. One word from God changed my life forever; I realized that prayer was my words to God, but He also spoke to me through His Word.

My prayer today is that your faith will soar, and you will realize that God can turn your pain into power, purpose, and passion. He stands ready to transform your test into a *testi*mony through the power of prayer.

AUGUST 17

When he had received the drink,
Jesus said, "It is finished."
With that, he bowed his head
and gave up his spirit.
(JOHN 19:30 NIV)

WHEN JESUS BREATHED His last and gave up the ghost, Matthew tells us that "the veil of the temple was rent in twain from the top to the bottom." (Matthew 27:51 KJV) The temple's high priest must have been terribly frightened. As he made his way into the Holy of Holies to sprinkle the blood for the evening sacrifice on the horns of the altar, the veil that separated man from God had been ripped from top to bottom.

Why was that important? It was a symbol that we no longer have to wait to be represented yearly by the high priest:

Seeing then that we have a great high priest, that is passed into the heavens, Jesus the Son of God, let us hold fast our profession. For we have not an high priest which cannot be touched with the feeling of our infirmities; but was in all points tempted like as we are, yet without sin. Let us therefore come boldly unto the throne of grace, that we may obtain mercy, and find grace to help in time of need. (Hebrews 4:14–16 KJV)

You, as a Believer, now have free access into the presence of God so that "by prayer and supplication with thanksgiving let [your] requests be made known unto God." (Philippians 4:6 KJV)

AUGUST 18

Pray without ceasing.
(1 Thessalonians 5:17 kjv)

PAUL WRITES that we are to "pray without ceasing." He is, quite obviously, not telling us to stay on our knees in a posture of prayer twenty-four hours each day. That would be nearly impossible. His admonition refers to a mindset of always being conscious of our Heavenly Father and living a life of surrender to Him and His will. It is an awareness of the truth that God should govern our every thought and action.

One writer proffered this advice:

When our thoughts turn to worry, fear, discouragement, and anger, we are to consciously and quickly turn every thought into prayer and every prayer into thanksgiving. In his letter to the Philippians, Paul commands us to stop being anxious and instead, "in everything, by prayer and petition, with thanksgiving, present your requests to God" (Philippians 4:6)....As we go through the day, prayer should be our first response to every fearful situation, every anxious thought, and every undesired task that God commands. A lack of prayer will cause us to depend on ourselves instead of depending on God's grace.[29]

To pray without ceasing is to reveal your total reliance on and dependence upon with your loving Father God.

AUGUST 19

He [God] saw that there was no man,
and wondered that there was no intercessor.
(ISAIAH 59:16 NKJV)

TWO OF THE SADDEST SCRIPTURES in the Bible can be found in Ezekiel and Isaiah, the one above, and:

So I sought for a man among them who would make a wall, and stand in the gap before Me on behalf of the land, that I should not destroy it; but I found no one. (Ezekiel 22:30 NKJV)

Today, God continues His search for that man, woman, young person, or child who will commit to stand in the breach and pray. Will you, like Isaiah, say, "Here am I! Send me." (See Isaiah 6:8.)

The children of Israel sinned in the wilderness, fashioning a golden calf, dancing before it, and denying God's sovereignty, and God threatened to destroy them. (See Exodus 32.) Moses fell on his face before Jehovah God to intercede.

God's Word is rife with examples of intercessors who prevailed against the Enemy, the prayer warriors of Hebrews 11 who subdued kingdoms, shut the mouths of lions, set armies to flight, raised the dead, and secured the promises of God—all through faith in God and prayer!

Will you accept the challenge to become an intercessor?

AUGUST 20

Hear my prayer, O God;
give ear to the words of my mouth.
(PSALM 54:2 KJV)

TODAY, THE CLARION CALL goes out to God-fearing people everywhere to man the battle stations and fight with prayer. We must not cower in fear inside the church walls; we must take the battle to the Enemy and defeat him through prayer in the name of Jesus!

Prayer is the only exploit that takes hold of eternity. It is the action that touches heaven, and moves earth. For a Christian, it is not the last resort ... it must always be the first line of defense!

Through prayer, we strive to do everything possible to overthrow kingdoms of darkness, shut the mouths of the lions of terror, and quench the flames of hell by the power of almighty God! How you and I respond to God's call will determine whether we succeed or fail. The people of God are still called to intercede for and to comfort the Jewish people.

Will you stand against the Enemy in prayer?

AUGUST 21

In the year that King Uzziah died,
I saw the Lord sitting on a throne,
high and lifted up,
and the train of His robe filled the temple.
(ISAIAH 6:1 NKJV)

GOD HAS ALWAYS sought volunteers to pray, to speak, and to perform His work on Earth with love and compassion. The story of Isaiah is a perfect example: King Uzziah had been a good king, a rare leader of God's people, and Isaiah was heartbroken when he died. It was at this time that God comforted Isaiah by showing him that the King of Kings was still on the throne.

When Isaiah realized that Jehovah God was still in control, when he glimpsed the One whose throne is elevated above every other, and who was still in charge, Isaiah was awed by the holiness of God and convicted of his own uncleanness. He fell on his face, repented, and the angel cleansed him of his iniquity.

Then one of the seraphim flew to me, having in his hand a live coal which he had taken with the tongs from the altar. And he touched my mouth with it, and said: "Behold, this has touched your lips; your iniquity is taken away, and your sin purged. (Isaiah 6:6–7 NKJV)

The prophet was cleansed of his iniquity, and was ready for his commission. Are you ready today?

AUGUST 22

For our sake he made him
to be sin who knew no sin,
so that in him we might
become the righteousness of God.
(2 CORINTHIANS 5:21 ESV)

THE SON OF MAN was so overcome in the Garden by the magnitude of what He was about to face that He prayed in desperation, yet He so desperately wanted to do the Father's will. He desired *that* more than He valued His own life.

Jesus was about to be crushed by the weight of sin just as the fruit of the olive tree was crushed by the stone press. Pressed from our Savior was not oil, but rather a perfect plan for our salvation fueled by a love that will not let us go.

The answer to Jesus' prayer of despair was the salvation of mankind. Jesus offered one sacrifice: Himself. He established the plan of forgiveness and reconciliation one time for all time! He had laid aside His robes of glory and donned a robe of flesh so that we might have access to God, the Father. Blood-bought, forgiven, redeemed, and delivered!

You and I are not saved by the *character* of the sacrifice; salvation only comes through the shed blood of Christ—the faultless and final price of atonement.

AUGUST 23

Father, if you are willing,
please take this cup of suffering away from me.
Yet I want your will to be done, not mine.
(LUKE 22:42 NLT)

THE EFFICACY OF OUR PRAYERS is not determined by our dexterity with whatever language we speak. It is not dependent on a prescribed repetitious prayer. God knows our hearts before we ever bow a knee and utter a word.

Many have asked the question: Why pray if God is omniscient—all-knowing? Prayer is not about imparting knowledge to God; it is about having fellowship with Him. We desire to spend time in communion with our heavenly Father and to seek His will. "Not my will, but thine, be done" was Jesus' prayer in the Garden of Gethsemane.

Prayer is an act of surrender to the will of God, of aligning ourselves with His plan and purpose for our lives. Surrender to Him today.

AUGUST 24

At the same time came the disciples unto Jesus, saying,
Who is the greatest in the kingdom of heaven?
And Jesus called a little child unto him, and set
him in the midst of them, and said, Verily I say unto you,
Except ye be converted, and become as little children,
ye shall not enter into the kingdom of heaven.
Whosoever therefore shall humble himself as this little child,
the same is greatest in the kingdom of heaven.
(MATTHEW 18:1–4 KJV)

THE DISCIPLES had asked Jesus a question, and in response Jesus turns around and sees a little boy walking by, or perhaps simply running down the street playing with some friends. Jesus says, "Child, come here." The boy stops and walks over to Jesus in obedience. Jesus takes the boy lovingly by the shoulders, turns him to face the disciples and says, "Whosoever shall humble himself as this little child, the same is greatest in the kingdom of heaven."

There have been times in my life when I knew I could do nothing in my own strength. I had no idea then that my desperate heart's cry was the fertile soil in which the glory of God could be manifested.

This is receiving the kingdom of God like a child. You can receive Him today.

AUGUST 25

Make every effort to keep the unity of the Spirit
through the bond of peace.
(EPHESIANS 4:3 NIV)

UNITY AND HARMONY were non-existent in my childhood home. Neither my parents nor my siblings enjoyed "unity of the Spirit." Not until I later began to study the Word of God did I realize just how important these words are.

Unity is the glue that holds a family, a Church, a nation together. The result of such harmony is a place where God's people are refreshed and strengthened by His Spirit. It is the place where His anointing flows! And it is the place where *zoe*—Hebrew for life, the eternal, God-kind of life—flows freely!

The Hebrew word for unity denotes a people drawn together for one purpose—to follow Jehovah, fulfill His plan and purpose, and to dwell together under the umbrella of His blessings.

Live under that umbrella today and enjoy God's best for you.

AUGUST 26

*That they all may be one; as thou, Father, **art** in me,*
and I in thee, that they also may be one in us:
that the world may believe that thou hast sent me.
(JOHN 17:21 KJV)

ONLY WHEN SELF is subjugated to Christ can we be one with God—and each other—to have this His unity in our lives. We will never be one by trying to agree with each other and putting aside differences of belief for the sake of unity alone.

You and I are to be one as Jesus and His Father are one. Only when Jesus is on the throne in each of our lives can we be in tune with His purpose and be one Body on earth able to work corporately, to bring true and lasting revival.

Only when Self is subjugated to Jesus will His "greater works" flourish as the body of Christ grows into His fullness and carries forth His kingdom on the earth.

Surrender to His will today.

*"Therefore do not worry, saying,
'What shall we eat?' or 'What shall we drink?' or
'What shall we wear?' For after all these things
the Gentiles seek. For your heavenly Father
knows that you need all these things.
But seek first the kingdom of God and
His righteousness, and
all these things shall be added to you."*

(MATTHEW 6:31-33 NKJV)

OFTEN, I THINK we are like little children—not so much hard of hearing as we are hard of *listening*. We *hear*, but do not necessarily *heed* His warnings.

Learning to hear God's voice from scripture—learning the way He expressed Himself to the men and women of old—teaches us how to distinguish the sound of His voice from our own and helps us avoid the deceptive whispers of the Enemy.

My journey to wholeness in Christ has been painful at times, but it is not an unfamiliar path. God tells us that in order to hear Him we must wait and seek and listen closely. Seeking first the Kingdom and His righteousness leads us to increased faith and less worry. Peace and worry cannot occupy the same space. One forces the other out.

Your daily prayer should be, "Help me to wait patiently for the very best You have for my life."

AUGUST 28

Then one of the crowd answered and said,
"Teacher, I brought You my son, who has a mute spirit.
And wherever it seizes him, it throws him down;
he foams at the mouth, gnashes his teeth, and becomes rigid.
So I spoke to Your disciples, that they should cast it out,
but they could not."
(MARK 9:17-18 NKJV)

IN MARK, CHAPTER 9, the disciples came to Jesus, frustrated and downcast. A father had brought his child to them for healing. The little boy had what his father described as a "mute spirit." After Jesus rebuked the spirit and the little boy was healed, the disciples privately asked Him why *they* could not heal the child. Jesus answered, "This kind can come out by nothing but prayer and fasting." (Mark 9:29)

September 11, 2001, was an assault from hell, planned and executed by evil spirits, just as have been other attacks worldwide—in Paris, London, San Diego, Boston, Las Vegas, New York. The continuing terrorist attacks in Israel, and indeed worldwide, are a result of the same dark spiritual powers. These powers cannot be defeated without prayer. Praying saints are God's agents to carry out His will on Earth.

If Jesus said that He could do nothing without prayer, then you and I surely cannot hope to accomplish anything of eternal value and significance without daily, fervent prayer.

AUGUST 29

Ask, and it will be given to you;
seek, and you will find;
knock, and it will be opened to you.
(MATTHEW 7:7 NKJV)

PRAYER is not for the faint of heart; it is hard work! As Scottish author and theologian Oswald Chambers wrote:

> We tend to use prayer as a last resort, but God wants it to be our first line of defense. We pray when there's nothing else we can do, but God wants us to pray before we do anything at all.[30]

My life has been bathed in prayer, protected by prayer, and guided by prayer. Blind English preacher William Walford wrote what may be the consummate hymn about prayer:

> Sweet hour of prayer! Sweet hour of prayer!
>
> That calls me from a world of care,
>
> And bids me at my Father's throne
>
> Make all my wants and wishes known.
>
> In seasons of distress and grief,
>
> My soul has often found relief,
>
> And oft escaped the tempter's snare,
>
> By thy return, sweet hour of prayer![31]

AUGUST 30

MANKIND cannot worship a holy God any other way—except through righteousness and holiness. Why? He requires that we worship according to His precepts. He is, after all, a God who demands order, and He reveals that to His people beginning in Genesis through the last chapter of Deuteronomy.

A holy God commands respect and veneration, reverence in worship, and devout consecration. But what does it mean to worship God in the beauty of His holiness? How can we mere mortals hope to be holy enough to worship Jehovah?

Dr. Jack Hayford, chancellor of The King's University in Van Nuys, California, provides an answer. He said:

> I would contend that what is on God's mind when we worship Him is not how many grandiose thoughts we have about Him, but how passionately our hearts desire Him.[32]

Worship God today in the splendor of His holiness.

AUGUST 31

Listen! Obedience is better than sacrifice,
and submission is better than offering the fat of rams.

(1 SAMUEL 15:22B NLT)

IN 1 SAMUEL 15, God gave specific instructions to King Saul to destroy the Amalekites—sparing no one and no animal. Saul *almost* fulfilled Jehovah's instructions; but being almost obedient is not being completely compliant.

When Samuel the prophet approached the Israelite encampment, he heard the lowing of cattle and the bleating of sheep. Marching into Saul's presence, Samuel demanded to know why the Israelite king had not followed God's direction. Like many a leader, Saul first blamed it on his troops.

Far from being pleased with Saul's response, Samuel had some harsh news for the ruler:

Rebellion is as sinful as witchcraft, and stubbornness as bad as worshiping idols. So because you have rejected the command of the LORD, he has rejected you as king. (1 Samuel 15: 23, 26b NLT)

Rebellion not only robbed Saul of his kingdom, it ultimately deprived the Israelites of their relationship with Jehovah. If you are in rebellion to God and His word, ask His forgiveness, and turn back to Him today.

SEPTEMBER

SEPTEMBER 1

Behold, when we come into the land,
you shall tie this scarlet cord in the window through
which you let us down, and you shall gather
into your house your father and mother, your brothers,
and all your father's household.

(JOSHUA 2:18 ESV)

THE ENCOUNTER between Rahab and the Israelite spies in Joshua 2 provides another illustration of the salvation offered by Jehovah.

The scarlet cord suspended from Rahab's window was symbolic of her faith in the God of the Israelites, representative of her belief in the stories she had heard of His power and deliverance. She had not only chanced the loss of her life, but those of her family by hiding the Hebrew spies and providing a way of escape for them. Her reward was a place in the lineage of Christ as the mother of Boaz, the great-great-grandfather of David.

There is a scarlet thread interwoven through the pages of the Old Testament. It, and the prophecies also contained therein, present an unimpeachable picture of the Messiah from birth to death and resurrection.

You have been offered cleansing and salvation through the blood of Christ. Accept that freely given gift today.

SEPTEMBER 2

Surely the Lord GOD does nothing,
unless He reveals His secret to His servants
the prophets.
(AMOS 3:7 NKJV)

GOD'S PLAN did not begin with the birth of a baby in Bethlehem; it began before He laid out the foundation of the world and spoke it into being. Jehovah provided a perfect picture of the plan when He gave Moses the design for the feast days to be observed by the Israelites.

God wanted them to see the shadow of what was to come, and revealed it to prophets, priests, and kings long before the angel appeared to a young virgin named Mary.

God's timing is never random, something left to the whim of mankind. No, it is the meticulous unfolding of a covenant plan that began in Genesis and will conclude with the last verse of Revelation.

In all sixty-six books of the Bible, you are presented with one snapshot after another of the revelation of Jehovah's grace and mercy and His plan of redemption through Jesus, the Messiah.

SEPTEMBER 3

Thus says the LORD: "About midnight
I will go out into the midst of Egypt;
and all the firstborn in the land of Egypt shall die,
from the firstborn of Pharaoh who sits on his throne,
even to the firstborn of the female servant
who is behind the handmill,
and all the firstborn of the animals."
(EXODUS 11:14-14 NKJV)

IN EXODUS 11, it is written that Moses and Aaron were sent to warn the Egyptian ruler of the last terrible plague that was to be poured out upon the land and its people.

Moses was vitally aware of what was about to befall the Egyptian people. Remember, as a baby he had been saved by Pharaoh's daughter because of an edict that demanded the deaths of all babies born to the children of Israel. Because of that action and the king's refusal to free God's people, a dire penalty would be exacted not only on Pharaoh's household but also on each family in the land of Egypt. Because God is a God of love, He made a way for the Israelites to escape the sentence of death that had been pronounced.

In Exodus 12, Moses delivered the instructions from Jehovah on the selection of the perfect lamb in preparation for the tenth and final plague. The animal, without spot or blemish, was to be chosen and removed from the flock on the tenth day of the month. The owner was to feed and lovingly care for the lamb. Imagine how carefully the lamb must have been chosen and with what regret it was slain!

Do you have a relationship with the perfect Lamb of Heaven that was slain for your salvation?

SEPTEMBER 4

Behold! The Lamb of God
who takes away the sin of the world!
(JOHN 1:29 NKJV)

PICTURE THE BODY of Jesus as it hung on the cross. The wounds He bore were in His head, His hands, and His feet—a depiction of the cross. When the Israelites observed the very first Passover, each head of the house applied blood to the lintel over the door and to the doorposts on either side, forming a cross. Jesus said, "I am the door."

When faced with a visit from the Death Angel, the only method of deliverance was through the blood of the lamb being applied to the doorposts of the home. John, the disciple, said of Jesus, "Religion doesn't take away the sin of the world."

Being charitable doesn't remove the stain of sin. Attending church or being baptized doesn't save anyone. The only way of salvation for you and me is through repentance and acceptance of the blood sacrifice of Jesus, the Lamb of God. He is the Way, the Truth, and the Life.

SEPTEMBER 5

*There are those who are clean in their own eyes
but are not washed of their filth.*
(PROVERBS 30:12 ESV)

WHILE WE MAY LAUGH at the *Peanuts* cartoon character Pigpen, who is always surrounded by a cloud of dust, and chuckle over scenes of people tumbling into a mud puddle or being splashed with dirty water, it would be distasteful for most not to have a daily bath or shower. Yet we eschew the spiritual cleanliness of which Solomon wrote in Proverbs, and James in the New Testament:

> Draw near to God, and he will draw near to you. Cleanse your hands, you sinners, and purify your hearts, you double-minded. (James 4:8 ESV)

As we watch, work, and wait, we, like the child Jesus, must be about our heavenly Father's business. (See Luke 2:49.)

Jesus charged His disciples with their task in John 9:4:

> We must quickly carry out the tasks assigned us by the one who sent us. The night is coming, and then no one can work. (NLT)

Not only must we listen for the sound of the trumpet, we must take time daily to reevaluate our relationship with our Lord, *before* the trumpet sounds.

Ask Him, through the *Ruach HaKodesh*—the Holy Spirit—to reveal any sin in your life, and pray for help to live the life God has called us to live in Him. His grace is sufficient in every situation and circumstance of your life.

SEPTEMBER 6

Aaron shall lay both his hands on the head of the live goat,
confess over it all the iniquities of the children of Israel,
and all their transgressions, concerning all their sins,
putting them on the head of the goat,
and shall send it away into the wilderness by the hand
of a suitable man.
(LEVITICUS 16:21 NKJV)

THE MENTION OF INIQUITIES, transgressions, and sins in
this verse is very specific. *Sin* means to "miss the mark." James
4:17 defines sin: "So whoever knows the right thing to do and fails
to do it, for him it is sin." (ESV)

Iniquity is more deep-seated; it is premeditated. Micah 2:1
warns:

> Woe to those who devise iniquity, and work out evil on their
> beds! At morning light they practice it, because it is in the power
> of their hand. (NKJV)

An example would be David's liaison with Bathsheba. The
planning that led to the death of Uriah, her husband, was well
thought out by David. When the king fell on his face before God
in repentance, he cried, "Wash me thoroughly from my iniquity,
and cleanse me from my sin!" (Psalm 51:2 ESV)

Transgressions are presumptuous sins—intentional disobedience. Samson committed such sins when he transgressed the
laws of God in his dalliance with Delilah and revealed the secret
of his strength.

David gave us hope in Psalm 32:1 when he wrote, "Blessed is
he whose transgression is forgiven, Whose sin is covered." (NKJV)

SEPTEMBER 7

For our sake he made him to be sin
who knew no sin,
so that in him we might become
the righteousness of God.

(2 CORINTHIANS 5:21 ESV)

JESUS OFFERED ONE SACRIFICE, Himself, and established the plan of forgiveness and reconciliation. He laid aside his robes of glory and donned a robe of flesh so that we might have access to God, the Father.

Blood-bought, forgiven, redeemed, and delivered! Believers are not saved by the character of the sacrifice; Salvation only comes through the shed blood of Christ—the one-time-for-all-time price of atonement. Zechariah foretold the efficacy of the sacrifice of Messiah:

Then I will pour out a spirit of grace and prayer on the house of David and the residents of Jerusalem, and they will look at Me whom they pierced. They will mourn for Him as one mourns for an only child and weep bitterly for Him as one weeps for a firstborn. (Zechariah 12:10 HCSB)

The words of a song written by poet and lyricist Fanny Crosby ring with praise:

Redeemed, how I love to proclaim it!

Redeemed by the blood of the Lamb;

Redeemed through His infinite mercy,

His child and forever I am.[33]

SEPTEMBER 8

He is not here, for he has risen, as he said.
(MATTHEW 28:6 ESV)

IT TOOK THE RENOWNED Florentine artist Buonarotti four years to recreate paintings of God's works at creation. We know him better as Michelangelo, and his artistry still today adorns the ceiling of the Sistine Chapel in the Vatican.

Three millennia before Michelangelo Buonarotti climbed the ladder to paint a history for all Mankind, God's story of deliverance was painted with the blood of a perfect Lamb on the doorposts of the houses of the children of Israel in the hot desert of Egypt.

The final eight days of the life of Jesus Christ were the culmination of that plan to save the lost. It was a period of time that would change the world forever, and it was accomplished through the sacrifice of another Lamb.

As the scenes unfolded, angels were moved to stand in silence as the beloved Son of God was viciously crucified. After three days bereft of hope, the joyous announcement of His resurrection was made!

It was a morning that would forever change the world and give hope to you, and to all who believe in Him.

SEPTEMBER 9

*...whereas you do not know what **will happen** tomorrow.*
*For what **is** your life? It is even a vapor*
that appears for a little time and then vanishes away.
(JAMES 4:14 NKJV)

ONE OF SATAN'S most effective tools is the word *tomorrow*. It was Thomas Jefferson who said, "Never put off until tomorrow what you can do today."

How much more important that is when dealing with the soul's salvation. No man knows the day or the hour when Jesus will return and set His feet once again on the Temple Mount.

On the day of His crucifixion, He was preparing to lay down His life so that those who would believe on Him in the ages to come will have no fear of tomorrow.

You have the promise that "whoever believes in Him should not perish but have everlasting life." (John 3:16 NKJV)

SEPTEMBER 10

And whenever you stand praying,
if you have anything against anyone,
forgive him, that your Father in heaven
may also forgive you your trespasses.
But if you do not forgive,
neither will your Father in heaven
forgive your trespasses.
(MARK 11:25–26 NKJV)

JESUS TAUGHT that there was a relationship between forgiving and receiving God's forgiveness. The prayer for forgiveness on the cross was not meant to be the last act of a dying man; it was an example for His followers. As they had been forgiven, so were they to forgive those who sinned against them. (See Matthew 6:9–13, the Lord's Prayer.)

God had a lesson, not only for Israel, but for all mankind: He loved them and each of us with an everlasting love. It was a mirror of God's constant love that reaches far beyond our sinfulness all the way to the cross, where Love hung between heaven and earth.

Your prayers are encumbered by unforgiveness. Conversely, your prayers are enabled by forgiveness; your faith is strengthened. Forgiveness is potent. Forgive today.

SEPTEMBER 11

For the word of God is living and powerful,
and sharper than any two-edged sword,
piercing even to the division of soul and spirit,
and of joints and marrow, and is a discerner
of the thoughts and intents of the heart.
(HEBREWS 4:12 NKJV)

KING DAVID SAID what God said! The words he spoke were the words of God—divinely inspired. He was praying what God said! Praying the Word is much more powerful than what you or I say.

"I am going through a horrendous time of terror, Mike," you might say to me. I know—I have been there many times. But remember, "Desperation is the mother of invention." If you're desperate, then you're hungry to do whatever it takes to change your situation.

As with the woman with the issue of blood who said, "If I may but touch His garment I shall be whole," (Matthew 9:20 KJV), you will transform your thinking through the power of the Word of God.

Your life journey of praying the Word of God begins with Psalm 20. Read it today, and pray the prayer of David.

SEPTEMBER 12

In him we live and move and have our being.
(ACTS 17:28 NKJV)

WHAT HAS GOD promised you? Do you have a vision for victory for your life? Speak the promises of God, meditate on His Word, and determine that you will allow nothing...nothing, to keep you from becoming everything God has created you to be. Then you will, indeed, develop a warrior spirit.

You will stand against the forces of darkness, look them squarely in the face, and encourage yourself in the Lord. David, in the midst of adversity, said, "I am going to pursue, overtake, and recover all." (See 1 Samuel 30.) And so will you!

The Bible says, "The people that do know their God shall be strong, and do exploits." (Daniel 11:32 KJV)

God did not choose King David to live in this end-time hour, but He has chosen you. Refuse defeat! Guard your words. Encourage yourself in the Lord. Remember that you are guaranteed victory from the creator of the universe because of what our Lord did at Calvary. You have to rise up and fight the fight of faith.

SEPTEMBER 13

*David became greater and greater
for the LORD God of hosts was with him.*
(2 SAMUEL 5:10, NASB)

DAVID RETURNED home to Ziklag one day to find that he and his men had lost everything. All was gone, taken by the Amalekites—their children and wives. His men were so angry that they wanted to stone David, but David knew that help was on the way, and he "strengthened himself in the LORD his God." (1 Samuel 30:6 NKJV)

David prayed, worshiped, and called on his priest Abiathar for counsel. He marched six hundred of his men fifteen miles to the brook Besor. Two hundred of the men stopped there because they were exhausted. The remaining four hundred joined him to hunt the Amalekites who had done this.

On the side of the road, David had found an Egyptian that had been left to die by the Amalekites. David had compassion on him, giving him food and water. The Egyptian knew where the enemy was, and because of David's kindness gave David this invaluable information. David's men followed and regained everything that the Amalekites had taken, and more.

The Prayer of David is called a *"Warrior's Psalm"* to be prayed before going into battle—a prayer for victory in battle. In what battles do you need victory? God is ready!

SEPTEMBER 14

May He remember all your gifts and
look favorably upon your burnt offerings.
(PSALM 20:3 NIV)

DAVID BEGAN HIS MINISTRY celebrating an offering that
Samuel had presented to God in Bethlehem. He did not know
that the greatest offering ever known would be born in a stable
in Bethlehem: the Lamb of God, pure and spotless.

Giving, for David, was an act of worship—ascribing worth to
the Lord.

Why would God want you to know that giving a tithe and an
offering to God is a holy act that commands a blessing on the
giver? Because when we give we are taking on the Nature of God.

God is an extravagant giver. He not only gave us the greatest
gift Heaven could afford—our Lord—He also blessed those in the
Bible who trusted Him! Giving is an act of love and obedience and
faith in God, virtues that the prince of this world does not have.
God challenges us to prove Him. What a challenge!

SEPTEMBER 15

Don't copy the behavior and customs of the world.
But be a new and different kind of person
with a fresh newness in all you do and think.
Then you will learn from your own experience
how His ways will really satisfy you.
(ROMANS 12:2 NLT)

WHEN GOD SAYS He will remember, it means more than recalling something. It's memorializing your offering or gift.

The offering was the basis in the Old Testament for answered prayer. Our Lord's offering became the basis of answered prayer for the world—a spotless Lamb.

We are admonished to present our bodies as an offering to God.

And so, dear friend, I plead with you to give your body to God. Let this be a sacrifice—holy—the kind He can accept. When you think of what He has done for you, is this too much to ask?

When you make Jesus Lord of everything, it is only then that you can be sure you have been with Jesus. You can expect a miracle, because you are no longer your own; you have surrendered all to Christ.

SEPTEMBER 16

The rain and snow come down from the heavens
and stay on the ground to water the earth.
They cause the grain to grow,
producing seed for the farmer and
bread for the hungry.
(ISAIAH 55:10 NLT)

THERE IS NO giver greater than God. He has *out-given* us all. He wants us to celebrate our giving and make it an act of worship. He wants us to plant our seeds and expect a miracle harvest.

Why? Because the more we are blessed, the more we can be a blessing, as long as our hearts are pure.

A seed is a container of life. Some seeds sit for decades with no growth until something pierces the outer shell so the seed can interact with the soil and water.

When a seed dies and sprouts, it can feed millions.

A woman came to Jesus with a costly box of perfume, or "nard," worth an entire year's wages. She broke that box directly over Christ's head so that He would be anointed with every drop of oil. The disciples grumbled that she had wasted money. But Christ was so moved that she had anointed Him for His death, He said that wherever His gospel was preached, the story of her offering would be told. (See John 12:3-7.)

God remembers your gifts.

SEPTEMBER 17

Then David fled from Naioth in Ramah
and came and said before Jonathan,
"What have I done? What is my guilt?
And what is my sin before your father,
that he seeks my life?"

(1 SAMUEL 20:1 ESV)

DAVID THE HERO, the king's son-in-law, was running for his life! He had defeated Goliath, the giant Philistine, but his second Goliath— Saul—was much more difficult to defeat.

The future king was now the hunted outlaw. Day and night for years, Saul dogged him, just waiting for the moment when David would become vulnerable. The desire of Saul's heart was to plunge his spear through David. Jealousy turns giants into jerks!

Saul had a golden opportunity to demonstrate greatness when the Israelites sang, "Saul has slain his thousands, and David his ten thousands." (1 Samuel 18:7 NKJV) He could have taken a bow for sending David into battle. He could have become bigger in the eyes of the people. Instead, he became bitter.

Did David fall into self-pity? Not this man of valor! He trusted Jehovah.

Have you ever found yourself in a pit of despair, hoping against hope that you would be left alone? Step out of the darkness into the brilliant light of God's Word!

SEPTEMBER 18

In thee, O Lord, do I put my trust;
let me never be ashamed:
deliver me in thy righteousness.
(PSALM 31:1 KJV)

Behold, God is mine helper,
the Lord is with them that uphold my soul.
(PSALM 54:4 KJV)

THE HOLY SPIRIT of God moved David to write Psalms 34 and 56 in the cave of Adullum and Psalms 31 and 54 in the cave of Ein Gedi.

David embraced God's word; Saul had rejected God's word. David put God first; Saul had put himself first. David presented offerings to Jehovah, while Saul hid that which God told him to destroy. David fell on his face before the angel of the Lord; Saul fell on his sword, and committed suicide.

Saul's enemy wasn't David; it was his own fleshly pride. There was no possibility that Saul could win in the spirit what he had already lost in the flesh. Saul's choice cost him not only his inheritance; it cost him everything.

David's passion in life was to dwell in the presence of the Lord, to provide a dwelling place in his heart and in Jerusalem. He had developed a heart attitude that moved God to action.

How is your attitude? Does God have first place in your heart and life?

SEPTEMBER 19

Most assuredly, I say to you,
he who believes in Me,
the works that I do he will do also;
*and greater **works** than these he will do,*
because I go to My Father.
(JOHN 14:12 KJV)

IMAGINE GOD ASKING YOU to give everything you owned to someone else who would do more with it than you would. Imagine giving up your talent, career, family, possessions, reputation—everything you have ever been.

That's exactly what Jesus did. He let go of everything—His power, His reputation, His name, His life, His history, His Words, His very Spirit, everything He'd ever been and everything He ever would be on this earth—and He gave it to us. Then Christ departed physically to sit at the Father's right hand in Heaven.

Jesus wants to establish His Kingdom in us and reign on the throne of our lives. Paul reminds us, "But we have this treasure in jars of clay, to show that the surpassing power belongs to God and not to us." (2 Corinthians 4:7 ESV)

Are His heart's desires yours; His plans yours? He will move heaven and earth if need be to accomplish His purposes through you.

SEPTEMBER 20

So that we may boldly say,
*The Lord **is** my helper, and I will not fear*
what man shall do unto me.
(HEBREWS 13:6 KJV)

THE EYES OF GOD are searching for hungry hearts willing to surrender to the person of the Holy Spirit and thirst to be with Jesus. Christ has determined that we will rule and reign with Him, not just when we get to Heaven, but while we are on this earth.

There is a place in Christ that will quench all the fiery darts of the Enemy, no matter the circumstance. With Self in charge, we meagerly try to contact God—flesh to Spirit. With Jesus on the throne of our lives as Lord and king, we experience a supernatural bond. While we stand in awe of God, we will never fear man.

When we have been with Jesus, we will never surrender that intimacy to dance to the world's song. But if we spend all of our time trying to be man-pleasers, we will ride a merry-go-round of repentance and regret.

When you allow the King to rule unchallenged in your life, your greatest passion will be to see God do His work through you—anywhere, anytime, in any way.

SEPTEMBER 21

But truly God has listened;
he has attended to the voice of my prayer.
(PSALM 66:19 ESV)

FULFILLING YOUR DESTINY comes through experiencing God's power. But you cannot have His power without His presence. We enter into God's presence through prayer!

The King of Glory is raising an army of mighty men and women who seek no temporal throne or temporal power, carry no carnal weapons of might, and do not stockpile the praises of men. Dead to Self, their only hope is to be seated in heavenly places with Christ, the hope of Glory. They alone terrify the demons of hell and torment principalities and powers, because they cannot be bought by ambition.

These soldiers of the King do not chase "superstars" of the faith hoping to get their Bible autographed. They see only One, Bright and Morning Star, Jesus, who has written His Name on the tablets of their hearts. They lay their plans at His feet and embrace His plan for their lives.

Embrace God's plan for your life today, and become a prayer warrior in His army.

SEPTEMBER 22

Now when they saw the boldness of Peter and John,
and perceived that they were uneducated,
common men, they were astonished.
And they recognized that they had been with Jesus.

(ACTS 4:13 ESV)

HAVE YOU BEEN WITH JESUS? Your family will know when you have. Your friends will know, and more importantly, the lost will know. When we've been with Jesus, a consuming fire burns in our bones. Idols are cast down. Anything that supersedes the lordship of Christ is gone.

Idols are destroyed because our pride is broken. Have you been with Jesus? If you have, the Word is alive—burning in your bones. Jeremiah the prophet cried:

> But if I say, "I will not mention his word or speak anymore in his name," his word is in my heart like a fire, a fire shut up in my bones. I am weary of holding it in; indeed, I cannot. (Jeremiah 20:9 NIV)

Have you been with Jesus? If you have, you no longer fear man. Yes, God is ready to move heaven and earth for you if you have been with Jesus.

SEPTEMBER 23

The battle is the Lord's.
(1 SAMUEL 17:47 KJV)

BANNERS FLYING were a part of military equipage, borne in times of war to assemble, direct, distinguish, and encourage the troops. They were used also for celebrations. The banner was also displayed to acknowledge His glory and to implore His favor.

The banners that are flying for the Believer today have the Name of our God, Yeshua (Jesus), on them. I believe their color is red for the power of the blood; the streamer adorning the flagpole is for the Gospel—the Good News.

Rejoice that all the giants in your life bend their knees to that mighty Name, for "it is not by sword or spear that the Lord saves: for the battle is the Lord's." (1 Samuel 17:47 NIV)

SEPTEMBER 24

See to it that no one takes you captive
by philosophy and empty deceit,
according to human tradition,
according to the elemental spirits of the world,
and not according to Christ.
(COLOSSIANS 2:8 ESV)

GOD DOES NOT CONSULT with you to determine His plan or purpose; it is your responsibility to consult with Him. You must be in His will; He has made no provision to be in your will. Our prayers can be answered as we understand this principle.

When self is on the throne of our lives, we can be sure that chaos will be the norm, no matter how religious or sincere we are. Chaos is a sure sign that we have not been with Jesus. Chaotic Christianity distorts the image of the living Savior.

The flesh desires to conquer the cross, ignore it, and disregard Christ's Lordship. The cross desires to conquer the flesh and eradicate its lordship!

How heartbreaking it is when we settle for tradition. When habits are formed, all too often, hunger is lost. Your hunger for God is the greatest indication of who is on the throne in your life.

SEPTEMBER 25

Anyone who refuses to obey will immediately
be thrown into a blazing furnace.
(DANIEL 3:6 NLT)

THE APPOINTED DAY set aside to unveil Nebuchadnezzar's image arrived. Off to one side of the king's dais was a reminder of the punishment for failure to bow down: the ovens into which those who refused to bow would be thrown.

The trio of Hebrews in the king's court had declared they could not bow; that Jehovah was their Lord and King—they would bow to no other. The king was infuriated by their answer. In vain, he ordered the musicians to play again. He then commanded the mightiest men in his army to bind the three men and toss them into the furnace. As the men who stood strong in His Name landed in the midst of the fire, Jehovah joined them, and as the fire lapped at the bindings of His servants, it lost the ability to devour.

Suddenly, the king's triumph turned to fear. He grew pale as he lurched from the throne and pointed toward the all-consuming flames. He stuttered, "Did we not cast three men bound into the midst of the fire? ... Look!...I see four men loose, walking in the midst of the fire; and they are not hurt, and the form of the fourth is like the Son of God." (Daniel 3:24-25 NKJV)

Do you have the courage to do what is right, to refuse to forfeit your integrity?

SEPTEMBER 26

Woe to the world because of offenses!
For offenses must come,
but woe to that man
by whom the offense comes!
(MATTHEW 18:7 NKJV)

YOU AND I LIVE in a less than perfect world. Rest assured, dear friend, you *will* be offended—it *will* come. The ideal response is to greet the offense with love and forgiveness.

Forgiveness begins with God, for His is the supreme pardon. It is seldom possible for man to forgive, but the Bible tells us that with God, "all things are possible." (Matthew 19:26 KJV)

"One of the secret causes of stress plaguing millions of people is unforgiveness," says Dr. Don Colbert, MD.[34] You and I must determine to avoid unforgiveness.

Just as a virus strikes a computer program and destroys it from within, so a lack of forgiveness can attack the body and cause physical and mental health problems. It is believed that stress levels rise when unforgiveness is harbored.

Refuse to lift and sip that poison. Choose instead to forgive. It can result in total healing of body, soul, and spirit.

SEPTEMBER 27

No, dear brothers and sisters,
I have not achieved it,
but I focus on this one thing:
Forgetting the past and looking forward
to what lies ahead...
(PHILIPPIANS 3:13 NLT)

THE ONE WHO FORGIVES pardons and moves on; not constantly rehearsing the wrong done. He or she doesn't hold on to past hurts and offenses, and doesn't hold pity parties or "poor little me" memorials. That only gives life to the past.

Unforgiveness is similar to walking a mile with a one-hundred-pound weight on your back. The apostle Paul cautioned that we should "lay aside every weight."

The subject of forgiveness cannot be complete without talking about forgiving yourself. You will never be able to move forward to a life of love and grace until you are able to forgive past mistakes. When allowed to fester, infection sets in and can eventually destroy you.

The Enemy uses unforgiveness as a stepping-stone to eat away at our faith in God's mercy and forgiveness. It is essential that you learn to forgive yourself for the sake of your spiritual health. Forgiving oneself is perhaps the hardest kind of Radical Forgiveness, but we must remember that Nehemiah wrote, "You are a God ready to forgive, gracious and merciful." (Nehemiah 9:17 NRSV)

SEPTEMBER 28

Anyone who does not love does not know God,
because God is love.
(1 JOHN 4:8 ESV)

AFTER THE DEATH of Joseph, the son of Jacob, there arose a Pharaoh that persecuted and enslaved the Hebrew people. God gave Pharaoh ten chances to let His people go, and ten times Pharaoh hardened his heart toward God and refused—until the tenth and most deadly plague was sent. The first-born male in every Egyptian home was slain by the Death Angel, including Pharaoh's son.

For every Hebrew son that had been drowned in the Nile River, an Egyptian boy died. For every Hebrew father who died at the oppressive hands of the overseers, an Egyptian father died.

Broken, Pharaoh released the children of Israel. But after they had gone, an angry, bitter Pharaoh gathered his terrified, demoralized troops and pursued the Hebrews. He led his army directly into the path of God's wrath... because of the choice to curse God's people rather than to bless them.

God has a protective hand upon you, child of God, because you are loved by the Lord of all creation!

SEPTEMBER 29

So he got up from the table, took off his robe,
wrapped a towel around his waist...
(JOHN 13:4 NLT)

THE SCENE: The Lord's Supper. In attendance: The disciples, including Judas.

When invited to a dinner, the lowest servant in the household drew the short straw and had to wash the dirty feet of the guests. We are not told why it was that as Jesus and the disciples arrived for the Passover meal, no one performed that odious task.

Because of that omission, Jesus had one more lesson to impart to his closest followers. Then the curtain is rolled back, and we see a stunning tableau as John 13:4 reveals his purpose: "Then he poured water into a basin and began to wash the disciples' feet and to wipe them with the towel that was wrapped around him." (NLT)

Even the feet of Judas, His betrayer! Would you do that—with love and humility give comfort to your worst enemy?

SEPTEMBER 30

Yes, a sword will pierce
through your own soul also...
(LUKE 2:35A NKJV)

AN ANONYMOUS ARTIST has painted a stunning picture of
Jesus as a child. The little One is playing with three large spikes
in Joseph's carpenter shop, and light streaming from the window
paints a cross on the floor behind the baby. Jesus was, literally,
born to die.

Singer/songwriter Barbara Mandrell wrote the words:

> It must have broken God's heart
>
> For the future He could see.
>
> Yet He formed the hands
>
> And feet knowing one day
>
> They'd be nailed to a tree.[35]

You and I, too, have been born with a purpose, and that is to
serve God. God loves us unconditionally and has provided a way
we can be rescued from eternal death.

OCTOBER

OCTOBER 1

And after the earthquake a fire,
but the LORD was not in the fire.
And after the fire
the sound of a low whisper.
(1 KINGS 19:12 ESV)

NOISE! We are daily beset by a cacophony of raucous sounds. When quietly blessing food in a noisy restaurant, a friend might ask, "Think God could hear that?" The more important question should, perhaps, be: Can we hear God?

Elijah was in fear for his life when Jehovah directed him to go to the brook Cherith where he would be provided with food and drink. There was little for him to do there, but rest and await further instructions.

When we find ourselves in a place of fear or despair, we often resort to telling God what He ought to do. Our urgent prayers, giving Him orders, often drown out the quiet whisper of God.

The Psalmist offered excellent advice: "Wait on the LORD; Be of good courage, And He shall strengthen your heart; Wait, I say, on the LORD!" (Psalm 27:14 NKJV)

OCTOBER 2

I am the vine, you are the branches.
He who abides in Me,
and I in him, bears much fruit;
for without Me you can do nothing.
(JOHN 15:5 NKJV)

SOMEONE ONCE SAID, "If a cucumber is separated from the vine, it will end up in a pickle." Funny analogy, but it is true in regard to our relationship with Jesus. If we want growth as Christians, we must be willing to be pruned, fertilized, and watered by a skilled gardener, or husbandman.

If we allow that process in our lives, we will have the presence of the Master Gardener always in our lives. Diseased branches will be removed; the soil around our roots will be loosened. We will begin to be productive, and love will blossom and grow.

The presence of the Farmer will assure that we are never alone. He shares our lives; He abides with us, nourishes us, and strengthens us.

Ask Jesus today to remove that which is useless in your life and you really can do everything through Christ who gives you strength.

OCTOBER 3

But as it is written:
"Eye has not seen, nor ear heard,
Nor have entered into the heart of man
The things which God has prepared
for those who love Him."
(1 CORINTHIANS 2:9 NKJV)

WHAT IS THE ONE THING designed to rob your joy? It is worry! Worry changes nothing—not our circumstances, not the bottom line on our bank account, not the diagnosis from the doctor. Prayer changes everything. When we lay our concerns at the feet of the omnipotent, omnipresent, omniscient Ruler of the Universe, we trust Him to answer as He sees fit.

British clergyman William Ralph Inge wrote: "Worry is interest paid on trouble before it comes due."[36] George MacDonald, Scottish author and minister said:

> No man ever sank under the burden of the day. It is when tomorrow's burden is added to the burden of today, that the weight is more than a man can bear.[37]

God has an answer to every problem that you and I could ever have imagined. He is all-powerful, all-knowing, and everywhere at all times! He knows what you need before you ask. You can trust Him fully.

OCTOBER 4

Hear a just cause, O LORD; attend to my cry!
Give ear to my prayer from lips free of deceit!
(PSALM 17:1 ESV)

MY FRIEND, luck has little, if anything, to do with success. You will likely find that a successful person is often a tireless and dedicated servant of God, a prayer warrior who seeks God's will at every turn. Missionary John Hyde discovered the key to powerful prayer:

> We need to be still before Him, so as to hear His voice and allow Him to pray in us—nay, allow Him to pour into our souls His overflowing life of intercession, which means literally: face to face meeting with God—real union and communion.[38]

Does it mean that the prayer warrior has never faced challenges or hard times? Not at all. It simply means that through the good times and bad, he or she has faithfully served God with the confidence that a loving Heavenly Father would grant them favor with both Him and man and turn every problem into an opportunity for blessing.

Don't hesitate to pray for God's favor; but while you pray, extend grace and favor to those you meet along the way.

OCTOBER 5

The angel went to her and said,
"Greetings, you who are highly favored!
The Lord is with you."
(LUKE 1:18 NIV)

AS A CHILD OF GOD, you are released to walk in the blessings of God—you are then free to bless others, but that does not mean you will not face adversity.

Mary, the mother of Jesus, was "highly favored," and yet she faced the scorn of her neighbors. She and Joseph undertook a trek from Nazareth to Bethlehem—Mary on the back of a donkey while nine months pregnant. She had no place to give birth to her Son except in a cave where animals were kept, yet she enjoyed the unheralded blessings of God.

Enjoying those blessings does not mean that you will not face challenges from the Enemy. Jesus was tested numerous times, but He persevered and was not defeated.

Because of God's unfailing favor and unmerited grace, you can, like the champions recorded in Hebrews 11, be ultimately successful.

OCTOBER 6

Call to me, and I will answer you,
and show you great and mighty things,
which you do not know.

(JEREMIAH 33:3 NKJV)

IN THE OLD TESTAMENT, the word "watchman" is often used for those called to intercessory prayer for their people. Just as the watchman in a city stood at the gate to warn the people of a coming enemy and was, therefore, the first line of defense, so intercessory prayer warriors are the first line of spiritual defense for our nations and communities. When the watchmen don't do their jobs, people perish.

The blood of Christians was on Paul's hands. So what did he say about it?

> Therefore I testify to you this day that I am innocent of the blood of all men. For I have not shunned to declare to you the whole counsel of God. (Acts 20:26-27 NKJV)

Paul repented and followed God. You and I must turn from apathy to steadfast prayer! God will do nothing without prayer. The fuel that moves the engine of humanity is prayer.

God has a purpose and a plan for your life. His ear has always been attuned to the sound of intercessory prayer from His children.

OCTOBER 7

For You will light my lamp;
The LORD my God will enlighten my darkness.
(PSALM 18:28 NKJV)

DARKNESS FLEES when we pray! Demons tremble when we pray. Heaven moves when we pray, and angels receive assignments when we pray. Prayer affects three realms: The divine, the angelic, and the human. Without it, demons rule uncontested. (See Ephesians 6.)

You and I cannot make contact with God without prayer. If we don't make that connection, no matter how sincere our intentions, we will not see a change in the circumstances of our lives.

God has stationed watchmen on the wall. I call them Esthers and Nehemiahs... hopefully, people such as you. Many people of this planet have figuratively been scratching their heads trying to find an answer to the crises that continually grip our world.

That answer is in your hands and mine—we just have to fold them together and beseech God in prayer.

OCTOBER 8

So I sought for a man among them who would make a wall,
and stand in the gap before Me on behalf of the land,
that I should not destroy it; but I found no one.
(Ezekiel 22:30 nkjv)

IN LIGHT OF what we are discovering about the power of prayer, here is another of the saddest scriptures in the Bible: He [God] saw that there was no man, And wondered that there was no intercessor. (Isaiah 59:16 nkjv [insert mine])

No one to stand in the gap. No one to intercede. What a tragedy! Today God is still looking for that man or woman, who will stand in the breach and pray.

When the children of Israel sinned in the wilderness and fashioned a golden calf, danced before it, and denied God's sovereignty, God threatened to destroy them. Moses fell on his face before Jehovah God, and the Psalmist wrote in Psalm 106:23:

Therefore He said that He would destroy them, Had not Moses His chosen one stood before Him in the breach, To turn away His wrath, lest He destroy them. (nkjv)

God's Word is rife with examples of intercessors that prevailed against the Enemy, and secured the promises of God—all through prayer! Will you take up the banner of prayer today?

OCTOBER 9

By this all will know that you are My disciples,
if you have love for one another.
(JOHN 13:35 NKJV)

WHEN LOVE IS ABSENT, all else is empty, without value. In his booklet *The Mark of a Christian*, based on John 13:35, theologian Dr. Francis A. Schaeffer wrote:

> Our love will not be perfect, but it must be substantial enough for the world to be able to observe or it does not fit into the structure of the verses in John 13 and 17. And if the world does not observe this among true Christians, the world has a right to make the two awful judgments which these verses indicate: That we are not Christians, and that Christ was not sent by the Father.... Love...is the mark Christ gave Christians to wear before the world.[39]

Your very grasp of God's Word has no worth if love is not present. Your discipleship can be called into question by the very world we are trying to influence if love is missing from all we say and do. It all has no value without God's agape—sacrificial love at work in your life.

OCTOBER 10

A new commandment I give unto you,
that ye love one another;
as I have loved you,
that ye also love one another.
(JOHN 13:34–35 KJV)

THE REASON God sent His Son to earth can be summarized in six words: For God so loved the world. Jesus came to earth because of love—the Father's love for His fallen creation. We can now be restored to a loving relationship with Jehovah-Yasha—the Lord my Savior—because of Jesus' death on the cross. Now we are no longer enemies, but beloved friends.

In 1882 a blind Scottish preacher published a song that spoke of longing for the One from whose loving hands we could not be removed. The cleric was George Matheson; his message as timely today as it was then:

> O Love that wilt not let me go,
>
> I rest my weary soul in thee;
>
> I give thee back the life I owe,
>
> That in thine ocean depths its flow
>
> May richer, fuller be.[40]

The heart of man begs to be loved despite our weaknesses and failures, to be completely accepted, highly esteemed, and to know that we have significance to someone. You and I want someone to be there to lift us up when we fail; to watch over us with kindness and compassion. That is the agape kind of love that God, the Father, has for you, His beloved child.

OCTOBER 11

Forgetting those things
which are behind and
reaching forward to those things
which are ahead.

(PHILIPPIANS 3:13 NKJV)

WHEN FACED WITH ADVERSITY, you and I can do one of two things—we can accept it as our lot in life, or we can overcome it through the peace of God and His Word. At a trying moment in my life I realized the Enemy was out to destroy me and my ministry. It was then that I did what God had told me to do: I traveled all the way to Israel to meet with the prime minister—Menachem Begin.

Doing God's will gave me the peace to overcome adversity. I began to worship God; to praise, to exalt my Creator. Praise dispelled the darkness and allowed the light of God's love to shine in and His peace to flood my being.

Peace is not the absence of conflict; it is having the courage to face the conflict and make the right choices. This is true in your life, too. Peace and worry cannot occupy the same space. One forces the other to vacate. Your prayer should be:

Help me to wait patiently for the very best You have for me. Help me not to be ruled by fear but to lay hold of Your peace.

OCTOBER 12

And let the peace that comes from Christ
rule in your hearts.
For as members of one body
you are called to live in peace.
And always be thankful.
(COLOSSIANS 3:15 NLT)

CHICAGO BUSINESSMAN Horatio Spafford wrote one of
the premier hymns about peace. On November 22, 1873, tragedy
struck when a ship carrying Mrs. Spafford and their four daughters to England collided with the British ship *Lochearn*. Anna
and the children's nanny struggled to get the children from their
staterooms to the deck of the ship. The lifeboats were unusable,
for they had been painted and had dried fast to the railing of
the ship. As panic seized those onboard, her daughter, Maggie,
stepped beside her mother and said, "Mama, God will take care
of us." Another daughter, Annie, added, "The sea is His and He
made it."[41]

Only twelve minutes after the two ships rammed, the *Ville
du Havre* sank to the bottom of the Atlantic, taking with it 226
people. Anna Spafford and fifty-six others survived. She was
found bruised and unconscious lying atop a board floating in the
Atlantic. The nanny, Nicolet, and the Spafford's' four daughters
were among those swept to a watery grave, their bodies never
recovered.

How can you have peace in the midst of the storms of life?
Peace is determined by your focus; if you focus on the problem,
then peace flees. If you focus on the Problem-solver, you will be
flooded with God's peace, which helps to calm your anxious heart.

OCTOBER 13

You keep him in perfect peace
whose mind is stayed on you,
because he trusts in you.
(ISAIAH 26:3 ESV)

UPON BEING NOTIFIED of the tragedy at sea, and the loss of his children, Horatio Spafford immediately set sail for Wales to be reunited with his heartbroken wife. Once at sea, Spafford asked the captain to point out exactly where the *Ville du Havre* had sunk.

When the ship crossed that fateful spot, the grief-stricken father sat with pen in hand and wrote what was to become one of Christendom's most beloved and long-lasting hymns, "It Is Well with My Soul":

> When peace, like a river, attendeth my way,
>
> When sorrows like sea billows roll;
>
> Whatever my lot, Thou has taught me to say,
>
> It is well, it is well, with my soul.
>
> Though Satan should buffet, though trials should come,
>
> Let this blest assurance control,
>
> That Christ has regarded my helpless estate,
>
> And hath shed His own blood for my soul.
>
> (*Refrain*)
>
> It is well, with my soul,
>
> It is well, it is well, with my soul.[42]

OCTOBER 14

Do not despise these small beginnings,
for the LORD rejoices to see the work begin.
(ZECHARIAH 4:10 NLT)

THE APOSTLE PAUL discovered on the road to Damascus that God had a plan for his life, one that he had never considered.

Paul truly met the God of the impossible—the One who was born as a baby, lived as a man, suffered death on the cross as the Lamb of God, rose again the third day and now sits at the right hand of the Father, making intercession for His beloved children.

The impossible often begins with one small step. When God wanted to create Adam, He began with a handful of dust. Moses was sent to challenge Pharaoh with a walking stick; Samson killed thousands of Philistines with the jawbone of a donkey (see Judges 15); Jesus fed the multitudes with a couple of fish and five loaves of bread. When He sent David to conquer a giant, the shepherd didn't take a cannon; he picked up five small stones. When God sent His Son to earth, He wasn't sent to a metropolis, but to the small, backwater hamlet of Bethlehem.

Do you think your ideas are too small to succeed? Give them to God and let Him anoint you for the impossible!

OCTOBER 15

Then the kingdom of heaven
shall be likened to ten virgins
who took their lamps and went out
to meet the bridegroom.
Now five of them were wise,
*and five **were** foolish.*
(MATTHEW 25:2 NKJV)

WHEN YOU and I have been born again, we are given a measure of the Holy Spirit that transforms our human spirit from spiritual death to spiritual life. (See John 20:22-23.)

But Paul writes that this is not enough. We must also "be filled with the Spirit." (Ephesians 5:18.) The form of the verb filled here is in present continuous, which means "to be filled" like wind filling a sail, making the ship move.

The foolish virgins had just enough of the Holy Spirit to get through normal times. When they reached the limit of what was needed to get along in the world, they had no more. The wise virgins had supplies in excess of what they needed.

It is not one filling at one time but a continuous, moment-by-moment filling, all the time, moving you forward in God's will for your life.

OCTOBER 16

Then the LORD God called to Adam
and said to him, "Where are you?"
So he said, "I heard Your voice in the garden,
and I was afraid because I was naked;
and I hid myself."
(GENESIS 3:9-10 NKJV)

WHAT HORROR Adam and Eve must have experienced when they immediately realized that something in their lives had changed. What do you think Eve might have given for a do-over? She and Adam had gone from being God-centered to being Self-centered. Before sin entered in, they conversed freely with God.

Suddenly, Adam realized that their holy covering had vanished; that now they were naked. The reaction was to cover their nudity with the leaves of the fig tree. The sanctity of the tabernacle in the garden had been breached by sin.

Having hurriedly fashioned aprons of fig leaves, Adam and Eve waited fearfully for their daily time of communion with God. The setting had not changed, but the two in the Garden had been changed forever.

Don't allow sin in your life to separate you from the holiness of Jehovah God. Repentance is available now.

OCTOBER 17

For in the day that you eat of it
you shall surely die.
(GENESIS 2:17B NKJV)

LITTLE HAS CHANGED since that long-ago evening in the Garden of Eden. Mankind continues to make excuses, shift blame, and refuse to accept responsibility for his/her actions. Little personal responsibility is accepted, only a guilt trip laid on the one who was insulted. Apologists admit little if any wrongdoing, following the tradition set by Adam and Eve.

The two inhabitants of the Garden would soon know firsthand that sin required a blood sacrifice. Beyond that, they had no idea of the door that had been opened and how one bite—just one bite of the fruit—would affect mankind from that moment forward.

Was God forced, then, to turn His back on His creation? He cannot look upon sin; therefore, God had to provide a way to impute righteousness to those who were separated from Him. No longer could Adam and Eve sit at the feet of Yahweh and commune with Him. But there in the Garden, God initiated the first sacrifice.

Only when you accept Christ and put on His righteousness will you be fully clothed to stand in the presence of Jehovah.

OCTOBER 18

The sacrifices of God are a broken spirit,
a broken and a contrite heart—these,
O God, You will not despise.
(PSALM 51:17 NKJV)

DAVID LONGED FOR the presence of God to surround him, and he craved the blessing of Jehovah on his life. He coveted the relationship he knew would come with spending time in His presence and valued above all the closeness he found with the Lord, his Shepherd.

It is so easy in this life to get sidetracked in the pursuit of things—wealth, fame, the perfect job, house, or mate—that we fail to stop and spend time in the presence of God.

David had learned the value of beholding the beauty of the Lord, of seeking Him. He knew that God wanted a man whose heart was submitted to Him. When David lost sight of that pursuit and sinned with Bathsheba, he suffered the consequences of his actions—the death of their first son. With his life dedicated to pursuing God, David finally understood exactly what God wanted: Total devotion.

You and I can rest assured that God rewards those who are totally devoted to Him.

OCTOBER 19

Then one of the seraphim flew to me
with a live coal in his hand,
which he had taken with tongs from the altar.
With it he touched my mouth and said,
"See, this has touched your lips;
your guilt is taken away and your sin
atoned for.

(ISAIAH 6:6–7 NIV)

AT THE TIME of Isaiah's vision in chapter 6, Israel was at a crossroads—the people were economically prosperous but spiritually bankrupt. As one writer noted, Isaiah dwelled in the midst of "fat and happy sinners."[43]

The prophet, in the presence of pure holiness, realized his unworthiness. He was concerned with his own impurity when seen under the microscope of God's purity. Isaiah realized he had no place to hide—he was doomed.

As he lay prostrate before the Lord God Almighty, he cried that he was a man of unclean lips and he lived among a people whose lips were unclean.

What is your reaction when we realize the holiness of God? A true encounter with God always brings inevitable change. Either your commitment to Him grows deeper, or you harden your heart and perish spiritually.

OCTOBER 20

Then Noah built an altar to the Lord,
and took of every clean animal
and of every clean bird,
and offered burnt offerings on the altar.
(GENESIS 8:20 NKJV)

DAY AFTER DAY Noah and his family had lived with the pounding of rain on the roof and waves against the hull of their huge vessel. Finally one morning Noah must have been awakened—not by the noise but by the quiet that reigned. He raced to the uppermost level of the craft, and threw open a window. The rains had stopped!

Noah began to fully comprehend what God had done in providing animals for food, clothing, and their very sustenance. In gratitude, Noah gathered stones and built an altar. He brought forth one of every type of clean animal and offered it as a sacrifice unto Jehovah. Noah had simply given back to God what he had been given, an offering in acknowledgment of Jehovah's gracious provision.

Offer a sacrifice of praise to God today in return for all He has given to you.

OCTOBER 21

Thou shalt not make unto thee
any graven image...
(EXODUS 20:4 KJV)

THE ONE THING many remember about the Ten Commandments is the "Thou shalt nots." All too often, those are shunned in favor of the Gospels. Our human nature would prefer to know the "dos" rather than the "don'ts" and all too often we focus on the latter when studying the ten laws handed down on Mount Sinai.

God went to great lengths to present His laws to the children of Israel, even writing them with His finger on the second set of tablets. It is indicative of His eternal love and care for us.

Jehovah is concerned about our very lives; thus, He gave instructions for every aspect of our relationship with Him—from how we are to love Him to how we are to treat our next-door neighbor. He did not set us on this journey and then abandon us.

Even more compelling: Jehovah still offers His unfathomable grace to those who have transgressed His laws through the shed blood of His Son, Jesus Christ.

OCTOBER 22

The path of the righteous is like the morning sun,
shining ever brighter till the full light of day.
(PROVERBS 4:18 NKJV)

PSALM 76:4 SAYS of Jehovah, "You are radiant with light, more majestic than mountains rich with game." Conversely, darkness is a simile for evil and sin. Isaiah 9:2 tells us, "The people walking in darkness [sin, evil] have seen a great light [Jehovah's righteousness]; on those living in the land of deep darkness a light has dawned." (NIV)

Of course, Jesus said in John 8:12: "I am the light of the world. Whoever follows me will never walk in darkness, but will have the light of life."

One small candle can illuminate the dark recesses of a room, chasing away the gloom and fear. Walk in His light, and you will escape the pitfalls of darkness.

OCTOBER 23

Therefore God exalted him to the highest place
and gave him the name that is above every name,
that at the name of Jesus every knee should bow,
in heaven and on earth and under the earth, and every
tongue acknowledge that Jesus Christ is Lord,
to the glory of God the Father.
(PHILIPPIANS 2:9-11 NKJV)

THE PRIESTHOOD of Jesus Christ resonates through the book of Hebrews. In chapter 3, verse 1; He is called "apostle and high priest." Again in chapter 4, verse 15, the writer refers to our Lord as "high priest." The commission of the high priest was to offer atonement for the sins of man—to bring man into a place of communion with God.

Jesus took on the role in order to open the way for man to approach Jehovah through the blood covenant of the cross. Christ presented not offerings, but Himself as a sacrifice to redeem fallen man. He had none of the frailties of earlier high priests; no longer a need to slay sheep and bullocks for forgiveness of sin. He was the sinless Son of God sent to take away the sins of the world—not to postpone them for another year.

When Jesus whispered, "It is finished," on Golgotha, the work that He had been sent to do had been completed. Now you can be free because of His sacrifice.

OCTOBER 24

For He Himself is our peace,
who has made both one,
and has broken down the middle
wall of separation...
(EPHESIANS 2:14 NKJV)

THE MAJORITY OF SACRIFICES offered to Jehovah in Old Testament times were not consumed by those making the offering. The peace offering was to be eaten after a portion had been burnt on the altar. The remainder of the offering was returned to the presenter and then distributed to the poor. It is a perfect illustration of Jehovah's provision—physically and spiritually; a picture of His matchless grace and kindness. The peace offering was a wonderful way to thank Jehovah-Jireh, our Provider whose grace is sufficient.

The peace offering was a foreshadowing of the One to come—the Messiah. The consistent instruction given throughout Scripture—beginning in Leviticus—is that praise springs forth from an offering that is completely satisfactory to God.

Your freedom of worship flows from the one truly acceptable offering: Jesus Christ our Lord, the matchless Son of God, the Lamb slain before the foundation of the world. (See Revelation 13:8.) Because of that sacrifice, not only can we worship God in "spirit and in truth" (John 4:24 KJV), we can receive forgiveness of sin through the blood of Christ.

OCTOBER 25

*Make every effort to keep yourselves
united in the Spirit,
binding yourselves together with peace.*
(EPHESIANS 4:3 NLT)

THE BUILDING RISING from the top of Mount Moriah was not just an ordinary house; it was God's House. It was the site from which sacrifices would be made; the covering for the Ark of the Covenant that would rest inside the Holy of Holies. This was the place where God would communicate with man.

Priests in white linen filed from the Holy Place just inside the temple doors. They joined musicians, also clad in white linen, as the trumpets began to resound. Soon they were accompanied by cymbals, harps, and psalteries and the assembled choir began to sing.

As the voices rose toward the heavens, something inexplicable happened—the Shekinah glory of God Almighty settled on the mountaintop and filled the temple. All came to a standstill. Instruments were silenced; the people fell prostrate to the ground in overpowering awe.

Only when God fills the house can there be such unity, such accord. Is God in control of your house today?

OCTOBER 26

*I have heard your prayer and have chosen this place
for myself as a temple for sacrifices.*
(2 Chronicles 7:12 NIV)

ONE NIGHT after the temple dedication, Solomon retired to his chambers where the Lord appeared to him to put His final stamp on the king's efforts. In one of the most oft-quoted verses of scripture, God encouraged Solomon that should the people sin against Him, there was hope:

> If my people, who are called by my name, will humble themselves and pray and seek my face and turn from their wicked ways, then I will hear from heaven, and I will forgive their sin and will heal their land. (2 Chronicles 7:14 NKJV)

God had given Solomon both the recipe for revival and the results, and that still holds true today.

This a beautiful picture of what can transpire when you are in one accord with God.

OCTOBER 27

These who have turned the world
upside down have come here too.
(ACTS 17:6B NKJV)

AS THE SON OF GOD, Jesus was to be the perfect example for all men. His baptism by John was not one of repentance; it was rather an act of public consecration. Today, the rite of baptism is to be an outward sign of the inward work of salvation. It is a powerful witness of God's work in an individual's life.

As the Son of Man emerged from the waters of the Jordan, Matthew tells us that the heavens were opened; a dove descended and alighted on Jesus. The Jews were awaiting a Messiah who would rescue them from the oppression of the Romans and establish His kingdom on earth—a warrior King. Instead, the Messiah was to be the loving Savior, Light of the World, Bread of Life, and Living Water.

Jesus would be rejected, in a sense, because He did not appear with tornadic might or the shaking of an earthquake or the destruction of a fire; He came as a still, small voice, a whisper.

Jesus came not to create chaos in the known world, but to stir your heart and mine.

OCTOBER 28

Then Jesus was led by the Spirit
into the wilderness to be tempted there
by the devil.
(MATTHEW 4:1 NLT)

HAVE YOU EVER FELT as if you were alone in a hot, dry place—tempted, tested, and tried? During His sojourn in the wilderness, Jesus was tempted in three different measures: body, soul, and spirit. It is important to understand the difference between *temptation* and *testing*.

Satan was not tempting Jesus in an attempt to discover who He was; Satan knew without a doubt that he was addressing the Son of God. He knew how that One might react; but would the Son of Man be more inclined to fall for the lies of the consummate Liar?

When God tests you, His child, it brings victory, strength, and goodness into your life. Obstacles overcome bring joy and reward to the one who overcomes.

OCTOBER 29

Eye has not seen, nor ear heard,
nor have entered into the heart of man
the things which God has prepared
for those who love Him.
(1 CORINTHIANS 2:9 NKJV)

THE FIRST "TEMPLE" where God walked with man was the Garden of Eden. Later, the Israelites watched as the tabernacle in the wilderness rose from the sands of the Sinai. Sadly, the awesome buildings that were the temples built by Solomon Herod's have vanished, still one temple remains.

Where is that temple? It is in the halls of heaven. The Scriptures are the only source of information about that temple. Glimpses can be caught through studying the tabernacle and the temples built in Jerusalem, which were but earthly reflections of the magnificence of heavenly grandeur. The book of Revelation does provide insight of a temple in heaven, a throne upon which God sits, with the Lamb of God.

What a precious promise for you, the overcomer! After all the struggles and strife, all the hardship and heartaches, God promises eternal fellowship with Him! No more crying; no more dying. No more pain; no more stain of sin...just love—full and unfathomable, and communion with God, the Father and the Son.

OCTOBER 30

And suddenly there came from heaven
a sound like a mighty rushing wind,
and it filled the entire house where
they were sitting.
(ACTS 2:2 ESV)

PETER, THE MUCH MALIGNED disciple because of his betrayal of Christ, changed. He had started out just like us. He knew Jesus. He experienced the love of Jesus. He believed upon Jesus and named Him as the Messiah. He personally experienced some miracles such as when he walked on the water with Jesus.

Peter received the full forgiveness and grace of Jesus after Jesus rose from the dead and appeared to him. He was blessed by Jesus. He ate and had fellowship with Jesus. He was taught by Jesus, Who took a personal interest in him.

No matter what he did, Peter was still Peter. He was embarrassed that he couldn't quite live up to the victorious Christian life. Peter felt like an outcast among the disciples because he had denied the Savior. He was embarrassed to show himself in the city where people knew who he was. But on the Day of Pentecost, something happened in Peter that was earth-shaking and life-changing.

That same change can happen in your life today if you surrender to the Holy Spirit, and ask Him to daily direct your walk with Christ.

OCTOBER 31

That Sunday evening the disciples
were meeting behind locked doors because
they were afraid of the Jewish leaders.
Suddenly, Jesus was standing there among them!
"Peace be with you," he said.

(JOHN 20:19 NLT)

PETER SAW JESUS after His resurrection. He knew Jesus was alive, but on the Day of Pentecost, Peter discovered that he also was alive in Christ as never before.

This was more than a "filling" with the Holy Spirit and power, more than a spiritual "high" that made him resolve to live his life in a better way. Peter was changed! This same Peter went into the city later and saw a man begging. "Look on me," he said.

Why did he draw attention to himself? What was there to see in Peter? He had been ashamed to show his face during Jesus' trial by the Sanhedrin. Nothing had changed in Peter's face or life, but man would now see Christ in Peter. The disciple had become Christ's representative fulfilling His mission and ministry on earth. What was so different? Nothing—except that Peter had been with Jesus and the life of Jesus now filled him.

Can people see that you have been with Jesus?

NOVEMBER

NOVEMBER 1

Happy is the one whose help is the God of Jacob,
whose hope is in the LORD his God.
(PSALM 146:5 CSB)

WHAT IS HAPPINESS? Webster defines it as "a state of well-being and contentment." Happiness is not the end product; it is a derivative of the ultimate pursuit: Jesus Christ.

Finding Jesus as Lord and Savior of your life is the ultimate and most profound joy. Have you read the acronym for "joy?" It is: Jesus, others, you.

Lyricist Oscar Hammerstein is credited with the quote, "Love's not love until you give it away."[44] To paraphrase that, "Joy is not joy until you give it away and share Jesus with others.

Nehemiah 8:10 reminds us that the "joy of the Lord is your strength." Pursue Jesus today and be blessed with true joy and happiness.

NOVEMBER 2

*For the wages of sin **is** death, but the gift of God **is**
eternal life in Christ Jesus our Lord.*
(ROMANS 6:23 NKJV)

AS LONG AS someone lives in sin, they are in prison. Sadly,
the greatest number of prisoners in chains today is those men and
women who have not surrendered to the Lordship of Jesus Christ.

As Paul instructs us in Romans 6:23, there are two ways to
be freed from the prison: One is the eternity of hell; the other is
eternity with God through the cleansing blood of Jesus. When
Jesus died on Calvary, He opened the life gate for all who would
receive His gift.

Which way have you chosen? Will you accept eternal life
through Christ, or will you turn your back on God's most gracious gift?

NOVEMBER 3

You, O LORD, remain forever;
Your throne from generation to generation.
(LAMENTATIONS 5:19 NKJV)

DO WE DISHONOR GOD to the point that He simply becomes our pal rather than the holy and righteous God? A true encounter with God always brings inevitable change. Either your commitment to Him grows deeper, or you harden your heart and perish spiritually. Psalm 93:2 reminds us that God's throne is everlasting—it always has been and forever will be.

What better assurance could we have than to know that God is on His throne, and beside Him sits the "Lamb slain from the foundation of the world?" (See Revelation 13:8.) It is a position of absolute power and command.

Nothing surprises God; He knows before a thought makes its way into your consciousness what you are going to do. He knows the answer even before you can form the question. He is aware of the solution even before you encounter the problem! Trust Him today with your future.

NOVEMBER 4

Teach us to number our days,
that we may gain a heart of wisdom.
(PSALM 90:12 NKJV)

POET WILLIAM ERNEST HENLEY wrote: "I am the master of my fate; I am the captain of my soul."[45]

Each of us struggles daily to allow God to sit on the throne of our life; to permit Him to steer our ship through the shoals and storms that confront us. The desire of our hearts is to allow the all-knowing, all powerful, ever-present God of the universe to take control, but we often fall short.

Contrary to what Henley wrote, you and I are not the masters of our fate. If we try to take over God's job, we will end up in the ditch of disaster.

Trust him for your today, your tomorrow, and your journey's end.

NOVEMBER 5

Jesus wept.
(JOHN 11:35 KJV)

ONLY TWO PLACES during His sojourn does the New Testament record Jesus weeping: At the tomb of his friend, Lazarus (John 11); and looking out over the city of Jerusalem (Luke 19). Could He have wept because Lazarus had died; after all, Jesus knew He was about to raise his friend from the dead. It could have been more from His compassion for the family and friends of Lazarus, or even due to the unbelief that gripped the mourners. Whatever the reason, Jesus showed us that tears are perfectly acceptable.

Should we as Christians always smile and be joyful? Circumstances along this road we walk will sometimes leave us bereft of happiness, our eyes filled with tears. See to it that your joy in the Lord never waivers.

The late Dr. Billy Graham wrote, "But joy is quiet confidence, a state of inner peace that comes from God."[46]

May the joy of the Lord be your strength today.

NOVEMBER 6

Yet in all these things we are more
than conquerors through Him who loved us.
(ROMANS 8:37 NKJV)

BENJAMIN FRANKLIN once said there were only two things certain in life: death and taxes. Enoch and Elijah might question the first, and someone in prison for tax evasion might question the second. I submit that there is only *one* thing in this life that is certain: The love of God for His creation.

The apostle Paul reassures us in Romans 8:38-39:

> For I am persuaded that neither death nor life, nor angels nor principalities nor powers, nor things present nor things to come, nor height nor depth, nor any other created thing, shall be able to separate us from the love of God which is in Christ Jesus our Lord. (NKJV)

You can rest today, child of God, in the knowledge that God loves you now and for all eternity.

*"A Message from God-of-the-Angel-Armies:
'I care!...I'm involved!'"*
(ZECHARIAH 8:1-2 MSG)

IT TAKES GREAT HUMILITY to become involved in the kind of situation Jesus describes in Luke 10:30-37, the story of the Good Samaritan. Many people today would have done exactly as the priest and the Levite did, heartlessly passing on the other side of the road.

Did these religious leaders feel they were too busy, too holy, or simply too important to come to the aid of a bleeding, naked, dying man? Did they think their elevated positions in society made it inappropriate for them to help someone of a lower class? Or was there some passage in the Torah they claimed would exempt them from getting their hands bloody?

Take a few moments to allow the Holy Spirit to search your heart. Are you willing to humble yourself to come to the aid of a person with serious needs? Are you willing to take the time to get your hands dirty and get involved? Or do you make excuses for why it's "someone else's" job to help?

NOVEMBER 8

He saved them for His name's sake,
that He might make His mighty power known.
(PSALM 106:8 NKJV)

SOMETIMES GOD does His greatest miracles during our most extreme times of testing. Even as Pharaoh's heart was hardening against the Israelites, the Lord told them, "I will...multiply My signs and My wonders in the land of Egypt." (Exodus 7:3 NKJV)

God's miracles in our life are a sign of His love and favor. He is a powerful, supernatural God, not limited by our human strength and ingenuity.

But God also performs signs and wonders to get the attention of the unbelieving world: "The Egyptians shall know that I am the Lord, when I stretch out My hand on Egypt and bring out the children of Israel from among them." (Exodus 7:5 NKJV)

What kind of miracle do you need in your life today? When God gives you a breakthrough in your family, your finances, your health, or your peace of mind, make sure to give Him the glory.

NOVEMBER 9

Live generously and graciously toward others,
the way God lives toward you.
(MATTHEW 5:48 MSG)

FORGIVENESS is something talked about much more often than it is practiced. It takes courage to exercise Radical Forgiveness when someone has hurt you deeply. But doing so will bring a new dimension into your life. It will free you to receive greater abundance and be healed both physically and emotionally.

Although great forgiveness was on full display at the cross, Jesus knew that the Father had been merciful and loving all along. God described Himself to Moses like this: "The Lord, the Lord, the compassionate and gracious God, slow to anger, abounding in love and faithfulness, maintaining love to thousands, and forgiving wickedness, rebellion and sin." (Exodus 34:6-7 NIV)

Pause to reflect on these words. Is this how you see the Lord, or has your view of Him been twisted by unscriptural religious traditions? Take time to thank Him for His mercy and forgiveness—then extend that forgiveness to others.

*A huge door of opportunity for
good work has opened up.*
(1 Corinthians 16:9 msg)

IF GOD PRESENTED you with an unexpected opportunity today, would you be prepared to make the most of it? Esther was. Her life began to take an unexpected turn when Persia's King Ahasuerus (also known as Xerxes) got upset with his beautiful queen, Vashti, and banished her from his presence.

The king's advisors decided Ahasuerus needed something to take his mind off Vashti, and a decree was issued: "Let beautiful young virgins be sought out for the king." (Esther 2:2 esv)

Just as a decree was sent out from King Ahasuerus in search of someone like Esther, King Jesus is searching for someone like you today! Can you hear His call? Are you spiritually fit and ready to respond?

Take a few moments to thank the Lord for the unexpected opportunities He is preparing for you. Then listen—really listen—for any instructions He has for you to obey on the road to your next assignment!

NOVEMBER 11

Humble yourselves under the mighty hand of God,
that He may exalt you in due time,
casting all your care upon Him, for He cares for you.
(1 PETER 5:6-7 NKJV)

DO YOU FEEL BURIED under the cares of life today? Have you been wounded by past failures or people's unkind words?

The good news is that God can lift you up and help you overcome whatever difficult circumstances you may be going through. But Radical Humility is needed to unleash this kind of favor: "Be clothed with humility, for 'God resists the proud, but gives grace to the humble'." (1 Peter 5:5-7)

Notice the vivid contrast: God resists—fights, confronts, and disregards—those who are proud and have an exaggerated view of their own importance. But He grants His grace and supernatural favor to those who humbly acknowledge their dependence on Him. So remember: *He's* God and you're not!

NOVEMBER 12

He comes alongside us
when we go through hard times.
(2 CORINTHIANS 1:4 MSG)

DURING YOUR TIMES of trial or persecution, you can find comfort and inspiration in the story of the Radical Obedience of Shadrach, Meshach, and Abednego.

Arthur Smith wrote a rousing spiritual about their miraculous deliverance, titled "The Fourth Man." The chorus reads:

> They wouldn't bend.
>
> They held onto the will of God so we are told...
>
> They wouldn't bow.
>
> They would not bow their knees to the idol made of gold...
>
> They wouldn't burn.
>
> They were protected by the fourth man in the fire.
>
> They wouldn't bend, they wouldn't bow, they wouldn't burn.

Despite his arrogance, even King Nebuchadnezzar had to admit that God had done an incredible miracle. These men were unharmed by their ordeal: "not a hair singed, not a scorch mark on their clothes, not even the smell of fire on them!" (Daniel 3:26-27 MSG) They lost the ropes that bound them!

This is the God you serve!

NOVEMBER 13

The one who blesses others is abundantly blessed;
those who help others are helped.
(PROVERBS 11:25 MSG)

THE BIBLE REVEALS GOD as a loving, generous Heavenly Father. When you choose to be generous, you are aligning yourself with the Father's heart.

Jesus says in Matthew 7:11, "If you then, being evil, know how to give good gifts to your children, how much more will your Father who is in heaven give good things to those who ask Him!" (NKJV)

Do you see what good news this is? As much as your earthly father may love you, your Heavenly Father loves you more...so much more. Your Father in heaven longs to give you good gifts. He longs to bless you. He longs to show you His kindness, approval, and favor.

Take time to thank Him today—and take steps of faith to be generous with others.

NOVEMBER 14

*I will turn their mourning to joy, will comfort them,
and make them rejoice rather than sorrow.*
(JEREMIAH 31:13 NKJV)

OFTEN PEOPLE who read the story of the Prodigal Son focus their attention on the son who went astray. This young man surely missed out on God's favor when he rebelliously ventured into "a far country" to fulfill his lustful desires. However, we see a beautiful depiction of God's grace and favor in action when this son returned home. (Luke 15:11-32)

The elder brother is quite a different story. He apparently thought his hard work and faithfulness to the family business would win him a life of favor. And he held his brother in disdain for walking away with an early inheritance, breaking their father's heart.

However, as the story concludes, the older brother still harbors unforgiveness. He heard the music and dancing in celebration of his sibling's return, but refused to embrace the forgiveness that would have released joy and favor in his life.

Don't turn your back on the Father; He loves you unconditionally.

NOVEMBER 15

Sanctify them by Your truth.
Your word is truth.
(JOHN 17:17 NKJV)

ARE YOU EXPERIENCING confusion or uncertainty in your life today? God's favor can help you cut to the heart of the issue you face, enabling you to discern the source of your battle and discover the Lord's prescription for victory.

This favor comes when you commit yourself to studying and obeying God's Word. Hebrews 4:12 declares:

The word of God is living and powerful, and sharper than any two-edged sword, piercing even to the division of soul and spirit, and of joints and marrow, and is a discerner of the thoughts and intents of the heart. (NKJV)

If you're going through a battle today in your health, family, finances, or emotions, you need a powerful sword to combat the lies of the enemy—"the sword of the Spirit, which is the word of God." (Ephesians 6:17 NKJV)

Let God's Word expose Satan's lies with the light of truth. Use it as a mighty sword to wage war for God's promised favor in your life!

NOVEMBER 16

My cup overflows.
(PSALM 23:5 NKJV)

WHAT IF YOU were walking in the woods one day and stumbled upon an ancient treasure chest? Suppose you could sense that great wealth must be hidden inside, but you needed a key in order to open it.

The Bible describes something like a heavenly treasure chest, complete with the keys for opening it: "The Lord will open to you His good treasure, the heavens, to give the rain to your land in its season, and to bless all the work of your hand." (Deuteronomy 28:12 NKJV)

While earthly treasure chests have a limited capacity, the blessings of heaven are unlimited. One of the keys for opening up this treasure trove of blessings is faithful, generous giving. When we are generous, God promises to "throw open the floodgates of heaven and pour out so much blessing that there will not be room enough to store it." (Malachi 3:10 NIV)

NOVEMBER 17

"The 'right time' is now.
Today is the day of salvation."
(2 Corinthians 6:2 NLT)

FORGIVENESS can be difficult, especially if the offense caused a deep wound in our heart or if we've allowed the wound to fester for a long time. Sometimes people spend nights in prayer, supplication, or weeping, often times imagining scenarios where they confront the one who harmed, insulted, embarrassed, or betrayed them.

It's not an easy process—it's usually just plain hard! Yet instead of focusing on how difficult it is to forgive, consider the incredible blessings released in your life when you choose Radical Forgiveness instead of hanging on to an offense. Forgiveness magnifies the image of God, activates the Word of God, and releases God's favor in your life. It brings God's blessings to your spirit, mind, emotions, body, finances, and relationships.

So what are you waiting for? Ask God to search your heart and reveal anyone you need to forgive today. Then do it now!

NOVEMBER 18

My God will supply all your needs
according to His riches in glory in Christ Jesus.
(PHILIPPIANS 4:19 NASB)

GOD DOESN'T LEAVE YOU to fend for yourself or rely upon your own strength or resources as you seek to be more conformed to His image. Through His incredible favor, the Lord will give you all the resources you need to have a transformed life and do what He has called you to do.

Do you have a vision for your life? Has God given you a clear picture of your calling? His favor will empower you, whether you are called to be a missionary or evangelist, a pastor or teacher, a salesman or CEO, a doctor or factory worker, a politician or stay-at-home parent caring for your family.

A critical key for receiving this kind of favor is to focus on God's kingdom in everything you do: "Seek first the kingdom of God and His righteousness, and all these things shall be added to you." (Matthew 6:33) Put the Lord first in your life!

NOVEMBER 19

Get all the advice and instruction you can,
so you will be wise the rest of your life.
(PROVERBS 19:20 NLT)

STRESS! At any moment, you can be overtaken by the cares of this world. Moses became overburdened with the task of advising and judging the children of Israel in the desert, and he needed some wise counsel. His father-in-law Jethro realized how desperate he was for assistance and asked: "Why are you trying to do all this alone while everyone stands around you from morning till evening...You're going to wear yourself out—and the people, too." (Exodus 18:14, 18:18 NLT)

Jethro proceeded to give Moses some wise and timely advice:

Select from all the people some capable, honest men who fear God and hate bribes...They should always be available to solve the people's common disputes, but have them bring the major cases to you...They will help you carry the load, making the task easier for you. (vs. 21-22)

Moses was floundering in his leadership role until he received this wise counsel from Jethro—just in time to save his sanity! Make sure you are always teachable and are open to receiving timely advice.

NOVEMBER 20

They delight in the law of the Lord,
meditating on it day and night.
(PSALM 1:2 NKJV)

ONE DAY JESUS asked some fair-weather disciples, "Why do you call Me 'Lord, Lord,' and not do the things which I say?" (See Luke 6:46.)

Like some professing Christians today, these people claimed to be following Jesus, but their lives bore no resemblance to His teachings.

If Jesus is truly your Lord, you need to make sure you are obeying Him. It means actually following Jesus in your daily life. It means paying attention to the teachings of the Bible and putting them into practice as a "doer" of the Word. (See James 1:22.)

A person who lives in obedience to Christ is given a wonderful promise from God: "This one will be blessed in what he does." (See James 1:25.)

Are you ready to be more blessed? Then make a commitment to put God's Word into practice through daily obedience.

NOVEMBER 21

"The Lord is my portion," says my soul,
"Therefore I hope in Him!"
(LAMENTATIONS 3:24 NKJV)

THE HUMBLE MAN or woman recognizes God as the Source of every good thing—life, health, opportunity, talent, and blessing. While our modern-day "me first" society seems to think we can take care of ourselves without God's help, the Bible says clearly, "Every good gift and every perfect gift is from above, and comes down from the Father of lights, with whom there is no variation or shadow of turning." (James 1:17 NKJV)

God reveals Himself in Scripture as "Jehovah Jireh," our Provider. (See Genesis 22:14.) As a shepherd, David discovered this aspect of God's character when he saw God's miraculous provision and protection for him and his flock. No wonder he could write the beautiful words of Psalm 23:1 (NLT): "The Lord is my shepherd; I have all that I need."

Pause and take a few minutes to acknowledge God's faithful provision in your life. Give Him praise for His promise to meet your every need.

NOVEMBER 22

He who has a generous eye will be blessed,
for he gives of his bread to the poor.
(PROVERBS 22:9 NKJV)

WHILE IT'S WONDERFUL to practice generosity toward your friends and relatives, it's much more profound to extend God's love, forgiveness, and favor to those who have mistreated you.

Solomon describes this well: "If your enemy is hungry, give him bread to eat; and if he is thirsty, give him water to drink; for so you will heap coals of fire on his head, and the Lord will reward you." (Proverbs 25:21-22 NKJV)

Notice the wonderful result set in motion when you practice such generosity—toward your enemies, in addition to your friends and family: "The Lord will reward you."

Pause for a few minutes now to pray and ask Him to show you ways you can be more generous—even toward those who have wronged you.

NOVEMBER 23

O Lord of Heaven's Armies,
what joy for those who trust in you.
(PSALM 84:12 NLT)

GOD IS SOVEREIGN, and the Bible teaches that He is the
One who determines the number of our days. The Lord holds us
in the palm of His hand, and we never need to see ourselves as
helpless victims.

In John 10:29 Jesus affirms the wonderful truth that no one
is able to snatch us out of the hands of our Heavenly Father. Do
you see what good news this is? When you give your life to Jesus
Christ, you can be secure in the knowledge that He is your Protector and Provider. No one can snatch you out of His hands or
separate you from His love.

Living in God's favor is not a matter of striving and struggling,
but rather a matter of resting securely in the Lord's amazing love
and goodness. Trust Him!

NOVEMBER 24

Today, if you will hear His voice:
Do not harden your hearts.
(PSALM 95:7-8 NKJV)

IN ORDER TO LIVE in God's favor, you must learn to walk by faith rather than feelings. As famed evangelist D.L. Moody once said, "Obedience means marching right on whether we feel like it or not. Many times we go against our feelings. Faith is one thing, feeling is another." The apostle Paul affirmed this when he wrote, "We walk by faith, not by sight." (2 Corinthians 5:7 NKJV)

When you've committed your life to Radical Obedience, you move when God says "Go" and stop when He says "Stop." Abraham exemplified this beautifully when he obeyed God's instruction to leave his homeland and set out for an unknown destination. God's call seems to have come when Abraham was going about his usual activities, and the Lord said: "Leave your native country, your relatives, and your father's family, and go to the land that I will show you." (Genesis 12:1 NLT)

What is God calling you to do today? Your obedience will unlock His blessings and His favor.

NOVEMBER 25

What is causing the quarrels and fights among you?
Don't they come from the evil desires at war within you?
(JAMES 4:1 NLT)

ARE YOU DEALING with relationship conflicts? If so, you are not alone. Even the Bible's greatest heroes of the faith had to deal with conflicts at times—and sometimes the conflicts were severe.

When Sarah saw Ishmael mocking Isaac one day, her anger reached volcanic level. She demanded that Abraham drive Hagar and her son from the encampment with only the bread and water the two could carry.

Abraham had to bear the pain, heartache, and tragedy of losing Ishmael as he complied with Sarah's demands. Despite God's forgiveness and favor, there were consequences to his actions. Nevertheless, God's plan for Abraham, Sarah, and Isaac—and also for Hagar and Ishmael—did not falter.

No matter how far you may have drifted from God, there is still time to humble yourself and discover His perfect plan for your life!

NOVEMBER 26

Sing to the Lord a new song!
For He has done marvelous things.
(PSALM 98:1 NKJV)

IN ORDER TO LIVE in God's favor, you must accept His forgiveness and restoration. And this means letting go of past failures and disappointments so you can move on to God's best for your life.

God tells us in Isaiah 43:18-19: "Do not remember the former things, nor consider the things of old. Behold, I will do a new thing, now it shall spring forth; shall you not know it?"(NKJV)

Just as you can't safely drive your car if all your attention is on the rearview mirror, so it is that God instructs you to forget the past and embrace the "new thing" He wants to do in your life today.

Take a few minutes to pause and reflect on anything from the past that you still need to release. Then ask God to give you a clear vision of the exciting things He's planning for your future!

NOVEMBER 27

Now I'm alert to God's ways;
I don't take God for granted.
(PSALM 18:21 MSG)

MOSES' HUMILITY sprang from the divine assurance that the Lord was in control. When he remained humble and obedient, he was assured of protection from his enemies.

Obedience to God's will is not an easy choice. Moses chose that pathway because of his love for the Lord and his recognition that His plans are best. While all the Israelites witnessed God's mighty acts, only Moses was shown His ways: "He made known His ways to Moses, His acts to the children of Israel." (Psalm 103:7 NKJV)

Like Moses, you can choose to obey or choose to walk away from God's plan and purpose for your life. But Moses chose the path of humility, obedience, and favor. He opened his heart to God's instruction at every turn.

NOVEMBER 28

No procrastination. No backward looks.
You can't put God's kingdom off till tomorrow.
Seize the day.
(LUKE 9:62 MSG)

HAVE YOU BEEN making up excuses to keep from obeying what God is calling you to do? Moses tried that, but it didn't work.

"Lord, I'm not very good with words," he pleaded. "I never have been, and I'm not now, even though you have spoken to me. I get tongue-tied, and my words get tangled." (Exodus 4:10 NLT)

But God rejects our excuses. "Who makes a person's mouth?" He replied to Moses. "Is it not I, the Lord? Now go! I will be with you as you speak, and I will instruct you in what to say." (vs. 11-12)

The Lord's answer to Moses' feelings of inadequacy was the same as He often must say to us when we try to make excuses: "I will be with you!" His plan for you is unchanging, so it's time to drop the excuses and make a commitment to Him!

NOVEMBER 29

Put on the new self, created to be like God
in true righteousness and holiness.
(EPHESIANS 4:24 NIV)

THERE ARE TWO SIDES to living in the abundance of God's favor. First, we must let go of the past and anything that is holding us back. Next, we must take active steps to enter into God's best for our life.

We see this pattern with the Israelites. God spoke to them about both sides of this process:

> Say therefore to the people of Israel, 'I am the LORD, and I will bring you out from under the burdens of the Egyptians, and I will deliver you from slavery to them, and I will redeem you with an outstretched arm and with great acts of judgment. (Exodus 6:6 ESV)

Take some time to assess where you are on this journey to God's favor. Have you left behind the toxic situations that were keeping you from enjoying God's blessings? Have you taken the needed steps of obedience to move into His will for your life?

NOVEMBER 30

With favor You will surround him as with a shield.
(PSALM 5:12 NKJV)

SOMETIMES GOD'S PEOPLE worry about conditions in the world or fluctuations in their nation's economy. However, when you are living fully in God's favor, you can rest secure in HIS protection and provision.

When Pharaoh hardened his heart and refused to let the Israelites leave Egypt, God sent terrible judgments upon the nation. And when the rest of Egypt was afflicted with swarms of flies and hailstorms, God's people were safe.

Psalm 91 promises that you can find protection "in the secret place of the Most High" and "under the shadow of the Almighty." (v. 1) Even though "a thousand may fall at your side... [terror] shall not come near you." (v. 7 NKJV)

So, go ahead and breathe a sigh of relief—God's favor can keep you safe!

DECEMBER

DECEMBER 1

*Repent...that times of refreshing may come
from the presence of the Lord.*
(ACTS 3:19 NKJV)

AFTER TIMES OF TRIAL and stress, we find ourselves needing rest and refreshment. This is what God provided for the Israelites after they left Marah: "the oasis of Elim, where they found twelve springs and seventy palm trees." (Exodus 15:27 NLT)

Imagine...finding a refreshing oasis in the middle of the wilderness! When everything around you is dry and barren, God provides you with a place of beautiful vegetation and shade.

But Psalm 84:6 (NLT) says we sometimes must pass "through the Valley of Weeping" in order to make it "become a place of refreshing springs."

Where are you in your pilgrimage today? In a barren wilderness? A Valley of Weeping? Or a place of refreshing springs like Elim? Rest in Him today and be confident He will take care of you all along the way.

DECEMBER 2

The righteous person faces many troubles,
but the Lord comes to the rescue each time.
(PSALM 34:19 NLT)

HOW WOULD YOU like to be visited by a mighty angel of God? Instead of immediately recognizing that this might be a sign of God's favor, "Mary was greatly troubled." (Luke 1:29 NIV) Gabriel sensed her apprehension and again assured her that his mission was one of favor and blessing: "Do not be afraid, Mary; you have found favor with God." (v. 30)

As the angelic message unfolded, Mary must have been even more baffled. Having a baby without even having had sexual relations? What?! A son who would be called "the Son of the Most High"? A child who would one day reign over Israel with a never-ending kingdom? Mary asked a very logical question in reply: "How will this be?" (v. 34)

Perhaps God has made promises to you that seem incredible. You look at your circumstances and wonder how things will ever change. If so, remember Mary. Trust God, and let Him take care of the *"how"* questions.

DECEMBER 3

Greetings, you who are highly favored!
The Lord is with you.
(LUKE 1:26-28 NIV)

LIFE WON'T BE necessarily easy just because you live in God's favor. When the angel Gabriel was sent to a young girl named Mary, her life got a lot harder—not easier—after his visit. Yet the angel assured her of God's great favor in her life: Before Gabriel's visit, Mary had a pretty ordinary, conventional life for a young Jewish girl. She was engaged to be married to a man of integrity who had his own carpenter shop. Life was good, and she had wonderful prospects for a happy future.

But everything was about to change. Not only was she going to give birth to a son without having sexual relations, but her baby would be called "the Son of the Most High." (v. 32)

If you face some complicated issues today, don't despair. So did Mary, and she was "highly favored."

DECEMBER 4

All the Lord's promises prove true.
(PSALM 18:30 NLT)

WHEN GOD MAKES A PROMISE to you, what does it take to actually believe it and receive its benefits? When Gabriel promised Mary amazing things about the birth and destiny of her son, he mentioned a "sign" that would confirm his message: Her relative Elizabeth, who had been childless, would "have a child in her old age." (Luke 1:36 NIV)

The Bible provides several examples of people like Moses and Gideon who were given supernatural signs to confirm God's veracity and His calling in their lives. But our ultimate trust must be in the faithfulness of God's Word, not just in some confirming sign. As Gabriel assured Mary, "No word from God will ever fail." (v. 37)

Pause for a moment to consider God's promises in your life. Are you waiting for some "sign" before you will believe what the Lord has told you? Or will you believe His Word, knowing it will never fail.

DECEMBER 5

Blessed is she who has believed that the Lord
would fulfill his promises to her!
(Luke 1:45 niv)

THE ANGEL GABRIEL had delivered a message that would have overwhelmed anyone. And although Mary initially questioned how the angel's message could possibly occur, she ultimately chose to believe and obey: "I am the Lord's servant," Mary answered. "May your word to me be fulfilled?" (Luke 1:38 niv)

First, Mary declared her willingness to be the servant of the Lord. Then she chose to believe God's message and participate in its fulfillment. Mary's response is reminiscent of Abraham, who also received unfathomable promises from God: "Abram believed the Lord, and he credited it to him as righteousness." (Genesis 15:6 niv)

Are you struggling to believe some promise the Lord has given you? Then remember the examples of Abraham and Mary. Humble yourself to become the Lord's servant, then trust Him to fulfill His promises—no matter how incredible they may seem!

DECEMBER 6

The LORD has done great things for us,
and we are filled with joy.
(PSALM 126:3 NIV)

YOU MAY OR MAY NOT be a good singer, but God puts a song of praise in your heart. This is exactly what happened to Mary as she saw God's goodness in her life:

My soul glorifies the Lord and my spirit rejoices in God my Savior, for he has been mindful of the humble state of his servant. From now on all generations will call me blessed, for the Mighty One has done great things for me—holy is his name." (Luke 1:46-49 NIV)

Take a few minutes to meditate on this beautiful testimony of God's favor. You may even want to write your own song of praise. Magnify the Lord, focusing on Him instead of on your problems. Rejoice in His goodness, and humble yourself in His presence. Thank Him that you are blessed because of the great things He has done for you.

DECEMBER 7

With my mouth I will make your faithfulness
known through all generations.
(PSALM 89:1 NIV)

WHEN WE READ the angel's proclamation that Mary would be blessed and highly favored (Luke 1:26-28 NIV), we might assume she would have an easy, carefree life. However, walking in God's favor doesn't mean you'll never face adversity.

Mary had to face the scorn of her relatives and neighbors. She and Joseph undertook the difficult trek from Nazareth to Bethlehem—Mary on the back of a donkey while nine months pregnant. She had no place to give birth except in a cave where animals were kept, and the family later had to hurriedly move to Egypt to find safety from King Herod. (See Matthew 2:13-23.)

Does this sound like an easy life to you? Yet despite many hardships, Mary enjoyed the unrivaled favor of God. She also recognized that her legacy would continue long past her own lifetime: "He took notice of his lowly servant girl, and from now on all generations will call me blessed." (Luke 1:48 NLT)

DECEMBER 8

Whoever calls on the name of the Lord shall be saved.
(ROMANS 10:13 NKJV)

JOSEPH, THE CARPENTER from Nazareth, faced a bewildering situation. He was betrothed to Mary, she was pregnant—and he knew he wasn't the father.

What could he do? He was planning to quietly break off the engagement.

But an angel appeared to Joseph and assured him that the baby had been conceived by the Holy Spirit, fulfilling the prophecy in Isaiah 7:14 that "the virgin will conceive a child." (Matthew 1:23 NLT)

Joseph was given a glimpse into Jesus' prophetic destiny as the One who would bring God's forgiveness to humankind: "You are to name him Jesus, for he will save his people from their sins." (v. 21 NLT)

John the Baptist would later confirm Jesus' identity as the "the Lamb of God who takes away the sin of the world." (John 1:29)

If you are dealing with a forgiveness issue such as guilt, shame, or addiction, there's only one solution: Turn to Jesus!

DECEMBER 9

*I am not ashamed of this
Good News about Christ.
It is the power of God at work,
saving everyone who believes.*
(ROMANS 1:16 NLT)

IT HAD BEEN just an ordinary day for the shepherds watching over their flocks near Bethlehem. But suddenly they received a message that would change their lives forever.

An angel of the Lord appeared to them, and the glory of the Lord shone around them, and they were terrified. But the angel said to them, "Do not be afraid. I bring you good news that will cause great joy for all the people." (Luke 2:9-10 NIV)

The silent, pitch-black night was suddenly interrupted by brilliant light and a loud angelic proclamation. The frightened shepherds were assured by the angel that his message was one of "good news that will cause great joy."

Even if you're going through a dark night, when God has seemed silent, everything can change in a moment of time. The breakthrough may not be as dramatic as the shepherds experienced, but the message will be the same: good news and great joy!

DECEMBER 10

This is the day the Lord has made.
We will rejoice and be glad in it.
(PSALM 118:24 NLT)

ON WHAT SEEMED like an ordinary night, the shepherds were awakened by quite an extraordinary message: "Today in the town of David a Savior has been born to you; he is the Messiah, the Lord." (Luke 2:11 NIV)

Hundreds of years before, God's people had been promised that one day their Savior and Messiah would come. They waited and waited, until many had given up hope. Could it be that the angel's message was true? After waiting so long, could *today* be the day when the prophecies would be fulfilled and the Savior would come?

There is a powerful lesson here for each of us. God has made many wonderful promises to us in His Word, yet sometimes we become weary while waiting for our breakthroughs. At such times, we must remember the shepherds. Little did they know that *today* would be the day when everything changed and light pierced the darkness with hope and favor.

DECEMBER 11

May the Lord show you his favor
and give you his peace.
(NUMBERS 6:26 NLT)

THE SHEPHERDS heard the angelic choir sing a powerful song of praise: "Glory to God in the highest heaven, and on earth peace to those on whom his favor rests." (Luke 2:13-14 NIV)

It was as if a doorway suddenly opened into the heavenly realm. Up until this time, the shepherds seem to have had a pretty drab and earthbound existence. But now "the highest heaven" had come down and touched the earth.

However, for many people, life was unchanged the night Christ was born. They didn't hear the angelic declaration or see any special star to signal the arrival of the newborn King.

The key was God's favor. The angels weren't proclaiming worldwide peace, but rather "peace to those on whom his favor rests" or "with whom God is pleased." (NLT) Out of millions of people on earth, the shepherds had been blessed by life-changing grace and favor from God.

DECEMBER 12

I speak only of what I know by experience...
There is nothing secondhand here, no hearsay.
(JOHN 3:11 MSG)

WHEN THE ANGELS told them about the newborn King, the shepherds could have just taken their word for it. But they concluded that they needed to act upon what they had heard: "Let's go to Bethlehem and see this thing that has happened, which the Lord has told us about." (Luke 2:15 NIV) They already had heard the news, but now they wanted to also "see this thing."

In the same way, many people have heard the message of Christ and His favor, but they've never taken the next step—to find out for themselves whether it's true. Their faith is secondhand, based on hearsay instead of firsthand experience.

Pause and ask yourself whether your relationship with God is backed by personal experience or just secondhand truths you've read in books or heard from preachers or friends. Go to "Bethlehem" and see for yourself what God has done!

DECEMBER 13

Don't procrastinate— there's no time to lose.
(PROVERBS 6:4 MSG)

THE SHEPHERDS wasted no time in pursuing firsthand knowledge of the newborn Savior they had heard about: "They hurried off and found Mary and Joseph, and the baby, who was lying in the manger." (Luke 2:16 NIV)

The angels had been telling the truth, of course, but it was crucial for the shepherds to take time to find out for themselves: "The shepherds returned, glorifying and praising God for all the things they had heard and seen, which were just as they had been told." (v. 20)

Too often, people miss out on the blessings of God because they procrastinate when the Lord tells them to do something. But the shepherds weren't like that. Instead of delaying, they took immediate action and "hurried off" to see the baby in the manger.

Remember: Delayed obedience is really disobedience. Listen for God's instructions today, and make sure to do them right away.

DECEMBER 14

The man went and spread the word,
proclaiming to everyone what had happened.
As a result, large crowds soon surrounded Jesus.
(MARK 1:45 NLT)

ONCE YOU KNOW THE SAVIOR, you will want to make Him known to others. This is exactly what happened to the shepherds after they encountered King Jesus in the manger: "When they had seen him, they spread the word concerning what had been told them about this child, and all who heard it were amazed at what the shepherds said to them." (Luke 2:17-18 NIV)

It's unlikely that these shepherds had ever thought of themselves as preachers or evangelists. But everything changed "when they had seen him." Once they had a firsthand experience with the newborn Messiah, they couldn't help but "spread the word."

Pause for a moment and ask yourself whether you are spreading the word about Jesus and the gospel. The more you see Him, the more you will want others to know Him. The more you experience His life-changing favor, the more you will want to share His grace and goodness with the people around you.

DECEMBER 15

Righteous your ways and true, King of the nations!
Who can fail to fear you, God, give glory to your Name?
(REVELATION 15:3-4 MSG)

WE DON'T KNOW the exact time frame of the journey made by "wise men from the East" in search of young King Jesus. (See Matthew 2:1-12.) It may have been several months or even a few years after Jesus' birth when they arrived at Herod's palace and asked, "Where is He who has been born King of the Jews?" (v. 1)

While some of the details of their journey are unclear, there's much we can learn from the wonderful example set by the Magi. Although they clearly were people of considerable education, esteem, and wealth, they went in search of the King of Kings. They were "wise men" indeed!

Make sure you put King Jesus first in your life!

DECEMBER 16

*Such people may seek you
and worship in your presence,
O God of Jacob.*
(PSALM 24:6 NLT)

THE "WISE MEN FROM THE EAST" (Matthew 2:1) were not just casual believers—they were committed believers. They came from a great distance and at great expense in order to have a personal encounter with the newborn "King of the Jews." When King Herod heard of their mission, "he was troubled" (v. 3), and their very lives were in danger as they continued their quest undeterred.

What a great example the Magi set for us today. These learned men were wise enough to prioritize the pursuit of God. At a great sacrifice of their time and treasure, they came to spend time in the presence of their young King.

How intentional and consistent is the time you spend in God's presence? What kind of priority have you made to be alone with Him each day?

DECEMBER 17

Whatever you do, do all to the glory of God.
(1 Corinthians 10:31 NKJV)

RIGHT FROM THE BEGINNING, the Magi made the purpose of their journey clear: "We have seen His star in the East and have come to worship Him." (Matthew 2:2 NKJV) They not only wanted to see the newborn King, they wanted to worship Him. These should be our focal points as well, yet modern-day life has numerous distractions and diversions. A life of worship cannot happen without intentionality and devotion.

Too often, when people hear the word "worship," they immediately think of church services and other kinds of public events. But the Bible makes it clear that our entire life should be a declaration of worship:

> I plead with you to give your bodies to God because of all he has done for you. Let them be a living and holy sacrifice—the kind he will find acceptable. This is truly the way to worship him. (Romans 12:1 NLT)

DECEMBER 18

You guide me with your counsel,
leading me to a glorious destiny.
(PSALM 73:24 NLT)

YOU DON'T GET TO CHOOSE the place of your birth—but God does. The Magi knew the town of Jesus' birth, because God had sovereignly arranged the circumstances to fulfill Micah's prophecy. (See Matthew 2:6, Micah 5:2.)

It had been prophesied long before that the Messiah would be born of the lineage of David. (See Acts 13:23.) And like David, He would be born in Bethlehem and would be a Shepherd of the people of God. But the Father not only had a plan for the life of His Son Jesus—He has a plan for your life too.

Just as He knew Jesus' birthplace in advance, He has preordained our "appointed times in history" and "the boundaries of [our] lands." (Acts 17:26 NIV)

So let's fulfill our destiny!

He guides me along right paths,
bringing honor to his name.
(PSALM 23:3 NLT)

A VITAL PART of living in the center of God's divine will is heeding His instructions and following His guidance. Knowing that we are in God's will should bring great joy to our lives, as we see with the Magi:

> Behold, the star which they had seen in the East went before them, till it came and stood over where the young Child was. When they saw the star, they rejoiced with exceedingly great joy. (Matthew 2:9-10 NKJV)

These men were intelligent and well read, yet they didn't trust their own wisdom or instincts when it came to their mission to find the Messiah. They needed God's supernatural guidance, and "rejoiced with exceedingly great joy" when it came.

Take a few moments to give God thanks for His great plan for your life. Ask Him to guide you by His Word and His Spirit, and commit yourself to obeying Him when He does.

DECEMBER 20

RIGHT FROM THE BEGINNING of their journey, the Magi had set out to worship the newborn King—and that's exactly what they did when they arrived at their destination. Then the Wise Men presented gifts to the Christ Child—gold, frankincense, and myrrh.

The sincerity of their worship was shown by their humility, as they fell down at the Child's feet in adoration. Rather than paying mere lip service, their worship included generous offerings. Our most treasured possession was addressed by the apostle Paul in Romans 12:1:

> And so, dear brothers and sisters, I plead with you to give your bodies to God because of all he has done for you. Let them be a living and holy sacrifice—the kind he will find acceptable. This is truly the way to worship him. (NLT)

If we have a genuine encounter with our Savior, the King of Kings, how can we not honor Him with our possessions?

DECEMBER 21

*God's Word warns us of danger
and directs us to hidden treasure.*
(PSALM 19:11 MSG)

WHEN GOD GIVES YOU a dream to pursue, you often will have to deal with a "King Herod" who tries to divert you from your intended purpose. However, the Magi truly proved to be "wise men," able to discern that King Herod had no intention of furthering their mission. (See Matthew 2:3-8.)

Again, these devout men were blessed by supernatural guidance from the Lord: "Being divinely warned in a dream that they should not return to Herod, they departed for their own country another way." (v. 12) Have you ever been "divinely warned"—whether from the Word of God or from His still small voice in your heart?

Notice that the Magi returned home "another way." Genuine worship will transform you and cause you to walk on a different path. As you worship the Lord today, He wants to instruct you, change your life, and give you a breakthrough of the favor you need!

DECEMBER 22

I will look on you with favor and make you fruitful.
(LEVITICUS 26:9 NIV)

OBTAINING GOD'S FAVOR is not a one-time proposition, but a daily journey. Jesus had His Father's favor at His birth, but He grew in that favor all along the way: "The child grew up healthy and strong. He was filled with wisdom, and God's favor was on him." (Luke 2:40 NLT)

Read this statement again and apply the principle to your own life. God wants you to grow up! He wants you to be healthy and strong. And most of all, He wants to fill you with wisdom so that His abundant favor can rest upon your life.

A few verses later, we see that Jesus not only grew in favor with God, but also with "all the people." (v. 52 NLT)

Take a few minutes to stop and thank God for His favor in your life. Then ask Him to also open new doors of favor with the people around you.

DECEMBER 23

With my whole heart I have sought You;
oh, let me not wander from Your commandments!
(PSALM 119:10 NKJV)

WE AREN'T GIVEN many specifics about Jesus' childhood, but Luke 2:41-52 (NIV) provides a story about Jesus and His parents journeying to the Feast of Passover when He was 12 years old. When the festival was over, His parents began their journey home, unaware that Jesus had stayed behind in Jerusalem.

This should serve as a warning to each of us not to go about our lives without including Jesus in all we do. If you realize you've done this, immediately stop what you're doing and go back, as Joseph and Mary did: "They went back to Jerusalem to look for him." (v. 45)

Mary and Joseph found Jesus "sitting among the teachers, listening to them and asking them questions." (v. 46) As the story ends, He willingly and obediently returned with His parents to Nazareth. Yes, even Jesus had to submit to authority. How much more should you and I submit to His directives.

DECEMBER 24

It is not the one who commends himself who is approved,
but the one whom the Lord commends.

(2 CORINTHIANS 10:18 NIV)

WHOSE AFFIRMING WORDS do you crave the most? Your spouse? Boss? Friend? Teacher? Pastor? When Jesus was about to begin His ministry, He received the most important affirmation a person could ever receive: the commendation of His Heavenly Father. (See Matthew 3:13-17.)

Our Lord had taken a step of Radical Humility—submitting Himself for baptism by John the Baptist. When John protested, He explained that "it is fitting for us to fulfill all righteousness." (v. 15) As Jesus came up out of the water, "the heavens were opened," and He heard the Father's affirming voice: "This is My beloved Son, in whom I am well pleased." (See Matthew 3:16-17.) In other translations, the Father says His Son "brings me great joy" (NIV) and is "marked by my love, the delight of my life." (MSG)

Pause for a moment and reflect on these words of affirmation. When you live in God's favor, this is what He is saying to you today!

DECEMBER 25

Anyone who believes in me
will do the same works I have done.
(JOHN 14:12 NLT)

IT IS NO COINCIDENCE that obedience, forgiveness, generosity, and humility are the very traits modeled by Jesus Himself: He humbled Himself in obedience to the Father. He gave His life so that we can experience forgiveness for sin.

Just as God's favor rests upon Jesus, it is released abundantly in our life when we follow in His footsteps. The Father bestows His favor so that we may be transformed and produce the fruits of His righteousness. When that happens, God is glorified and we are blessed beyond measure.

The psalmist wrote: "The Lord God is a sun and shield; the Lord will give grace and glory; no good thing will He withhold from those who walk uprightly." (Psalm 84:11 NKJV)

When you, as God's child, grasp this essential principle, you are released to walk in His blessings—then you are free to bless others.

DECEMBER 26

I lift you high in praise, my God, O my King,
and I'll bless your name into eternity.
(PSALM 145:1 MSG)

GOD WANTS to bless you and make you a blessing during your sojourn on earth. But His favor goes far beyond this lifetime. As David observed, our earthly life is just a drop in the bucket compared to eternity: "My entire lifetime is just a moment to you; at best, each of us is but a breath." (Psalm 39:5 NLT)

Jesus described the eternal home being prepared for us: "Let not your heart be troubled; you believe in God, believe also in Me. In My Father's house are many mansions; if it were not so, I would have told you. I go to prepare a place for you. And if I go and prepare a place for you, I will come again and receive you to Myself; that where I am, there you may be also." (John 14:1-3 NKJV)

Jesus promised His followers a place of eternal favor in heaven.

DECEMBER 27

Be very glad!
For a great reward awaits you in heaven.
(MATTHEW 5:12 NLT)

THE BEST OF God's favor is yet to come, because His favor is not limited to this lifetime. But how we live our lives here on earth has a direct relationship to what we'll find awaiting us in heaven.

Paul the apostle quotes Isaiah the prophet on this: "Eye has not seen, nor ear heard, nor have entered into the heart of man the things which God has prepared for those who love Him" (1 Corinthians 2:9 NKJV)

Artists who try to paint the splendor of heaven always come up short, simply because it's impossible for the human mind to conceive the grandeur of God's house. And one reason it's impossible to do justice to the majesty of heaven is that its beauty is totally overshadowed by the presence of God Almighty.

What majesty and joy await you!

DECEMBER 28

You are famous, God, for welcoming God-seekers,
for decking us out in delight.
(PSALM 5:11-12 MSG)

THE APOSTLE PAUL was lifted all the way to the third heaven, but he never attempted to describe the tree of life, pearly gates, and streets of gold. And although John the Revelator wrote about heaven, he gave us only a scant description of its beauty.

When you've lived a life for Christ, you will be greeted with these wonderful words of favor: "Well done, good and faithful servant; you were faithful over a few things, I will make you ruler over many things. Enter into the joy of your Lord." (Matthew 25:21 NKJV)

Pause for a moment to read these powerful words again, reflecting on how they apply to your life. Are you a "faithful servant," humbly obeying your Master? Have you been a good steward of the "few things" He has given you? Now's the time to get ready!

DECEMBER 29

There's more life to come—an eternity of life!
You can count on this.
(TITUS 3:7-8 MSG)

ONE OF THE MOST life-changing revelations you can ever have is to understand that this world is not your ultimate home:

> There's far more to life for us. We're citizens of high heaven! We're waiting the arrival of the Savior, the Master, Jesus Christ, who will transform our earthy bodies into glorious bodies like his own. He'll make us beautiful and whole with the same powerful skill by which he is putting everything as it should be, under and around him. (Philippians 3:20-21 MSG)

Take time to read these words again, applying each phrase to your life. No matter how much of God's favor you may be experiencing today, it's good to know "there's far more to life for us," because you are a citizen of heaven!

When Jesus returns He not only will "transform our earthly bodies," but He will also put everything else in order under His loving lordship.

DECEMBER 30

Those who love their life in this world will lose it.
Those who care nothing for
their life in this world will keep it for eternity.
(JOHN 12:25 NLT)

UNDERSTANDING YOUR heavenly destiny will transform your life on earth. Yet as British author C. S. Lewis correctly observed, "It is since Christians have largely ceased to think of the other world that they have become so ineffective in this one."[47] The Lord wants us to "see things from his perspective" (Colossians 3:2 MSG), as Paul describes:

> Set your hearts on things above, where Christ is, seated at the right hand of God. Set your minds on things above, not on earthly things...When Christ, who is your life, appears, then you also will appear with him in glory. (Colossians 3:1-4 NIV)

So, where is your focus today—on "things above" or on "earthly things"? If you want to walk in blessings, you must learn to set your mind on the things of God. Instead of being focused on pleasing yourself, you must put your attention on the Lord and discover "a spacious, free life." (Romans 8:5-8 MSG)

DECEMBER 31

For the time is coming when I will restore
the fortunes of my people of Israel and Judah.
I will bring them home to this land that I gave
to their ancestors, and they will possess it again.
I, the LORD, have spoken!"

(JEREMIAH 30:3 NLT)

JOHN SAW AMAZING visions of eternity: a new heaven, a new earth, New Jerusalem, a new river of life, and a new tree of life (Revelation 21 and 22). He saw a day when the curse of pain and death would be gone, tears would be wiped away, and the leaves of the Tree of Life would bring healing to the nations. Best of all, we will see the Lord face to face!

The theme of this heavenly vision is found in Revelation 21:5: "Behold, I make all things new." (KJV) Pause a moment and let those words sink in. He doesn't promise to make just some things new—He says "all things!"

As you consider your life and a New Year, what are some of the things you want God to "make new"? Your health? Your finances? Your marriage? Your children? Your emotions? Although John's vision focuses on a future day, the renewal process in your life can start today!

ENDNOTES

1   Squire Parsons, Beulah Land, http://www. gospelsonglyrics.net/b/beulah-land.htm; accessed March 2018.

2   http://thinkexist.com/quotation/there_is_a_god_ shaped_vacuum_in_the_heart_of/166425.html; accessed March 2018.

3   John 10:10

4   Originally from *Our Daily Bread*, the original concept for this story is found online at: http://www. christianglobe.com/Illustrations/theDetails.asp?which One=p&whichFile=protection.

5   See Psalm 1:1

6   G. Campbell Morgan, "The Gospel According to Matthew," Chapter Nine, Copyright 1929, http://www. baptistbiblebelievers.com/LinkClick.aspx?fileticket= voDoiuSWN3I%3d&tabid=322&mid=1057; accessed August 2017.

7   Matthew 5:44, NKJV

8   C. S. Lewis, *The Problem of Pain*, https:// www.biblegateway.com/devotionals/cs-lewis-daily/2014/06/19; accessed August 2014.

9   David Wilkerson, http://sermons.worldchallenge.org/ node/1035; accessed July 2014.

10 http://en.wikipedia.org/wiki/Mission:_Impossible; accessed August 2014.

11 Elisabeth Elliott, *A Chance to Die: The Life and Legacy of Amy Carmichael*, quoted at http://www. goodreads.com/work/quotes/121523-a-chance-to-die-the-life-and-legacy-of-amy-carmichael; accessed August 2014.

12 Thomas à Kempis, http://izquotes.com/quote/243132/.

13 http://biblegodquotes.com/sometimes-god-calms-the-storm/; accessed August 2014.

14 http://www.quotegarden.com/optimism.html; accessed December 2014.

15 Stephanie Sarkis, "50 Quotes on Beauty," *Psychology Today*, April 30, 2012, http://www.psychologytoday. com/blog/here-there-and-everywhere/201204/50-quotes-beauty; accessed January 2015.

16 J. Dobson & Gary Bauer, *Children at Risk*, (Nashville, TN: Word Publishing, 1990), 187–188.

17 John Piper, "Blessed Are the Meek," February 9, 1986, ©2015 Desiring God Foundation, http://www. desiringgod.org/sermons/blessed-are-the-meek; accessed January 2015.

18 Dr. Lance Wallnau, "Favor," 1989, audiocassette, http://www.amazon.com/FAVOR-DR-LANCE-WALLNAU/dp/B001DK08EO/ref=sr_1_18? s=books&ie=UTF8&qid=1421873646&sr=1-18&keywords=lance+wallnau; accessed January 2015.

19 Zechariah 4:6, paraphrased

20 https://www.brainyquote.com/quotes/pat_ summerall_308278?src=t_humility; accessed May 2018.

21 Merriam-Webster Online, http://www.merriam-webster.com/dictionary/favor; accessed September 2012.

22 Earl Jabay, *The Kingdom of Self,* (Logos International, 1980.)

23 Ellis J. Crum,"He Paid a Debt He Did Not Owe," http://www.digitalsongsandhymns.com/songs/4203; accessed June 2018.

24 https://sermons.faithlife.com/sermons/62635-a-man-fell-into-a-pit-.ser-illustration; accessed May 2018.

25 Mosie Lister, "Then I Met the Master," http://www. namethathymn.com/hymn-lyrics-detective-forum/ index.php?a=vtopic&t=6490; accessed May 2018.

26 https://www.goodreads.com/author/quotes/84278. Booker_T_Washington; accessed May 2018.

27 https://missionbibleclass.org/songs/english-songs/ anytime-songs/im-in-the-lords-army-song/; accessed May 2018.

28 https://www.brainyquote.com/quotes/ saint_augustine_105351God

29 "What does it mean to pray without ceasing?" Got Questions Ministries, https://www.gotquestions.org/ pray-without-ceasing.html; accessed October 2017.

30 Ibid.

31 Public Domain.

32 Dr. Jack Hayford, "Getting to the Heart of Worship," https://www.jackhayford.org/teaching/articles/getting-to-the-heart-of-worship/, accessed February 2018.

33 Words by Fanny Crosby, http://wordwisehymns. com/2013/09/30/redeemed-how-i-love-to-proclaim-it/; accessed June 2018.

34 Duong Sheahan, "Unforgiveness, a Deadly Virus," http://ezinearticles.com/?Unforgiveness---A-Deadly-Virus&id=784282; accessed July 2012.

35 Barbara Mandrell, Born to Die, https://elyrics. net">http://elyrics.net</a>; accessed May 2018.

36 https://www.brainyquote.com/quotes/william_ralph_ inge_; accessed May 2018.

37 http://thinkexist.com/quotation/no-man-ever-sank-under-the-burden-of-the-day-it/362964.html; accessed May 2018.

38 Francis McGaw, *John Hyde, The Apostle of Prayer* (Minneapolis, MN: Bethany House Publishers1970), 44.

39 Francis A. Schaeffer, *The Mark of the Christian* (Downers Grove, IL: InterVarsity Press), 25, 35.

40 http://www.cyberhymnal.org/htm/o/l/oltwnlmg.htm; accessed August 2014.

41 Bertha Spafford Vester, *Our Jerusalem: An American Family in the Holy City 1881–1949* (Jerusalem: Ariel Publishing House, 1988), 34.

42 Public Domain; words by Horatio Spafford, score by Phillip P. Bliss, 1873; http://www.cyberhymnal.org/ htm/i/t/i/itiswell.htm. Note: Phillip Bliss died in a train accident shortly after completing the score.

43 Johnold Strey, "Three Lessons About the Triune God," http://pastorstrey.wordpress.com/2009/06/08/sermon-on-isaiah-6/; accessed June 2018.

44 https://www.goodreads.com/quotes/71281-a-bell-s-not-a-bell-til-you-ring-it--; accessed June 2018.

45 https://www.poetryfoundation.org/poems/51642/ invictus; accessed June 2018.

46 Billy Graham, *Hope for Each Day (Words of Wisdom and Faith)* (Nashville, TN: J. Countryman, a division of Thomas Nelson, Inc., 2002), 338.

47 C.S. Lewis, https://www.christiancafe.com/blog/2993/ cslewis-christian-quotes; accessed June 2018.

MICHAEL DAVID EVANS, the #1 *New York Times* best-selling author, is an award-winning journalist/Middle East analyst. Dr. Evans has appeared on hundreds of network television and radio shows including *Good Morning America, Crossfire* and *Nightline*, and *The Rush Limbaugh Show*, and on Fox Network, *CNN World News*, NBC, ABC, and CBS. His articles have been published in the *Wall Street Journal, USA Today, Washington Times, Jerusalem Post* and newspapers worldwide. More than twenty-five million copies of his books are in print, and he is the award-winning producer of nine documentaries based on his books.

Dr. Evans is considered one of the world's leading experts on Israel and the Middle East, and is one of the most sought-after speakers on that subject. He is the chairman of the board of the ten Boom Holocaust Museum in Haarlem, Holland, and is the founder of Israel's first Christian museum located in the Friends of Zion Heritage Center in Jerusalem.

Dr. Evans has authored a number of books including: *History of Christian Zionism, Showdown with Nuclear Iran, The Visionaries, Why Was I Born?*, and *Israel Reborn*. His body of work also includes the novels *The Locket, Born Again: 1967, Netanyahu*, and *Shimon Peres: A Friend of Zion*.

✦　✦　✦

Michael David Evans is available to speak or for interviews.
Contact: EVENTS@drmichaeldevans.com.